Transnational Spaces

Social relations in our globalizing world are increasingly stretched out across the borders of two or more nation-states. Yet, despite the growing academic interest in transnational economic networks, political movements and cultural forms, too little attention has been paid to the transformations of space that these processes both reflect and reproduce.

Transnational Spaces takes an innovative perspective, looking at transnationalism as a social space that can be occupied by a wide range of actors, not all of whom are, themselves, directly connected to transnational migrant communities. Drawing on examples from around the world – including Britain, Canada, India, Singapore and the US – and from a range of disciplinary perspectives, this book investigates how:

- Transnationalism involves the flow of human and economic capital, commodities and ideas, with transformative effects on both source and destination regions.
- Gender relations and notions of ethnic, racial and national identity are transformed through the forces of transnationalism.
- Transnationalism is an ideological and discursive practice that can be deployed in various ways and can be embedded in a variety of political processes.

This international, interdisciplinary volume provides fresh insights into the nature of transnational space via a series of theoretically informed studies, thoroughly grounded in detailed empirical research. It will be of interest to anthropologists, sociologists, political scientists and geographers interested in the study of transnationalism.

Peter Jackson is Professor of Human Geography at the University of Sheffield. **Philip Crang** is Reader in Human Geography at Royal Holloway, University of London. **Claire Dwyer** is Lecturer in Geography at University College London.

Transnationalism
Series editor: Steven Vertovec, *University of Oxford*

'Transnationalism' broadly refers to multiple ties and interactions linking people or institutions across the borders of nation-states. Today myriad systems of relationship, exchange and mobility function intensively and in real time while being spread across the world. New technologies, especially involving telecommunications, serve to connect such networks. Despite great distances and notwithstanding the presence of international borders (and all the laws, regulations and national narratives they represent), many forms of association have been globally intensified and now take place paradoxically in a planet-spanning yet common arena of activity. In some instances transnational forms and processes serve to speed-up or exacerbate historical patterns of activity, in others they represent arguably new forms of human interaction. Transnational practices and their consequent configurations of power are shaping the world of the twenty-first century.

This book forms part of a series of volumes concerned with describing and analysing a range of phenomena surrounding this field. Serving to ground theory and research on 'globalization', the Routledge book series on 'Transnationalism' offers the latest empirical studies and ground-breaking theoretical works on contemporary socio-economic, political and cultural processes which span international boundaries. Contributions to the series are drawn from Sociology, Economics, Anthropology, Politics, Geography, International Relations, Business Studies and Cultural Studies.

The series is associated with the Transnational Communities Research Programme of the Economic and Social Research Council (see http://www.transcomm.ox.ac.uk).

The series consists of two strands:

Transnationalism aims to address the needs of students and teachers and these titles will be published in hardback and paperback. Titles include:

Culture and Politics in the Information Age
A new politics?
Edited by Frank Webster

Transnational Democracy
Political spaces and border crossings
Edited by James Anderson

Routledge Research in Transnationalism is a forum for innovative new research intended for a high-level specialist readership, and the titles will be available in hardback only. Titles include:

* Also available in paperback

Transnational Spaces

Edited by
Peter Jackson, Philip Crang
and Claire Dwyer

Routledge
Taylor & Francis Group

LONDON AND NEW YORK

First published 2004
by Routledge
11 New Fetter Lane, London EC4P 4EE

Simultaneously published in the USA and Canada
by Routledge
29 West 35th Street, New York, NY 10001

Routledge is an imprint of the Taylor & Francis Group

© 2004 Peter Jackson, Philip Crang and Claire Dwyer for selection
and editorial matter; individual contributors for their contributions

Typeset in Times by
Florence Production Ltd, Stoodleigh, Devon
Printed and bound in Great Britain by
MPG Books Ltd, Bodmin, Cornwall

British Library Cataloguing in Publication Data
A catalogue record for this book is available
from the British Library

Library of Congress Cataloging in Publication Data
Transnational spaces/editors, Peter Jackson, Philip Crang,
and Claire Dwyer.
    p. cm.
    Includes bibliographical references and index.
1. Transnationalism.   2. Emigration and immigration – Social aspects.
3. Human geography.   I. Jackson, Peter, 1955–   II. Crang, Philip, 1964–
III. Dwyer, Claire.
JV6225T7 2004
305.8–dc22   2003023383

ISBN 0–415–25419–1

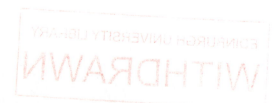

Contents

Illustrations

Figures

Table

Contributors

Parminder Bhachu, Department of Sociology, Clark University, Worcester, MA

Philip Crang, Department of Geography, Royal Holloway, University of London

Claire Dwyer, Department of Geography, University College London

Peter Jackson, Department of Geography, University of Sheffield

David Ley, Department of Geography, University of British Columbia

Katharyne Mitchell, Department of Geography, University of Washington, Seattle

Alisdair Rogers, School of Geography and Environment, University of Oxford

Roger Rouse, Department of Anthropology, University of California-Davis

Margaret Walton-Roberts, Department of Geography, Wilfrid Laurier University, Ontario

Johanna Waters, Department of Geography, University of Liverpool

Katie Willis, Department of Geography, Royal Holloway, University of London

Brenda Yeoh, Department of Geography, National University of Singapore

Preface and acknowledgements

Despite the growing academic interest in transnational economic networks, political movements and cultural forms, too little attention has been paid to the transformations of space that these processes both reflect and reproduce. This international, interdisciplinary volume addresses this problem via a series of theoretically informed studies, thoroughly grounded in detailed empirical research.

Until recently, research on transnationalism has been dominated by studies of transnational migration and by the sociological analysis of transnational communities. *Transnational Spaces* takes a different perspective. As outlined in the Introduction and illustrated by all of the contributors, transnationalism is a complex and multidimensional field – a social space that can be occupied by a wide range of actors, not all of whom are, themselves, directly connected to transnational migrant communities. Drawing on examples from around the world (including Britain, Canada, India, Mexico, Singapore and the US) and from a range of disciplinary perspectives (including anthropology, geography and sociology), this book seeks to expand our understanding of transnationalism by exerting our collective geographical imagination.

Most of the chapters were first presented at a special session of the annual meeting of the Association of American Geographers (AAG) in Pittsburgh in April 2000. The session was sponsored by the journal *Environment and Planning D: Society and Space*. We are also grateful to the UK Economic and Social Research Council (ESRC) for funding the participation of Roger Rouse and to the AAG's Enrichment Fund for sponsoring Parminder Bhachu's participation. Several of the participants (Crang, Dwyer, Jackson, Yeoh, Willis and Rogers) were funded by, or otherwise associated with, the ESRC's 'Transnational Communities' research programme, while several others (Ley, Mitchell, Walton-Roberts and Waters) were funded by, or associated with, the Canadian 'Metropolis' programme. We would like to acknowledge the University of Toronto Press for permission to reprint Roger Rouse's chapter, originally published in *Diaspora: A Journal of Transnational Studies* (vol. 1, 1991, pp. 8–23) and Routledge for permission to publish a revised version of Katharyne Mitchell's paper, originally published in *Economy and Society* (vol. 30, 2001, pp. 165–89). We would like to thank Michael Watts who served as a provocative and inspiring discussant at the conclusion of the AAG session at which most of these papers were first presented. Peter Jackson would like to thank Graham Allsopp for providing expert technical assistance and Gill Johnson and Kate Schofield for sorting out his endless word-processing problems and for their intimate knowledge of the world's most temperamental photocopier. Finally, we are all grateful to our editors at Routledge (Heidi Bagtazo, Craig Fowlie and Grace McInnes) for their skill and patience in seeing this book through to publication.

Introduction

The spaces of transnationality

*Peter Jackson, Philip Crang and
Claire Dwyer*

This book aims to provide a new perspective on the study of transnationality. In this Introduction and in related work (Crang *et al.* 2003), we argue that most current work in this rapidly expanding field has underestimated the significance of space in the constitution of various forms of transnationality. Previous studies have emphasized the importance of transnational corporations and business networks (Dicken 1986; Yeung 1998; Beaverstock and Boardwell 2000). They have examined the scope of transnational urban politics and social movements (Smith and Guarnizo 1998; Smith 2001) and explored the significance of newly emerging transnational cultural forms (Appadurai 1986, 1996; Hannerz 1996). But, in our collective view, such studies of the economic, political and cultural dimensions of transnationalism have characteristically under-played *the transformation of space* that is involved in the evolution of transnational social forms. Rather than taking space as a passive backdrop to transnational social relations, we argue that space is *constitutive of transnationality* in all its different forms.

The case can be made in a number of ways. First, within academia itself, different models of transnationality have been developed in *different geographical spaces*. So, for example, the kinds of arguments made about transnational migration in the context of the US–Mexican border are very different from those made in the context of the Asia-Pacific rim. In the former, transnational migrants are seen as a threat to national (US) stability, while relatively impoverished immigrants provide an economically valuable source of cheap labour but one that is subject to constant surveillance, regulation and control. In the latter case, transnational migration is often promoted by both sending and receiving countries, as an active strategy for nation-building and/or as a source of capital investment and skilled labour (see Chapters 1 and 7 of this volume). Other contexts have also produced their own transnational geographies, so that, for example, European transnationalities might be distinguished from those of the Americas (as Alisdair Rogers argues in Chapter 8 of this volume). So, transnationality varies over time and space.

Furthermore, these different transnational formations can, themselves, be distinguished by their different geographies, their *particular spatialities*. Here, Robin Cohen's overview of 'global diasporas' is exemplary (Cohen 1997). It is organized through an explicitly 'inexact' typology of different types of diaspora: victim/refugee; imperial/colonial; labour/service; trade/business/professional; cultural/hybrid/postmodern. Cohen's concern is less assigning particular groups to these categories – he notes how the Jews could, over time, be 'regarded as a victim, labour, trade and cultural diaspora' (Cohen 1997: 179) – and more about using the taxonomy to suggest different diasporic forms, experiences and geographies. This becomes particularly apparent in his suggestive use of horticultural metaphors to characterize his typology. So, the victim/refugee diaspora is linked to the gardening term 'weeding' (the identification of aliens and their 'cleansing' or expulsion); the imperial/colonial diaspora to 'sowing' (the scattering or distribution of seed); the labour/service diaspora to 'transplanting' ('digging up and replanting'); the trade/business/professional diaspora to 'layering' (as a method of vegetative rather than seminal propagation, taking cuttings, and replanting in new soil but only detaching them from the parent plant once they are established); and the cultural/hybrid/postmodern diaspora to 'cross-pollinating' (the travel of pollen borne by various media). Cohen is understandably cautious about the illustrative role of these metaphors and, of course, a variety of other metaphorical distinctions have also been mobilized in this context (including horticultural, biological and culinary ones). What interests us here is not the specifics of this metaphorical scheme, but its use to express different diasporic spatialities. At the heart of the gardening terms deployed by Cohen are distinctions regarding the character of movement and relations to space and place. Different diasporas are characterized by different geographies that go beyond simple oppositions between the national and the transnational, the rooted and the routed, the territorial and the de-territorialized. Diaspora is not only an inherently spatial term. Its particular historical forms evidence particular and distinctive spatialities. The same, we suggest, is true of the transnational.

Third, our argument is not limited to the different forms of transnationality that have emerged in different places, nor is it restricted to the geographies of transnational migrant communities themselves. Rather, we wish to argue that more and more people throughout the world are experiencing different forms of transnationality and that, as a social force and ideological formation, transnationalism now readily applies beyond the social worlds of those who define themselves as transmigrants or who are the members of ethnically identified migrant communities, all of whom can trace their origins to some more-or-less distant place of origin. We wish to suggest that increasing numbers of people participate in transnational space, *irrespective of their own migrant histories or 'ethnic' identities*. Our argument here parallels that advanced by Avtar Brah in her study of the

Cartographies of diaspora (1996). Brah's book uses the concept of diaspora to offer a critique of discourses of fixed origins while taking account of a 'homing' desire (as distinct from a desire for a specific 'homeland'). More particularly, Brah advances the concept of *diaspora space* to describe cultural geographies that are 'inhabited' not only by diasporic subjects but equally by those who are represented as 'indigenous' (Brah 1996: 16):

> In other words, the concept of diaspora space (as opposed to that of diaspora) includes the entanglement, the interwining of the genealogies of dispersion with those of 'staying put'. The diaspora space is the site where the native is as much a diasporian as the diasporian is the native.
>
> (Brah 1996: 209)

To take an example:

> In the diaspora space called 'England' . . . African-Caribbean, Irish, Asian, Jewish and other diasporas intersect among themselves as well as with the entity constructed as 'Englishness', thoroughly re-inscribing it in the process.
>
> (Brah 1996: 209)

So, the notion of diaspora space highlights how the diasporic is not limited only to diasporic communities but, rather, reconfigures attachments to and distancings from places much more widely.

In the course of this book, we advance an equally expansive notion of transnational space. Our use of the term encompasses all of those engaged in transnational cultures, whether as producers or consumers. It includes not just the *material geographies* of labour migration or the trading in transnational goods and services but also the *symbolic and imaginary geographies* through which we attempt to make sense of our increasingly transnational world. Transnational space is, we argue, *complex, multidimensional and multiply inhabited* (cf. Crang *et al.* 2003). People from various backgrounds enter its spaces with a whole range of investments and from various positionalities. They may occupy its spaces momentarily (during the consumption of a meal, for example) or for a lifetime (as members of ethnically defined transnational communities). They may have residual affinities to the transnational identities of earlier migrant generations or emergent identities as a result of their own current transnational experiences. Focusing on the spaces of transnationality, rather than just identifiable transnational communities distinguished from other (and often still normative) national communities, opens up ways of exploring this multiplicity of transnational experiences and relations.

We have argued, then, that a spatial focus usefully foregrounds the contextual specificity of transnational forms, the different transnational geographies associated with different transnational communities, and the multiplicity of transnational experiences and relations that extend beyond narrowly defined transnational populations. Fourth, and finally, we also believe that this spatial focus is important in making explicit what is central but sometimes under-theorized in transnational studies; namely, that transnationality is a geographical term, centrally concerned with *reconfigurations in relations with place, landscape and space*. Because this is so obvious, there is a danger that the vocabulary of transnationality operates as a simple geographical cipher, opposed to the national. So, the national is about place, territory, landscape, rootedness, belonging; the transnational connotes space, de-territorialization, other global cultural '-scapes' like mediascapes (Appadurai 1996), uprooting, rootlessness and routes of travel, and exclusion and longing. Substantive historical and geographical research has shown these neat oppositions break down in actually existing transnational cultures, economies and polities. Foregrounding the spaces of transnationality highlights the need for comparable theoretical work in developing spatial vocabularies that can sensitize us to these complexities in ways of being in space and place. We return to these ideas later in this Introduction. We begin, though, by reviewing the existing literature on transnationality, highlighting areas of agreement and disagreement in the field.

Approaching transnationality

'Transnationality' – and perhaps even more so 'transnationalism' (which for us conveys some sort of ideological commitment to the transnational, but is often used more neutrally to describe social, cultural and economic forms) – has become a vogue term in the social sciences within recent years. Yet, the condition to which it refers – 'multiple ties and interactions linking people or institutions across the borders of nation-states' (Vertovec 1999: 447) – has a much longer history. Indeed, critics of the term dispute its alleged novelty and challenge the implication that the nation-state has diminished in significance as a unit of social analysis. As Nancy Foner argues: 'Transnationalism is not new, even though it often seems as if it were invented yesterday' (1997: 355). On the basis of her comparison of transnationalism in nineteenth- and late twentieth-century New York, Foner argues that technological change has facilitated more frequent and closer transnational connections; that economic links are easier to maintain; that dual nationality facilitates some forms of transnationality; and that there may now be greater tolerance of ethnic pluralism in society at large – but that historically the differences are easily over-stated (ibid.: 362).

While transnationalism may have radical implications for our understanding of contemporary citizenship and nationhood, the nation-state continues to play a key role in defining the terms in which transnational processes are played out. As Nina Glick Schiller argues in her critique of some of the more celebratory studies of transnational identity formation:

while borders may be cultural constructions, they are constructions that are backed by force of law, economic and political power, and regulating and regularizing institutions. What they come to mean and how they are experienced, crossed or imagined are products of particular histories, times, and place.

(1997: 159)

Geographies of transnational space must clearly recognize the continuing power of nation-states in defining the framework and setting the terms within which transnational social relations take place.

This collection's focus on transnational space is clearly influenced by anthropological sources as well as by our own inherently transnational discipline of geography. Inspirational, for example, was Arjun Appadurai's injunction that in order to understand 'the social life of things' – the circulation of commodities in everyday life – 'we have to follow the things themselves, for their meanings are inscribed in their forms, their uses, their trajectories ... it is the things-in-motion that illuminate their human and social context' (1986: 5). Together with other anthropologists (such as Hannerz 1996), Appadurai has provided a searching critique of the 'globalization as homogenization' thesis. Beginning from the premise that there are many centres of modernity rather than a single source (reducible to the hegemonic force of 'Americanization'), Appadurai has explored the financial, social, political, cultural and media links that connect our increasingly transnational world. From this perspective, Appadurai declares: 'The United States is no longer the puppeteer of a world system of images but is only one node of a complex transnational construction of imaginary landscapes' (1996: 31). 'World systems, regarded especially from the cultural point of view, now emerge as much from Bombay, Tokyo, Rio de Janeiro and Hong Kong as they do from Los Angeles, New York, London and Paris' (Appadurai and Breckenridge 1988: 2). Appadurai also argues that even the most 'global' forces are subject to 'local' inflection in specific sites of consumption: 'at least as rapidly as forces from various metropolises are brought into new societies they tend to become indigenized in one way or another' (Appadurai 1996: 32). A more dialectical view of the links between 'the global' and 'the local' is now commonplace (Kearney 1995; Miller 1995, 1997). For, as Grewal and Kaplan maintain: 'How one separates the local and the global is difficult to decide when each thoroughly infiltrates the other' (1994: 11).

Transnational studies characteristically begin from the premise that social and cultural practices now regularly exceed the boundaries of individual nation-states. As Gupta and Ferguson argue, the emergence of a transnational public sphere has 'rendered any strictly bounded sense of community or locality obsolete' (1992: 9). When American sports logos for the Chicago Bulls, the LA Lakers or the New York Knicks turn up in even the remotest towns and villages of Belize in Central America, a process of de-territorialization might well be thought to be in train. But, according to the research from which this example is taken (Miller Matthei 1998), such findings cannot be taken as evidence of a generalized 'Americanization' process (much less an abstract process of 'globalization'). Instead, as Miller Matthei insists, it is the product of specific inter-personal networks of Belizean migrants in the US, re-establishing the particularities of place even when space itself appears to have been transcended. So, too, argues Michael Watts, from a geographical perspective, processes of de-territorialization may be accompanied by simultaneous and equally forceful processes of *re-territorialization*. While it might at first appear that 'The whole world watches Oprah and drinks Coca-Cola', Watts' own work in West Africa leads him to suggest that 'globalization does not so much mark the erasure of place but in a curious way contributes to its revitalization. Globalization here implies less the erosion of place than a sensitivity to how location, identity, and community are refashioned in incompletely globalized sites' (Watts 1996: 63–5).

Kong's (1999a, 1999b) work on globalization and Singaporean trans-migration also provides strong evidence of the dialectical nature of transnationalism, provoking a strongly nationalist response. The Singapore government's attempt to construct a national identity coincided with attempts to encourage its citizens to 'globalize' through economic invest-ment and temporary sojourns in China, for example (as further discussed by Yeoh and Willis in Chapter 7). Migration to China has had the para-doxical effect of enhancing Singaporean transmigrants' sense of national identity rather than contributing to its demise. This is not merely a reflec-tion of the Singaporean government's hegemonic project of state formation but also a result of the way that Singaporean transmigrants themselves negotiate their sense of national identity. While ministers of state empha-size the pragmatic advantages of a strong sense of Singaporean national identity as a kind of 'competitive advantage' in a globalizing economy, Singaporean citizens living in China actively reinforce their own sense of national identity through a variety of cultural strategies.

Our own work reaches similar conclusions (Cook and Crang 1996; Crang 1996; Dwyer and Crang 2002; Dwyer and Jackson 2003). While particular goods may appear to be 'de-territorialized' in the sense that they are sourced from places that may be very distant from where they are consumed, their meanings are 're-territorialized' both through distinctive local contexts of consumption and through product 'placements' that emphasize specific geographical contexts (even where those geographies are purely imaginary). We therefore treat with some scepticism the bold assertion that 'Culture is becoming increasingly deterritorialized' (King 1991: 6). While borders and boundaries are, in some places and for some people, becoming increasingly porous, we are sympathetic to Arturo Escobar's (2001) argument that, for most people, most of the time, culture still 'sits in places'. We must not let the often elite ideology of transnationalism blind us to the practical and emotional importance of attachments to and in place.

Of course, the question is how we can think about the relations to contextuality – the belonging – that Escobar characterizes as 'sitting in place', and how can we do so in ways that move beyond the dichotomies such as de- and re-territorialization. In part this involves thinking through refigurations of the geographies of place, settlement and belonging. We belong in place partly through the kind of sitting Escobar evokes. We engage with our surroundings, we develop competencies in relationship to them, and this means sometimes we can be 'settled'. This is too easily dismissed in concerns about breaking neat – and politically conservative – connections between culture and place. But our surroundings, our places of settlement, our belongings in the literal sense of material culture, are all constituted through much wider flows and circuitries. The fabrics we touch, the foods we eat, these homely things all also inhabit distanciated systems of exchange. And then, of course, belonging is not only an embodied, practical state, but an emotional state and imaginative manoeuvre, as regulated through moral and political institutions and practices. So, to sit in place is also always to be 'displaced' (Crang 1996) in the sense of inhabiting threefold geographies: of immediate contextuality; of flows and circuits, that in turn constitute those contexts; and of imaginative geographies, that characterize those contexts and flows and our relations to them.

Other figures than 'displacement' have been used to express the complexities of transnational relations to place. Thus, Steven Vertovec (1999) speaks of 'triadic' geographies of belonging, through relations to places of residence, myths of homelands, and imaginations of diasporic communities, and there is much profit to be had – and good work already being done – from not only employing this schema but in working across it. Thus, how is transnationality configured by embodied visits to and stays in (mythical) homelands; how are those homelands themselves transformed by such physical contacts; how are imaginations of global diasporic communities rooted in and routed through particular sites of residence; and how are places of residence transformed by diasporic imaginations (cf. Brah 1996)? We might also look to work that seeks to move beyond accounts of imaginative geographies in which 'Self' and 'Other' are constituted in processes of discursive projection. Here physical processes of dwelling, becoming and transculturation are highlighted. For example, Ella Westland (2002) narrates the novelist D.H. Lawrence's time in the British county of Cornwall in part through his imbrication in Edwardian imaginaries of its Celtic otherness. But she also highlights his little acts of dwelling – his descriptions of the landscape just outside his door; his work on the neighbouring farm – and his plans for a diasporic artists' community there (later imaginatively relocated to Canada). She concludes that Lawrence's stay in Cornwall represents the sort of serially monogamous relations to place that many have in the precarious, modern world.

Focusing on the spaces of transnationality, therefore, highlights how a range of transnational studies have sought to refigure the relations between subjectivity, culture and place. In so doing they argue against the hyperbolic equation of transnationality only with discourses of flow, movement, flight and smooth space. But they also suggest that these hyperboles are not best countered by invoking opposed qualities of settlement, grounding and the like. This is a false opposition, both ontologically and epistemo-logically. Transnationality is constituted through the dialectical relations of the grounded and flighty, the settled and the flowing, the sticky and the smooth.

Transnationalism from 'above', 'below' and 'in between'

Our perspective on transnational space leads us to doubt the usefulness of the common distinction between geographies of transnationalism 'from above' and 'from below'. The former is often couched in terms of a very one-dimensional reading of globalization (e.g. Falk 1993), focusing on the increasing transnational mobility of capital. By contrast, those who argue for an understanding of transnationalism 'from below' tend to emphasize (and sometimes over-emphasize) the human agency or 'adaptive strategies' of transnational migrants (e.g. Ballard 1994). While studies of trans-nationalism 'from above' emphasize the (negative) human consequences of technological change, the hyper-mobility of capital and the concomitant need for increasingly 'flexible' labour practices, those who champion trans-nationalism 'from below' assert that a social process of this magnitude cannot be all one-sided: 'By its very momentum, the process is likely to trigger various reactions giving rise to counter-vailing structures' (Portes 1997: 2).

Studies of transnationalism 'from above' are associated with global capital flows and supranational political institutions, while transnationalism 'from below' is usually understood in terms of various forms of local resist-ance (via the informal economy, 'ethnic' nationalism and grassroots activism, for example). The range of practices that can be encompassed within such a definition of resistance is extremely diverse, including the transnational business practices of 'ethnic entrepreneurs' as well as various forms of cultural hybridity, multipositional identities and border crossings by marginalized Others (Guarnizo and Smith 1998: 5). Indeed, as Portes has suggested, popular resistance to global restructuring 'does not emerge in opposition to broader economic forces but is driven by them' (1997: 9). From this perspective, what is commonly referred to as transnationalism 'from below' should not be seen as a form of resistance to global capitalism but as an adaptation to it.

Our own preference is to avoid the binary thinking that characterizes the very language of 'above' and 'below'. We concur with Michael Peter Smith's analysis of transnationalism 'from between', where globalization is understood as an unfinished product of politically and culturally constructed social practices (2001: 184–6). Like Smith, we aim to transcend the binary thinking of 'above' and 'below', following people, goods and ideas as they cross and re-cross national boundaries (cf. Wilson and Dissanayake 1996). We see transnationalism as neither imposed from above nor produced by some anonymous and disembodied force of 'resistance' from below. Rather, paralleling Giddens' theorization of globalization, we see transnationalism not as an 'out there' but as an 'in here' phenomenon, involving 'transformations in the very texture of everyday life' (1996: 367–8).

We also wish to challenge those who celebrate transnationalism as a force of cultural creativity that is invariably progressive in its political consequences. Katharyne Mitchell (1997a) launched a particularly effective attack on this tendency within the literature which she labels 'the hype of hybridity', arguing that all such assertions should be tempered by an understanding of the material forces and social inequalities that typify most forms of transnationalism. Without literal empirical data related to the actual movements of things and people across space, Mitchell argues:

> theories of anti-essentialism, mobility, plurality and hybridity can quickly devolve into terms emptied of any potential political efficacy . . . It is through the contextualization of concepts such as hybridity and margins, and the deconstruction of concepts such as capitalism and modernity that theories of transnationalism can best serve a progressive politics of the future.
>
> (1997b: 110–12; cf. Mitchell 1993)

Caren Kaplan (1995) provides a valuable intervention in this debate, arguing that while transnational cultural forms may be a means of resisting the practices of modernity and their associations with various forms of nationalism and imperialism, there is nothing intrinsically progressive about transnationalism. Taking various examples (including Ralph Lauren's 'Safari' perfume, National Geographic, American Express and The Body Shop), Kaplan demonstrates that their insistence on 'a world without boundaries' can serve as a simple means of managing cultural difference, mystifying historical and contemporary forms of exploitation, and promoting a form of 'feel-good capitalism' which she associates with an equally problematic 'fuzzy geopolitics' (1995: 59).

We share Kaplan's reservations about the politics of transnational culture and Mitchell's concern that studies of transnational cultural creativity should be grounded in an understanding of the social relations of production. In this respect, too, we follow Smith and Guarnizo's emphasis on 'grounding' transnationalism (1998: 11). It is clear, for example, that transnational practices remain 'embedded in enduring asymmetries of domination, inequality, racism, sexism, class conflict and uneven development' (ibid.: 6), forces that are all too easily elided in empirically ungrounded studies of cultural hybridity where it may be implied that cultures 'mix and match' on remarkably equal terms. As Steven Vertovec argued at the start of the recent ESRC 'Transnational Communities' research programme, 'there is immediate need for more in-depth and comparative empirical studies of transnational human mobility, communication, social ties, channels and flows of money, commodities, information and images' (1999: 456) – a need which this book aims to address.

Aiwa Ong and Donald Nonini have launched an excoriating critique of certain strands within the Cultural Studies literature, accusing them of ungrounded speculation (or 'lite anthropology'). In their words:

> The earlier promise of ethnographies investigating the cultural and social effects of transnational identities in third world societies . . . has lately been diluted by an American cultural studies approach that treats transnationalism as a set of abstracted, dematerialized cultural flows, giving scant attention either to the concrete, everyday changes in people's lives or the structural reconfigurations that accompany global capitalism . . . [W]hat has often dropped out of this approach is an interest in describing the ways in which people's everyday lives are transformed by the effects of global capitalism, how their own agencies are implicated in the making of these effects, and the social relationships in which these agencies are embedded.
>
> (1997: 13)

While their argument may be over-stated, it does point to certain methodological imperatives for transnational research. According to George Marcus, for example, it implies a commitment to multi-sited ethnography: 'tracing a cultural formation across and within multiple sites of activity' (1995: 96). Marcus advocates an approach that follows the people (especially migrants); the thing (commodities, gifts, money, works of art and intellectual property); the metaphor (including signs and symbols or images); the plot, story or allegory (narratives of everyday experience or memory); the life or biography (of exemplary individuals); or the conflict (issues contested in public space). Appadurai's attempt to trace the flow of people, technologies, finance, information and ideology through a number of different 'dimensions' (termed ethnoscapes, mediascapes, technoscapes, financescapes and ideoscapes) reflects a similar methodological agenda, following chains, paths, threads, conjunctions, or juxtapositions of locations (1996). The same logic of tracing flows and connections across space and time is illustrated in James Clifford's (1997) work on travel and translation and in Nicholas Thomas's (1991) explorations of the mutual 'entanglement' of material objects and post-colonial histories. Nina Glick Schiller (1997: 160) advances a similar case, arguing that 'we need to develop key words that reflect dynamics of interconnection', citing LiPuma's (1997) work on 'encompassment' as an example of one such useful neologism which, we would suggest, can be taken in relation to others such as 'transculturation' (Pratt 1992), creolization and the like.

For Michael Peter Smith, the challenge of transnationalism is 'to develop an optic and a language capable of representing the complexity of trans-national connections', including 'the dynamics of cross-border networks, and the shifting spatial scales at which agency takes place' (2001: 174). Smith supports the need for multi-locational research in fluid trans-localities. Specifically, he recommends comparing different transnational networks in the same city, different network practices across space, and the different ways in which the neo-liberal project of globalization is localized in different places. While this goes some way beyond the aims of the present book, it provides a useful introduction to some of our specific concerns with transnational space and with the previous ways in which such spaces have been understood.

Transnational spaces: issues and debates

While transnational connections have been a characteristic feature of capi-talist economies throughout history, there is general agreement that the speed and extent of such connections have intensified in recent decades (Castells 1989, 1996; Hannerz 1996). Paraphrasing Portes *et al.* (1999), Vertovec concludes that it is the 'scale of intensity and simultaneity of current long-distance, cross-border activities – especially economic transac-tions – which provide the recently emergent, distinctive and, in some contexts, now normative social structures and activities which . . . merit the term "transnationalism"' (Vertovec 1999: 448). While there are continuities with the past, transnationality is emerging as a phenomenon of ever-greater intensity and scope.

Despite historical continuities, there is a growing consensus that contem-porary transnational connections are different from the past in terms of range and depth (Goldberg 1992: 205), density and significance (Jones 1992: 219). For Kearney, too, it is the recent increase in the volume and velocity of transnational flows of information, symbols, capital and commodities that justifies the current interest in transnationalism (1995: 547). Such flows have disrupted the significance of national boundaries, though (as discussed earlier) they have not rendered obsolete the power of the nation-state. As Roger Rouse asserts:

> the comfortable modern imagery of nation-states and national languages, of coherent communities and consistent subjectivities, of dominant centers and distant margins no longer seems adequate . . . [D]uring the last 20 years, we have all moved irrevocably into a new kind of social space.
>
> (Rouse 1991: 8)

While we might question the extent to which this 'comfortable imagery' was ever an accurate representation of the modern world or whether we do indeed *all* now have a common experience of these new social spaces, we share Rouse's interest in exploring these transnational spaces and clarifying their social significance.

Rouse argues that transnational social fields are articulated via the agency of transnational migrants and by the far-reaching effects of transnational corporations. He refers specifically to the 'circuits' of migrant labour, evoking 'the continuous circulation of people, money, goods and information, the pseudo-institutional nature of the arrangement (over purely individual ties), and the qualified importance of place (over purely social linkages)' (1991: 20).

Several other authors, besides Rouse, have referred to transnationality as a 'social field'. In the context of their work on Caribbean (St Vincentian and Dominican) and Filipino transnationals in the US, Nina Glick Schiller *et al.* argue that within this transnational social field:

> The constant and various flows of ... goods and activities have embedded within them relationships between people. These social relations take on meaning within the flow and fabric of daily life, as linkages between different societies are maintained, renewed, and reconstituted in the context of families, of institutions, of economic investments, business, and finance and of political organisations and structures including nation-states.
>
> (1992: 11)

Basch *et al.* (1994) develop these ideas further, arguing that for these transnational migrant groups at least, the link between geographic space and social identity has been disrupted. Their work seeks to develop the notion of a 'dialectical anthropology', based on four premises:

- transnational migration is inextricably linked to the changing conditions of global capitalism and must be analysed within the context of global relations between capital and labour (ibid.: 23);
- transnationalism is a process by which migrants, through their daily life activities and social, economic, and political relations, create social fields that cross national boundaries (ibid.: 27);
- bounded social science concepts such as 'ethnic group', 'race', and 'nation' can limit the ability of researchers first to perceive and then to analyse the phenomenon of transnationalism (ibid.: 30); and
- by living their lives across borders, transmigrants find themselves confronted with and engaged in the nation-building processes of two or more nations. Their identities and practices are configured by hegemonic categories such as race and ethnicity that are deeply embedded in the nation-building processes of these nation-states (ibid.: 34).

Geographers have been particularly attracted to the idea of understanding transnationalism as a social field involving webs of connection between distant places. Recent work by Bailey *et al.* (2002), for example, explores the transnational social field that spans El Salvador and several northern New Jersey towns. Their work suggests that the migrants' uncertain legal status permeates every aspect of their daily lives, leading them to employ practices of 'strategic visibility' within a situation that they characterize as 'permanent temporariness'. Bailey *et al.* draw on Henri Lefebvre's (1991) ideas about the 'production of space'. They refer to the constitutive role of transmigration and emphasize the extent to which Salvadorans have formed households with members of other ethnic groups. But there is relatively little emphasis on the transformations that Salvadoran migrants have caused to the meaning of space *for non-Salvadoran residents* in New Jersey.

Adopting the idea of transnationality as a social field can, however, have transformative effects on what and how we study. It can, as we have already suggested, encourage the development of more encompassing notions of transnationality including those who are not themselves transnational migrants. This has not been common in most previous studies of the transnational. Even where researchers have spoken of the impact of transmigration on a wider social field – as in references to the 'Dominicanization' of New York City (Nyberg Sørensen 1998) – or where they have expanded the definition of transnationalism to include those who do not, themselves, migrate (e.g. Mahler 1998), the analysis can still have a very restricted scope. In her analysis of an advertisement for Dominican rum, for example, Nyberg Sørensen (1998) restricts herself to an interpretation of the ad's reception among Dominicans in New York and in the Dominican Republic (excluding non-Dominican interpretations of the ad in either place). The ad's content includes an ironic representation of Americans' alleged inability to understand *merengue* or to talk Spanish (*'Ay americana, no sabe nada'*). But the transnational field to which the ad alludes could clearly be cast more widely to include those non-Dominican New Yorkers whose grasp of the Dominican vernacular is the subject of such derision. Similarly, while Mahler raises questions about transmigrants as agents of change 'across entire transnational fields' (1998: 94), she is still preoccupied with members of particular (ethnically defined) transnational communities rather than with the transformations they may be effecting across a wider transnational social field.

Clearly, then, our approach to transnational space is much wider in scope than most existing studies of transnational communities. Such a widening of the scope of transnationalism raises its own problems. As transnational studies have proliferated, there have been increasingly strenuous attempts to police the boundaries of the field and to provide a firmer institutional identity for transnational studies. So, for example, one of the leading figures in the field, Alejandro Portes, has objected to the re-labelling of 'immigrants' as 'transmigrants', arguing that it adds nothing to what is already known. He also argues that the term 'transnational' should be reserved for 'activities of an economic, political, and cultural sort that require involvement of participants on a regular basis as a major part of their occupation' (1997: 17). Such activities should, moreover, be of a near-instantaneous character across national borders and long distances, involving substantial numbers of people. Once a critical mass is reached, Portes argues, such activities tend to become normative (ibid.: 18). Thus, for Portes at least, the membership of transnational communities should be tightly defined to include people who are 'at least bilingual, move easily between different cultures, frequently maintain homes in two countries, and pursue economic, political, and cultural interests that require a simultaneous presence in both' (Portes 1997: 16). As is evident from the preceding comments, our own ambitions are clearly rather different.

Steven Vertovec (1999) has voiced similar concerns about the 'conceptual muddle' that has resulted from the recent rush of studies on transnationalism – encompassing transnational communities, capital flows, trade, citizenship, corporations, intergovernmental agencies, non-governmental organizations, politics, services, social movements, social networks, families, migration circuits, identities, public spaces and public cultures. In response to this undisciplined profusion, Vertovec provides a useful typology of transnationalism(s), distinguishing between transnationalism as social morphology, type of consciousness, mode of cultural reproduction, avenue of capital, site of political engagement and reconstruction of 'place' or locality (cf. his previous attempt to clarify the definition of 'diaspora': Vertovec 1997).

Nina Glick Schiller (1997: 155) also feels that there is much confusion as to the scope of transnational studies, covering work on global communications, media, consumerism and public culture, globalization and global cities and transnational migration. In order to discipline this field, she argues that 'the study of cultural representations must be linked to explorations of the structures of inequality' (ibid.: 155–6), arguing for a greater emphasis on the specification and location of agency; the relationship between transnational processes and states; and the historical simultaneity of (and interaction between) global, transnational, national and local social fields.

Portes *et al.* (1999) go even further, providing some 'conceptual guidelines' for future research in the field, urging researchers to: *establish the phenomenon*; *delimit the phenomenon* (which in their terms restricts the term 'to occupations and activities that require regular and sustained social contacts over time across national borders for their implementation', ibid.: 219); *define the unit of analysis* (distinguishing, for example, between individuals, networks, communities and institutional structures); *distinguish types* (economic, political and socio-cultural, further categorized by level of institutionalization); and *identify necessary conditions* (e.g. technology).

Given our interest in mapping the wider spaces of transnationalism, there is something too prescriptive about such 'guidelines'. Rather than seeking to delimit the field of transnational studies, restricting analysis to the study of migration flows and diasporic populations, we seek to extend the field to encompass a wider range of other cultural practices and social processes. Specifically, we wish to extend the study of transnationality beyond the confines of still-bounded-but-displaced 'ethnic communities' to encompass a more multidimensional, materially heterogeneous social field, characterized by multiple inhabitations and disjunctions (cf. Crang *et al.* 2003).

Such a perspective has the potential to transform our understanding of other key concepts. So, for example, with our emphasis on the permeable borders of transnational space, the meaning of 'ethnicity' becomes a highly contested signifier rather than an explanation for particular cultural forms or business practices (cf. Dwyer and Crang 2002). Several recent studies of transnationality follow a similar line of argument. In Ong and Nonini's account of Chinese transnationalism, for example, 'Chineseness' is understood as 'an inscribed relation of persons and groups to forces and processes associated with global capitalism and its modernities' (1997: 3–4). Similarly, in Lily Kong's work on Singaporean transmigrants, a 'Chinese' identity is described as a 'resource' that can be mobilized for economic gain but which can also elicit negative treatment (1999b: 233).

Outline of the book

The chapters that follow use the concept of 'transnational space' in several different ways, but all share our commitment to a more encompassing, and transformative, definition. We begin by reprinting Roger Rouse's classic essay on the social spaces of transnationalism. In place of the static world of centres and peripheries, Rouse's ethnography of Mexican migrants in the US seeks to develop 'an alternative cartography of social space'. These cartographic spaces are etched through the continuous movement of people, money, goods and information. Taken together, these transnational movements have come to constitute 'a single community spread across a variety of sites' or what Rouse calls a transnational migrant circuit. This transnational circuit, Rouse insists, is not simply the product of American corporate capital. It is also being forged by the way Mexican workers (from the rural village of Aguililla, where Rouse's study is set, and in Redwood, California, some 2,000 miles distant) have, themselves, responded, actively creating transnational circuits and support networks of their own. Significantly, for Rouse, the juxtaposition of these different social worlds has not resulted in either homogenization or synthesis. Notions of 'circuit' and 'border zone' enable Rouse to begin to sketch a wider social landscape 'found throughout Mexico and the United States' (an argument that he pursued in later work, e.g. Rouse 1995). In a statement that comes very close to the position outlined in this Introduction,

Rouse concludes that 'The forces shaping Aguilillans' lives are . . . coming to affect *everyone* who inhabits the terrain encompassed by Mexico and the United States' (1991: 18; emphasis added).

The chapters by Bhachu and Dwyer probably provide the best examples of the more encompassing notion of transnational space that we have advanced in this Introduction. Parminder Bhachu examines the significance of the *salwaar-kameez* (or Punjabi suit) for women of South Asian origin and descent in various parts of the diaspora (including Britain and North America as well as the Indian sub-continent). From her ethnography, however, it is also clear that many other women who would not define themselves as having a close personal connection to South Asia or any immediate connection to South Asian communities in the diaspora also participate in this particular transnational commodity space. Whether through the appropriation of 'South Asian' garments or through music, film, food and other cultural practices, consumers of diverse backgrounds have come to participate in the spaces of 'South Asian' commodity culture, engaging on different terms and with varying degrees of investment. Such practices are not simply cultural 'imports', wrested from one point of origin and passively consumed in another locality distant from its source. Commodities such as the *salwaar-kameez* are constituted transnationally in the sense that their meaning is actively re-worked in different cultural contexts as the goods are themselves manufactured and moved around the world. For, as Bhachu argues, it is not just the members of British-Asian communities in places like Southall or Wembley for whom the 'Punjabi suit' is of contemporary cultural significance. Prominent members of the 'white' British establishment, like Jemima Goldsmith-Khan and the late Diana, Princess of Wales, have publicly adopted the *salwaar-kameez*, and both Cherie Blair and Ffion Hague, as wives of the Labour and (former) Tory party leaders, have worn saris to South Asian events in Britain as gestures of symbolic identification with their audiences. During the 1990s, examples of the fusion of British-Asian style became widespread in popular culture, pioneered by celebrities like David Beckham and Madonna, wearing sarongs and *mendhis* (henna tattoos). As Bhachu argues, for a period of time it was 'hip to be Asian', as white British audiences listened to British-Asian bands like Cornershop, danced to the hybrid sounds of *bhangra* and wore 'Asian'-inspired fashions, bought from high-street retailers rather than from specialist 'ethnic' retailers. The cultural significance of such relatively short-lived trends can, of course, be debated (cf. Hutnyk 2000). But they are representative of a much wider set of transnational geographies than those conventionally associated with any specific 'minority' group.[1]

Claire Dwyer's chapter provides an even wider reading of the nature of contemporary transnational space, including the *symbolic and imaginary geographies* that people bring to the consumption of transnational commodities. She provides case-study evidence from a number of firms in the fashion industry whose transnationalities are multidimensional, including their personal biographies, their business practices and networks, the 'stylization' of their clothing (as 'ethnic', 'Indian', 'traditional', etc.) and the way that consumers relate to their products. The transnational spaces she examines are multiply inhabited by a range of social actors with variable investments in 'South Asianness'. It is a lived social field that extends well beyond the membership of specific British-Asian ethnic communities. By focusing on transnational commodity culture, Dwyer's work offers fresh insights into the study of transnationality, while simultaneously using the lens of transnationality to throw new light on the workings of contemporary commodity culture.

Margaret Walton-Roberts provides a rich account of two villages in Punjab, India which, through a history of long-term out-migration, have been part of a wider transnational space for over a century. In one case, the 'global village' of Palahi, villagers use internet and telephone links to connect to relatives overseas in Britain and Canada. The other village, Dhesian Kahna, has benefitted from the patronage of its Non-Resident Indians who have invested in the creation of a park and the draining of a pond with funding from Vancouver (Canada) and Bradford (England). These transnational links are maintained through the flow of remittances, international travel and cultural interactions and have led to wider transformations in both source and sending regions. A transnational social field has been created whose influence extends to other regions of India where a process of uneven development has arisen, differentiating those places that have transnational connections from those that do not. Walton-Roberts concludes that it is no longer valid to study 'immigrant settlement' (in Britain or Canada) as a separate academic field from 'development studies' (in India).

The next two chapters examine a very different kind of transnational migration, encouraged by the destination country (in this case Canada) as a way of attracting the capital and entrepreneurial skills of overseas business elites (in this case from Hong Kong and Taiwan). David Ley and Johanna Waters examine the rhetoric of a borderless world, characterized by a friction-less 'space of flows', as advanced by globalization theorists such as Manuel Castells (1989). Their own work on Hong Kong business migrants in Vancouver demonstrates that there is still considerable 'friction' involved in the transfer of entrepreneurial skills to Canada. Faced with higher taxation and tougher labour, environmental and consumer regulations, many Hong Kong business migrants have taken early retirement on arriving in Canada or have scaled down their business activities in favour of a more relaxed pace of life. Indeed, most of Ley and Waters' interview sample migrated for political reasons (based on their anxieties over the future of Hong Kong and Taiwan) or for their children's education. This evidence effectively challenges stereotypical images of the Hong Kong businessman as an economically driven profit maximizer (*Homo economicus*). Ley and Waters also show that the development of 'astronaut' households – where one family member returns to East Asia to maximize their earnings while the rest of the family remain in Canada – has a range of implications (in terms of gender and family relations, for example) that go well beyond a narrowly defined economic strategy.

Katharyne Mitchell's chapter addresses a related topic, extending her previous work on the migration of Hong King business-people to Canada to explore the consequences of this state-sponsored migration for the extension of Canadian neo-liberalism as a material practice and an ideological discourse. She argues that the wealthy Hong Kong immigrants attracted to Canada by its Business Immigration Programme supported the development of 'shadow state' welfare organizations, such as the United Chinese Community Enrichment Services Society (SUCCESS) in Vancouver. The extension of such services, Mitchell argues, enabled the Canadian government to pursue its neo-liberal agenda of deregulation, privatization and the withdrawal of direct social service provision. Mitchell's work demonstrates the transformative capacity of transnational migration, where the exodus of wealthy business-people and capital has had widespread effects on both source and destination countries, deepening the grip of neo-liberalism within Canada and shifting the nature of state–society relations, with consequences that extend well beyond the migrant community itself.

Brenda Yeoh and Katie Willis examine another form of state-sponsored transnational migration: the Singapore government's 'go regional' policy that is designed to expand the transnational field of Singaporean capital investment and entrepreneurial activity throughout South and East Asia. While the economic motivation is clear, Yeoh and Willis argue that this expansion of transnational space has a variety of other effects, including the reshaping of gender relations and identities at home and abroad. Most studies of the gendered nature of transnational migration have focused on the role of women in supporting transnational families and networks. Here, instead, Yeoh and Willis explore the consequences of transnational migration for the men who set off 'on the regional beat'. They argue that the stretching of gender relations across transnational space reinforces rather than destabilizes traditional forms of patriarchy. In this case, transnational migration is conceived of as a process of toughening up young Singaporean businessmen, a kind of masculine *rite de passage*, the rigours of which are best endured alone or with the backing of a supportive wife. The situation contrasts with Hong Kong business migrants in Vancouver (discussed by Ley and Waters in Chapter 5) where transnational migration can be transformative of conventional gender relations, with increased independence for some transmigrant women in Canada whose partners are working in Hong Kong.

In the final chapter, Alisdair Rogers advocates a macro-regional approach to the study of transnationalism, examining the differences between Europe and the Americas. Using the concepts of 'migration order' and 'migration configuration', he also distinguishes 'Eastern' and 'Western' European forms of transnationalism and the possible emergence of a single European mobility order. Focusing on the case of Abdullah Ocalan, the exiled leader of the Kurdish Workers' Party, Rogers demonstrates the geographical extent of the Kurdish diasporas (encompassing parts of Central Asia, Australia and the Philippines as well as many parts of Europe) and the transnational politics to which such diasporas have given rise. Rogers identifies a number of forms of transnationalism within Europe associated with forced, transit and labour migration as well as with tourism, trading and trafficking. According to Rogers, European transnational space will, in future, be shaped by the politics of mobility and security as much as by economic forces, and by wider forces such as geopolitical change and demographic ageing.

Individually and collectively, the contributors bring a wealth of empirical detail and conceptual sophistication to bear on the nature of transnational space. In conclusion, we would like to draw attention to some of the issues that remain unresolved by the work presented here. These include issues of methodology and politics. Several of the chapters employ an ethnographic approach, implying a commitment to long-term, first-hand fieldwork, aiming to grasp the meaning of social action 'in the round'. Such a method has clear advantages in terms of the depth of knowledge it can uncover. But it is particularly exacting in the context of transnational research, implying an in-depth engagement with multiple field sites where contact is maintained, more-or-less simultaneously, through both face-to-face contact and by means of a variety of information technologies (email, fax and phone). What are the challenges in terms of research design for further investigating these complex transnational spaces (cf. Marcus 1995)? And what are the possibilities for how ethnography is, itself, recast? Does transnational research demand even more commitments of time and personnel than the traditional, located ethnography? Does it suggest thinking of many placed ethnographies connecting together into a transnational collection? Or should the entire practice of ethnographic work be transformed to reflect transnational connections with other times and spaces?

Likewise, the preceding chapters all imply a more complex form of political engagement than can be grasped in the rather two-dimensional language of a dominant culture 'exploiting' or 'appropriating' a less powerful subordinate one (cf. hooks 1992; Root 1996). Questions of authority and authenticity, voice and position, have all been alluded to in the empirical work reported here. These are complex issues since we are never wholly able to appreciate the position from which we approach our research, or to judge the full effects of our research on those we study (Rose 1997). Moreover, those involved in transnational networks and social practices also occupy complex and shifting positionalities that might be best approached by researchers attempting to specify different 'degrees of reflexivity' (Mauthner and Doucet 2003).

Yet, we remain uncertain about how best to uncover (and challenge) the unequal 'power geometries' (Massey 1994) that characterize the circuits and flows of transnational space. We have argued that transnational space is multiply inhabited, but how can the politics of that multiplicity be expressed? Perhaps it is a matter of developing notions that can convey the differences in relations to transnational spaces: of position and positionality; of differing levels, forms and practices of investment in transnationality. Perhaps it will involve developing forms of representation that can express not only heterogeneity but also relationality (Crang 1992). Research on transnational space is still in its infancy. By outlining some of the complex geographies that inhere within transnational space, we are aware of how much yet remains to be done.

Note

1   Marie Gillespie's (1995) ethnographic work in Southall applies a similar argument to the consumption practices of young Punjabi Londoners who regularly appropriate such archetypally 'global' brands as Coca-Cola and McDonalds. Gillespie's work shows that the meaning of such goods is thoroughly re-worked in this particular space of consumption, taking on a range of culturally specific meanings that cannot be reduced to any simple notion of 'Americanization'.

References

Appadurai, A. ed. 1986. *The social life of things*. Cambridge: University of Cambridge Press.
Appadurai, A. 1996. *Modernity at large: cultural dimensions of globalization*. Minneapolis: University of Minnesota Press.
Appadurai, A. and Breckenridge, C.A. 1988. Why public culture? *Public Culture* 1: 5–9.
Bailey, A.J., Wright, R.A., Mountz, A. and Miyares, I.M. 2002. (Re)-producing Salvadoran transnational geographies. *Annals, Association of American Geographers* 92: 125–44.
Ballard, R. ed. 1994. *Desh Pardesh: the South Asian presence in Britain*. London: C. Hurst.
Basch, L., Glick Schiller, N. and Szanton-Blanc, C. 1994. *Nations unbound: transnational projects, postcolonial predicaments and deterritorialized nation-states*. Langhorne, PA: Gordon & Breach.
Beaverstock, J.V. and Boardwell, J.T. 2000. Negotiating globalization, transnational corporations and global city financial centres in transient migration studies. *Applied Geography* 20: 277–304.
Brah, A. 1996. *Cartographies of diaspora: contesting identities*. London: Routledge.
Castells, M. 1989. *The informational city*. Oxford: Basil Blackwell.
Castells, M. 1996. *The rise of the network society: the informational age: economy, society and culture, vol. I*. Oxford: Basil Blackwell.
Clifford, J. 1997. *Routes: travel and translation in the late twentieth century*. Cambridge, MA: Harvard University Press.

Cohen, R. 1997. *Global diasporas: an introduction*. London: UCL Press.

Cook, I. and Crang, P. 1996. The world on a plate: culinary culture, displacement and geographical knowledges. *Journal of Material Culture* 1: 131–53.

Crang, P. 1992. The politics of polyphony: on reconfigurations in geographical authority. *Environment and Planning D: Society and Space* 10: 527–49.

Crang, P. 1996. Displacement, consumption and identity. *Environment and Planning A* 28: 47–67.

Crang, P., Dwyer, C. and Jackson, P. 2003. Transnationalism and the spaces of commodity culture. *Progress in Human Geography* 27: 438–56.

Dicken, P. 1986. *Global shift*. London: Harper & Row.

Dwyer, C. and Crang, P. 2002. Fashioning identities: the commercial spaces of multi-culture. *Ethnicities* 2: 410–30.

Dwyer, C. and Jackson, P. 2003. Commodifying difference: selling EASTern fashion. *Environment and Planning D: Society and Space* 21: 269–91.

Escobar, A. 2001. Culture sits in places: reflections on globalism and subaltern strategies of localization. *Political Geography* 20: 139–74.

Falk, R. 1993. The making of global citizenship, in J. Brecher, J.B. Childs and J. Cutler eds. *Global visions: beyond the new world order*. Boston: South End Press, 39–50.

Foner, N. 1997. What's new about transnationalism? New York immigrants today and at the turn of the century. *Diaspora* 6: 355–75.

Giddens, A. 1996. Affluence, poverty and the idea of a post-scarcity society. *Development and Change* 27: 365–77.

Gillespie, M. 1995. *Television, ethnicity and cultural change*. London: Routledge.

Glick Schiller, N. 1997. The situation of transnational studies. *Identities* 4: 155–66.

Glick Schiller, N., Basch, L. and Blanc-Szanton, C. 1992. Transnationalism: a new analytical framework for understanding migration, in N. Glick Schiller, L. Basch and C. Blanc-Szanton eds. *Towards a transnational perspective on migration*. New York: New York Academy of Sciences, 1–24.

Goldberg, B. 1992. Historical reflections on transnationalism, race and the American immigrants saga, in N. Glick Schiller, L. Basch and C. Blanc-Szanton eds. *Towards a transnational perspective on migration*. New York: New York Academy of Sciences, 201–16.

Grewal, I. and Kaplan, C. eds. 1994. *Scattered hegemonies: postmodernity and trans-national feminist practices*. Minneapolis: University of Minnesota Press.

Guarnizo, L.E. and Smith, M.P. 1998. The locations of transnationalism, in M.P. Smith and L.E. Guarnizo eds. *Transnationalism from below*. New Brunswick, NJ: Transaction Publishers, 3–34.

Gupta, A. and Ferguson, J. 1992. Beyond 'culture': space, identity, and the politics of difference. *Cultural Anthropology* 7: 6–23.

Hannerz, U. 1996. *Transnational connections*. London: Routledge.

hooks, b. 1992. *Black looks: race and representation*. London: Turnaround.

Hutnyk, J. 2000. *Critique of exotica: music, politics and the culture industry*. London: Pluto.

Jones, D. 1992. Which migrant? temporary or permanent?, in N. Glick Schiller, L. Basch and C. Blanc-Szanton eds. *Towards a transnational perspective on migration*. New York: New York Academy of Sciences, 217–24.

Kaplan, C. 1995. 'A world without boundaries': the Body Shop's trans/national geographics. *Social Text* 43: 45–66.

Kearney, M. 1995. The local and the global: the anthropology of globalization and transnationalism. *Annual Review of Anthropology* 24: 547–65.

King, A.D. ed. 1991. *Culture, globalization and the world-system.* Binghampton: State University of New York Press.

Kong, L. 1999a. Globalisation, transmigration and the renegotiation of ethnic identity, in K. Olds, P. Dicken, P.K. Kelly, L. Kong and H. Wai-chung eds. *Globalisation and the Asia-Pacific: contested territories.* London: Routledge, 219–37.

Kong, L. 1999b. Globalisation and Singaporean transmigration: re-imagining and negotiating national identity. *Political Geography* 18: 563–89.

Lefebvre, H. 1991. *The production of space.* Oxford: Basil Blackwell.

LiPuma, E. 1997. History, identity and encompassment: nation-making in the Solomon Islands. *Identities* 4: 213–44.

Mahler, S.J. 1998. Theoretical and empirical contributions toward a research agenda for transnationalism, in M.P. Smith and L.E. Guarnizo eds. *Transnationalism from below.* New Brunswick, NJ: Transaction Publishers, 64–100.

Marcus, G.E. 1995. Ethnography in/of the world system: the emergence of multi-sited ethnography. *Annual Review of Anthropology* 24: 95–117.

Massey, D. 1994. *Space, place and gender.* Cambridge: Polity.

Mauthner, N.S. and Doucet, A. 2003. Reflexive accounts and accounts of reflexivity in qualitative data analysis. *Sociology* 37: 413–31.

Miller, D. ed. 1995. *Worlds apart: modernity through the prism of the local.* London: Routledge.

Miller, D. 1997. *Capitalism: an ethnographic approach.* Oxford: Berg.

Miller Matthei, L. 1998. Boyz 'n the 'Hood? Garifuna labor migration and transnational identity, in M.P. Smith and L.E. Guarnizo eds. *Transnationalism from below.* New Brunswick, NJ: Transaction Publishers, 270–90.

Mitchell, K. 1993. Multiculturalism, or the united colors of capitalism? *Antipode* 25: 263–94.

Mitchell, K. 1997a. Different diasporas and the hype of hybridity. *Environment and Planning D: Society and Space* 15: 533–53.

Mitchell, K. 1997b. Transnational discourse: bringing geography back in, *Antipode* 29: 101–14.

Nyberg Sørensen, N. 1998. Narrating identity across Dominican worlds, in M.P. Smith and L.E. Guarnizo eds. *Transnationalism from below.* New Brunswick, NJ: Transaction Publishers, 241–69.

Ong, A. and Nonini, D.M. eds. 1997. *Ungrounded empires: the cultural politics of modern Chinese transnationalism.* London: Routledge.

Portes, A. 1997. *Globalization from below: the rise of transnational communities.* ESRC Transnational Communities Programme Working Paper No. 1 (available at http://www.transcomm.ox.ac.uk).

Portes, A., Guarnizo, L.E. and Landolt, P. 1999. Introduction: pitfalls and promise of an emergent research field. *Ethnic and Racial Studies* 22: 217–37.

Pratt, M.L. 1992. *Imperial eyes: travel writing and transculturation.* London: Routledge.

Root, D. 1996. *Cannibal culture: art, appropriation, and the commodification of difference.* Oxford: Westview Press.

Rose, G. 1997. Situating knowledges: positionalities, reflexivities and other tactics. *Progress in Human Geography* 21: 305–20.

Rouse, R. 1991. Mexican migration and the social space of postmodernism. *Diaspora: A Journal of Transnational Studies* 1: 8–23.

Rouse, R. 1995. Questions of identity: personhood and collectivity in transnational migration to the United States. *Critique of Anthropology* 15: 351–80.

Smith, M.P. 2001. *Transnational urbanism: locating globalization.* Oxford: Basil Blackwell.

Smith, M.P. and Guarnizo, L.E. eds. 1998. *Transnationalism from below.* New Brunswick, NJ: Transaction.

Thomas, N. 1991. *Entangled objects: exchange, material culture and colonialism in the Pacific.* Cambridge, MA: Harvard University Press.

Vertovec, S. 1997. Three meanings of 'diaspora', exemplified among South Asian religions. *Diaspora* 6: 277–99.

Vertovec, S. 1999. Conceiving and researching transnationalism. *Ethnic and Racial Studies* 22: 447–62.

Watts, M.J. 1996. Mapping identities: place, space, and community in an African city, in P. Yaeger ed. *The geography of identity.* Ann Arbor: University of Michigan Press, 59–97.

Westland, E. 2002. D.H. Lawrence's Cornwall: dwelling in a precarious age. *Cultural Geographies* 9: 266–85.

Wilson, R. and Dissanayake, D. eds. 1996. *Global/local: cultural production and the transnational imaginary.* Durham, NC: Duke University Press.

Yeung, H.W.-C. 1998. *Transnational corporations and business networks.* London: Routledge.

1   Mexican migration and the social space of postmodernism†

Roger Rouse

In a hidden sweatshop in downtown Los Angeles, Asian and Latino migrants produce automobile parts for a factory in Detroit. As the parts leave the production line, they are stamped 'Made in Brazil'.[1] In a small village in the heart of Mexico, a young woman at her father's wake wears a black T-shirt sent to her by a brother in the United States. The shirt bears a legend that some of the mourners understand but she does not. It reads, 'Let's Have Fun Tonight!' And on the Tijuana-San Diego border, Guillermo Gómez-Peña, a writer originally from Mexico City, reflects on the time he has spent in what he calls 'the gap between two worlds':

> Today, eight years after my departure, when they ask me for my nation-ality or ethnic identity, I cannot answer with a single word, for my 'identity' now possesses multiple repertoires: I am Mexican but I am also Chicano and Latin American. On the border they call me 'chilango' or 'mexiquillo'; in the capital, 'pocho' or 'norteño', and in Spain 'sudaca'. ... My companion Emily is Anglo-Italian but she speaks Spanish with an Argentinian accent. Together we wander through the ruined Babel that is our American postmodernity.[2]

I

We live in a confusing world, a world of crisscrossed economies, inter-secting systems of meaning, and fragmented identities. Suddenly, the comforting modern imagery of nation-states and national languages, of coherent communities and consistent subjectivities, of dominant centres and distant margins no longer seems adequate. Certainly, in my own discip-line of anthropology, there is a growing sense that our conventional means of representing both the worlds of those we study and the worlds that we ourselves inhabit have been strained beyond their limits by the changes that are taking place around us. Indeed, the very notion that ethnographers and their subjects exist in readily separable domains is increasingly being called into question.[3] But the problem is not confined to a single discipline, nor

† This paper was originally published in 1991.

even to the academy at large. As Fredric Jameson has observed, the gradual unfolding of the global shift from colonialism and classic forms of dependency to a new transnational capitalism has meant that, during the last 20 years, we have all moved irrevocably into a new kind of social space, one which our modern sensibilities leave us unable to comprehend. With appropriate dramatic flair, he calls this new terrain 'postmodern hyperspace'.[4]

Jameson suggests that, in order to locate ourselves in this new space, we must make two moves. First, to understand why the crisis in spatial representation exists, we must identify as clearly as possible the broad politico-economic changes that have undermined the verisimilitude of existing images, and second, to understand where we are and where we can go from here, we must develop new images, new coordinates, a series of new and more effective maps. Jameson seeks to construct these alternative images through a critical reading of aesthetic forms such as novels, buildings, paintings, and films. But his focus seems unduly narrow. Given the ubiquity of the changes he describes and the profundity of their influence, the raw materials for a new cartography ought to be equally discoverable in the details of people's daily lives. And, from a radical perspective, the most significant materials surely lie in the circumstances and experiences of those working-class groups whose members have been most severely affected by the changing character of capitalist exploitation.[5]

In this chapter, I will develop these ideas by drawing on my work with rural Mexicans involved in migration to and from the United States. After outlining the images conventionally used to map the social terrain they inhabit, I will first build on their experiences to suggest new images better suited to charting their current circumstances and then indicate how these images may, in fact, be increasingly useful to us all as we try to map social landscapes found throughout Mexico and the United States.

II

Two socio-spatial images have dominated the modern discourse of the social sciences concerning the people of rural Mexico. I claim neither novelty nor insight for recognizing their influence. By underlining their importance and delineating their attendant assumptions, however, I hope to make it easier to understand both the nature of their limitations and the significance of the alternatives I shall propose.

The first image is one to which I shall attach the label 'community'.[6] The abstract expression of an idealized nation-state, it has been used concretely at numerous different levels, from the peasant village to the nation itself. It combines two main ideas.[7] First, it identifies a discriminable population with a single, bounded space – a territory or place. In so doing, it assumes that the social relationships in which community members participate will be much more intense within this space than beyond. It also assumes that members will treat the place of the community as the principal environment to which they adjust their actions and, correspondingly, that they will monitor local events much more closely than developments further afield. Second, the image implies a certain commonality and coherence, generally expressed either in the functionalist dream of an entity whose institutional parts fit together neatly to form an integrated whole or in the structural-functionalist vision of a shared way of life that exists not only in a multiplicity of similar actions but, more profoundly, in a single and internally consistent set of rules, values, or beliefs. From the perspective that these two ideas establish, the heterogeneities and complexities of the worlds we actually encounter are normally understood in terms of either superficial interactions between distinct communities or transitional moments in the movement from one form of integrity and order to another.

The second image is one that I shall label 'centre/periphery'.[8] The abstract expression of an idealized imperial system, it too has been realized concretely at many different levels, from the rural town to the entire world system. This image involves three main ideas. First, it suggests that differences are organized concentrically around a dominant core. Thus, power and wealth are greatest at the centre and diminish gradually as one moves outwards through a series of surrounding zones, and different locations are associated with different ways of life according to the zone in which they are found. Second, the image implies a process of change in which the centre exercises a privileged capacity to shape outcomes, whether it is extending its influence to the margins or moulding people from the periphery who enter its terrain. And third, it suggests that fields ordered in this way are autonomous: each peripheral site is orientated to a single centre and each centre is independent of all others at the same level.

In many ways, these images are opposed. Formally, the idea of community tends to privilege homogeneity and stasis while the idea of centre/periphery privileges variation and change. And, in practice, they have frequently been used against one another, community being the principal socio-spatial image invoked by modernization theory and centre/periphery, of course, serving as a crucial counter-image for dependency theory and the world systems approach. But their opposition should not be exaggerated. In many works they have been used in tandem and, in fact, the key tension between modernization theory and its critics lies less in frictions over spatial imagery than in disagreements about the intentions of the centre and the nature of its influence.[9] Indeed, even when the two images have been in conflict, they have supported one another negatively, each being treated as the only viable alternative to the other. Opposed, combined, or alternating, they have long dominated work on rural Mexico with the casual authority of the commonsensical.

Migration has always had the potential to challenge established spatial images. It highlights the social nature of space as something created and reproduced through collective human agency and, in so doing, reminds us that, within the limits imposed by power, existing spatial arrangements are always susceptible to change. In practice, however, academics dealing with Mexican migration have rarely used it as the basis for a critical reappraisal of existing images. Instead, with a few notable exceptions, they have simply adapted the existing repertoire to make it fit the peculiarities of a mobile population. This is particularly apparent in the way they have used frameworks derived from the image of community to understand the experiences of the migrants themselves.

First, because migration is self-evidently a movement between places, it has commonly been treated as a movement from one set of social relationships to another. Thus, numerous studies have sought to gauge the changes that migrants have undergone by comparing the systems of family organization, kinship, and friendship dominant in their places of origin with those they have developed in the places to which they have moved.[10]

Second, as a movement between places, migration has also commonly been treated as a shift from one significant environment to another. Within a bipolar framework variously organized around oppositions between the rural and the urban, the traditional and the modern, and Mexico and the United States, many studies have examined how migrants take practices and attitudes adjusted to their original 'niche' or setting and adapt them to the new locale in which they find themselves.[11]

And third, as a move between communities identified with distinct ways of life, migration has normally been seen as a process in which the migrants and their descendants experience a more or less gradual shift from one ordered arrangement to another, either fully converting to the dominant way of life or forging their own form of accommodation in an ordered synthesis of old and new. Such a perspective does recognize that contradictions can arise when people combine attitudes and practices associated with the place to which they have moved with others linked to their place of origin, but it has generally dealt with these in ways that sustain the primacy of order, treating them either as incongruities in form that disappear when viewed in terms of function or as temporary features peculiar to transitional situations. In the latter case, it has been particularly common to locate the contradictions within a widely used model of generational succession according to which the migrants themselves retain much of what they learned while growing up, they and their children balance traditional attitudes and practices maintained in intimate arenas such as the home and the ethnic neighbourhood with others more appropriate to participation in the wider society, and a consistent socio-cultural orientation appears only in the third generation.[12]

These ways of construing migration have faced a qualified challenge from accounts that treat it principally as a circular process in which people remain orientated to the places from which they have come. Under such circumstances, the patterns of social and cultural adjustment are clearly different.[13] But it is important to stress that the basic socio-spatial assumptions remain the same. As in accounts that emphasize a unidirectional shift, migrants are held to move between distinct, spatially demarcated communities and, in the long run, to be capable of maintaining an involvement in only one of them.

III

In recent years, however, this mobilization of modern socio-spatial images has become increasingly unable to contain the postmodern complexities that it confronts. Symptomatic of the unfolding shift to transnational capitalism, migration between rural Mexico and the United States since the Second World War, and especially since the mid-1960s, has been obliging us ever more insistently to develop an alternative cartography of social space. I can elaborate this argument most effectively by drawing on the case that I know best, the United States-bound migration that has been taking place since the early 1940s from the rural *municipio* of Aguililla in the southwest corner of the state of Michoacán.[14]

At first sight, Aguililla seems to be an isolated community dedicated to small-scale farming and manifestly part of the Mexican periphery. The *municipio* is located in the mountains that form the southern limit of the west-central region; its administrative centre, also known as Aguililla, lies at the end of a poor dirt road, one of those points where the national transport system finally exhausts itself; the land has been used principally for the subsistence-orientated production of basic foodstuffs and the raising of livestock; and trade with the interior has been limited. It is the kind of place onto which urban dwellers find it easy to project their fantasies of difference and danger.

But appearances can be deceptive. Aguililla's growing involvement in transnational migration has profoundly changed both its economic orientation and its socio-spatial relationships. By the early 1980s, when I carried out fieldwork in the *municipio*, it had come to operate largely as a nursery and nursing home for wage-labourers in the United States. Almost every family had members who were or had been abroad; the local economy depended heavily on the influx of dollars; and many of the area's small farming operations continued only because they were sustained by migrant remittances. Concomitantly, the *municipio* has become part of a transnational network of settlements and, in so doing, has significantly modified its status as a marginal site within a purely national hierarchy of places. Over the years, migrants have established several outposts in the United States, by far the largest being the one they have formed amidst a rapidly growing Latino neighbourhood in Redwood City, an urban area on the northern edge of California's famous Silicon Valley. There they now work principally in the service sector, as janitors, dishwashers, gardeners, hotel workers, house cleaners, and child minders – proletarian servants in the paragon of 'postindustrial' society. Some Aguilillans have settled in Redwood City for long periods, but few abandon the *municipio* forever. Most people stay in the United States relatively briefly, almost all of those who stay longer continue to keep in touch with the people and places they have left behind, and even those who have been away for many years quite often return.

This pattern of migration must be understood as symptomatic of the way in which broad politico-economic developments involved in the unfolding of transnational capitalism have refracted themselves through the specificities of local circumstance. For many years, Aguilillans have placed a heavy emphasis on the capacity to create and maintain small-scale, family-run operations, ideally based in land, and, in relation to this goal, the broad developments have exerted contradictory pressures.

In the *municipio*, the nationwide diversion of capital to industry and commercial agriculture that has taken place since the 1940s has left the local economy without needed infrastructure, while the concentration of what government spending there has been in health and education has encouraged population growth and the broadening of people's horizons. As a result, it has become impossible for most Aguilillans to approach the realization of their goals solely through access to local resources. At the same time, however, the lack of large-scale land acquisitions in the *municipio* by commercially orientated owners, the periodic provision of small amounts of government aid to the area's farmers, and the entrepreneurial opportunities provided by the influx of dollars have all impeded full proletarianization. This, in turn, has meant that the old goals have not been abandoned and that migration has been seen principally as a way of raising outside funds to finance their local realization.[15]

Meanwhile, in the United States, the growing polarization of the labour market has created a mounting demand for Mexican workers to fill the bottom layers in agriculture, deskilled assembly, and, above all, services. Yet various factors have discouraged most Mexicans from staying permanently. In the case of Aguilillans, their cultural emphasis on creating and maintaining independent operations has led them to have deep-seated reservations about many aspects of life in the United States, prominent among them the obligation of proletarian workers to submit to the constant regulation of supervisors and the clock. In addition, the disappearance of many middle-level jobs and the attendant change in the shape of the labour market – from pyramid to hourglass – have made it increasingly difficult for people to see chances of upward mobility for themselves or, perhaps more significantly, for their children. And finally, the economy's steady downturn since the mid-1960s has markedly increased both the hostility and the legal restrictions that many of the migrants face.[16]

Influenced by these contradictory developments, Aguilillans have forged socio-spatial arrangements that seriously challenge the dominant ways of reading migration. First, it has become inadequate to see Aguilillan migration as a movement between distinct communities, understood as the loci of distinct sets of social relationships. Today, Aguilillans find that their most important kin and friends are as likely to be living hundreds or thousands of miles away as immediately around them. More significantly, they are often able to maintain these spatially extended relationships as actively and effectively as the ties that link them to their neighbours. In this regard, growing access to the telephone has been particularly significant, allowing people not just to keep in touch periodically but to contribute to decision-making and participate in familial events even from a considerable distance.

Indeed, through the continuous circulation of people, money, goods, and information, the various settlements have become so closely woven together that, in an important sense, they have come to constitute a single community spread across a variety of sites, something I refer to as a 'transnational migrant circuit'. Although the Aguilillan case undoubtedly has its local peculiarities, there is evidence that such arrangements are becoming increasingly important in the organization of Mexican migration to and from the United States.[17] Just as capitalists have responded to the new forms of economic internationalism by establishing transnational corporations, so workers have responded by creating transnational circuits.[18]

At the same time, as a result of these developments, it has become equally inadequate to see Aguilillan migration as a movement between distinct environments. Today, it is the circuit as a whole rather than any one locale that constitutes the principal setting in relation to which Aguilillans orchestrate their lives.[19] Those living in Aguililla, for example, are as much affected by events in Redwood City as by developments in the *municipio* itself, and the same is true in reverse. Consequently, people monitor what is happening in the other parts of the circuit as closely as they monitor what is going on immediately around them. Indeed, it is only by recognizing the transnational framework within which Aguilillans are operating that we can properly appreciate the logic of their actions. Thus, people in the United States may spend large amounts of time and money trying to obtain papers without ever seeking citizenship because it is as Mexican citizens with the right to 'permanent residence' that they will be best equipped to move back and forth between the two countries. And they may send their children back to Mexico to complete their education or to visit during school vacations at least in part because they want to endow them with the bilingual and bicultural skills necessary to operate effectively on both sides of the border.

Finally, it is a mistake to see Aguilillan experiences in terms of an inexorable move towards a new form of socio-cultural order. Although transnational migration has brought distant worlds into immediate juxtaposition, their proximity has produced neither homogenization nor synthesis. Instead, Aguilillans have become involved in the chronic maintenance of two quite distinct ways of life. More importantly, the resulting contradictions have not come simply from the persistence of past forms amid contemporary adjustments or from involvement in distinct lifeworlds within the United States. Rather, they reflect the fact that Aguilillans see their current lives and future possibilities as involving simultaneous engagements in places associated with markedly different forms of experience. Moreover, the way in which at least some people are preparing their children to operate within a dichotomized setting spanning national borders suggests that current contradictions will not be resolved through a simple process of generational succession.

The different ways of life that Aguilillans balance can be understood partly by reference to spatially demarcated national or local cultures, but they should also be understood in terms of class. In numerous combinations, Aguilillans have come to link proletarian labour with a sustained attachment to the creation of small-scale, family-based operations; and even though these ways of making a living may be reconcilable economically, in cultural terms they are fundamentally distinct, involving quite different attitudes and practices concerning the use of time and space, the conduct of social relationships, and the orchestration of appearances.[20] Indeed, one of the main considerations preserving the polarized relationship between Aguililla and Redwood City has been the fact that the latter has offered Aguilillans so few opportunities to create independent operations while the former, partly through the continued influx of remittances, has remained a place in which such opportunities are still available.

Obliged to live within a transnational space and to make a living by combining quite different forms of class experience, Aguilillans have become skilled exponents of a cultural bi-focality that defies reduction to a singular order. Indeed, in many respects, Aguilillans have come to inhabit a kind of border zone, especially if we follow Américo Paredes in recognizing that a border is 'not simply a line on a map but, more fundamentally, . . . a sensitized area where two cultures or two political systems come face to face'.[21] Socio-economically, the relationship between Aguililla and Redwood City is strikingly similar to the relationship along the international border between twinned cities such as Ciudad Juárez and El Paso or Matamoros and Brownsville. They are mutually implicated in numerous ways, but the line between them never disappears. And culturally, life within the circuit corresponds closely to the situation that Gómez-Peña describes for the border linking Tijuana and San Diego: 'In my fractured reality, but reality nonetheless, live two histories, languages, cosmogonies, artistic traditions, and political systems dramatically opposed – the border is the continuous confrontation of two or more referential codes'.[22] For many years, the United States–Mexican border seemed like a peculiar space, a narrow strip quite different from what lay at the heart of the two countries. But this is no longer the case. Ties such as those between Aguililla and Redwood City, places two thousand miles apart, prompt us to ask how wide this border has become and how peculiar we should consider its characteristics.

IV

Socio-spatial frames derived from the image of the community no longer serve to represent the local terrain that Aguilillans inhabit. It seems that images such as those of the circuit and the border zone may be more appropriate. But these claims do not apply solely to small-scale settlements.

Partly as a result of the migration that Aguilillans exemplify, they are becoming increasingly relevant to social landscapes found throughout Mexico and the United States.

It is scarcely a revelation to suggest that Mexico's dependent status renders problematical any assumption of functional integration or the presence of a singular socio-cultural order. However, the shift to transnational capitalism has both intensified and changed the nature of national disarticulation, particularly during the last 20 years. Foreign capital plays a more significant role in Mexico than ever before, and, more critically, thanks to the rising use of offshore plants that carry out only a part of the production process and the growing ease with which these plants can be transferred to other underdeveloped countries, the ties linking foreign capital to the rest of Mexican society are becoming progressively weaker. Moreover, as the massive flight of domestic capital during the last few years illustrates only too well, the Mexican bourgeoisie is also orchestrating its actions increasingly within a transnational framework. At the same time, the growing institutionalization of migration to the United States through the medium of transnational circuits means that more of the Mexican population is orientated to developments outside the country and that this orientation is becoming steadily more pronounced. And finally because of the expansion of a television system that carries numerous US programmes, the mounting of satellite dishes that tune directly into US broadcasts, and the increasing exposure to US ways of life through migration, foreign cultural influences are becoming rapidly more pervasive. The black T-shirt with its English exhortation, defying any attempt to read the wake as the textual expression of a coherent local culture, is emblematic of a process pervading rural Mexico.

What is perhaps more striking is that a similar kind of disarticulation is beginning to appear in the United States, particularly in its major cities. The United States economy, long dominated by domestic capital, is now increasingly influenced by transnationally orchestrated foreign investment, especially from Britain, Canada, Germany, the Netherlands, and Japan.[23] As regards labour, although immigrant workers have been an important factor for many years, they are today arriving under circumstances that distance them much more fully from the rest of society. In particular, the declining availability of those middle-level jobs that once encouraged hope of upward mobility, the increased scapegoating and legal restrictions that have accompanied economic decline since the mid-1960s, and the related development of transnational circuits are all serving to subvert the older possibilities of assimilation to a single national order. And partly as a result, ways of life commonly identified with the Third World are becoming increasingly apparent in a country often treated as the apogee of First World advancement. Extreme poverty, residential overcrowding and homelessness, underground economies, new forms of domestic service, and sweatshops exist side by side with yuppie affluence, futuristic office blocks, and all the other accoutrements of high-tech post-industrialism.

Los Angeles is by no means typical, but the situation that had developed there by the mid-1980s offers a suggestive outline of emerging possibilities. In the downtown area, 75% of the buildings were owned wholly or in part by foreign capital, and as much as 90% of new multi-storey construction was being financed by investment from abroad.[24] In the larger conurbation, 40% of the population belonged to ethnic 'minorities', many of them migrants from Asia and Latin America (estimates suggest that the figure will approach 60% by the year 2010).[25] And throughout the region, the growing contrasts between rich and poor and their increasingly apparent juxtaposition were prompting journalists to speculate about the 'Brazilian-ization' of the city.[26] The hidden sweatshop in the heart of the metropolis, defying any attempt to claim a comfortable distance between Third World and First, calls attention to a trend that is gradually if unevenly affecting the whole of the country.[27]

Thus, in the United States as well as in Mexico, the *place* of the putative community – whether regional or national – is becoming little more than a *site* in which transnationally organized circuits of capital, labour, and communications intersect with one another and with local ways of life. In these circumstances, it becomes increasingly difficult to delimit a singular national identity and a continuous history, and the claims of politicians to speak authoritatively on behalf of this imagined community and its purported interests become increasingly hollow. But it is not just the image of the community which is compromised. The image of centre and periphery is also coming under increasing strain. United States capital increasingly intersects with capital from other core countries not only in peripheral areas such as Mexico but also in the United States itself. The growing influence of foreign investment means that, in both countries, people must accommodate themselves to a capital that is increasingly heteroglot and culturally diverse. And the concentric distribution of differ-ences in power, wealth, and ways of life is breaking down, in large part because the United States no longer works as effectively to transform those who enter its terrain. Alongside the more familiar tale of capitalist penetration in the periphery, we are beginning to witness what Renato Rosaldo has called 'the implosion of the Third World into the first', or what Saskia Sassen-Koob calls 'peripheralization at the core'.[28]

One of the results of these developments is that we are seeing a prolifer-ation of border zones. The international border is widening and, at the same time, miniature borders are erupting throughout the two countries. In Mexico, the provisions granting special tariff dispensations to offshore production have stretched and distended the border for capital, especially now that the offshore plants, first established in the northern part of the country, are steadily moving southwards. At the same time, in the United States, the provisions regarding employer sanctions in the new immigration law have exploded the border for labour and relocated it in a multitude of fragments at the entrance to every workplace, while the recent amnesty has encouraged transnationally orientated migrants to extend their presence

throughout the country. Moreover, the most readily dramatized juxtapositions of citizens and migrants are no longer confined to major urban sites
such as downtown Los Angeles. They are also beginning to appear on
the margins of suburbia as members of the native middle classes, scared
by the real and imagined violence of these inner-city border zones, are
developing residential enclaves in rural areas long inhabited by migrant
farm workers.

Conditions in northern San Diego County illustrate the last of these
trends in a particularly vivid way. Here, against the background of a
burgeoning military-industrial economy, rapidly expanding middle-class
suburbs have recently encroached on areas long filled with the ramshackle
encampments of Latino migrants. In the words of the *Los Angeles Times*,
the result has been a world where 'squalid, plywood and cardboard hooches
sit in the shadow of million-dollar mansions, where the BMW and Volvo
sets rub elbows at the supermarket with dusty migrants fresh from the
fields'. Put more pithily by an academic familiar with the area, 'What you
have . . . is the first of the First World intermixing with the last of the Third
World. It's Nicaragua versus Disneyland'. Or, as one local suburban
resident observed, 'It's like we're living in the Third World here. It doesn't
seem to me that this is part of the American Dream'.[29]

But these collisions and complaints are not the only markers of a newly
emerging border zone. One man in a local trailer park, offended by migrants
taking water from his spigot, put barbed wire on the chain-link fence behind
his trailer, installed a set of floodlights, and armed himself with a 12-gauge
shotgun.[30] Other residents have hunted migrants with paint-pellet guns
and run them down with trucks. And, in November 1988, a local youth
went one step further, shooting and killing two Latinos after confronting
them near the camps. Asked to explain his actions, he said simply that he
hated Mexicans.[31] This is Nicaragua versus Disneyland, then, not simply
as Latino versus Anglo or Third World versus First but as the savage
implosion of frontline violence within the sanitized dream-worlds of
middle-class escape.

V

The forces shaping Aguilillans' lives are thus coming to affect everyone who inhabits the terrain encompassed by Mexico and the United
States. Throughout this fractured territory, transnationalism, contradictions
in development, and increasingly polarized economies are stretching
images of community beyond their limits, bringing different ways of
life into vivid, often violent juxtaposition, and encouraging the chronic
reproduction of their incongruities. The impact of these changes clearly
varies with the circumstances of the people they affect, but their reach
is increasingly broad.

Under such circumstances, images such as the circuit and the border zone
may help us understand not only the specificities of Aguilillan experience

but social landscapes increasingly familiar to us all. If this is true, it adds weight to the idea that, in our attempts to orientate ourselves amidst the complexities of postmodern hyperspace, we should look not only to art and literature but also to the lives of those 'ordinary' people who inscribe their transient texts in the minutiae of daily experience. And this, in turn, suggests a pleasing irony with which to conclude, for it implies that, as in the case of Aguilillans and others like them, people long identified with an unworkable past may in fact be those from whom we have most to learn as we try to chart our way through the confusions of the present towards a future we can better understand and thus more readily transform.

Acknowledgements

The first version of this paper was written in early 1988 while I was a visiting research fellow at the Center for US–Mexican Studies, University of California, San Diego. It draws on fieldwork carried out between 1982 and 1984 under a doctoral fellowship from the Inter-American Foundation. I am grateful to both organizations for their support. Many of the ideas contained in the paper were developed in a study group on postmodernism organized with colleagues from the center. My principal thanks – for comments, criticisms, and immensely pleasant company – go to the group's members: Josefina Alcazar, Alberto Aziz, Roger Bartra, Luin Goldring, Lidia Pico, Claudia Schatán, and Francisco Valdés. I have also benefited from Khachig Tölölyan's sensitive reading of the text.

Notes

1 See Lockwood and Leinberger (1988: 35). The assertion of a false point of origin is apparently used so that the manufacturers can participate in foreign delivery contracts. See Soja (1989: 217).
2 'Hoy, ocho años de mi partida, cuando me preguntan por mi nacionalidad o identidad étnica, no puedo responder con una palabra, pues mi "identidad" ya posee repertorios múltiples: soy mexicano pero tambien soy chicano y latinoamericano. En la frontera me dicen "chilango" o "mexiquillo"; en la capital "pocho" o "norteño" y en España "sudaca." . . . Mi compañera Emilia es angloitaliana pero habla español con acento argentino; y juntos caminamos entre los escombros de la torre de Babel de nuestra posmodernidad americana' (Gómez-Peña 1987, my translation).
3 See, for example, Clifford (1986: 22) and Rosaldo (1989: 217).
4 Jameson (1984: 83). Like Jameson, I find it useful to follow Ernest Mandel in arguing for the emergence since the Second World War of a new phase in monopoly capitalism, but I prefer to label this phase 'transnational' rather than 'late' partly to avoid the implication of imminent transcendence and, more positively, to emphasize the crucial role played by the constant movement of capital, labour, and information across national borders.
5 See Davis (1985) and Lipsitz (1986–7, esp. 161).
6 It is important to stress that I am concerned not with the various meanings of this particular term but, instead, with the image itself. The term serves merely as a convenient marker.
7 See Williams (1976: 65–6).

8 Williams (1976: 65–6).
9 The combination of these images is readily apparent in the classic works on rural social organization by Robert Redfield and Eric Wolf (*The little community and peasant society and culture*, 1966 and 'Types of Latin American peasantry', 1955), both of whom draw heavily on Mexican materials, and can also be seen in Immanuel Wallerstein's tendency (in *The capitalist world economy*, 1979) to use nation-states as the constituent units of his world system, at least in the core.
10 This approach has been used in two related but different kinds of study. In work focusing on migration itself – especially on migration within Mexico – changes have commonly been gauged by comparing the forms of organization found in the points of destination with arrangements revealed by detailed research in the specific communities from which the migrants have come. See, for example, Butterworth (1962), Kemper (1977), and Lewis (1952). In work on communities known to contain a significant number of migrants and descendants of migrants – and especially in work on Mexican and Chicano communities in the United States – it has been more common to compare forms of organization found in these communities with arrangements discovered secondhand through reading literature on the general areas or types of society from which the migrants have come. See, for example, Achor (1978), Horowitz (1983), Humphrey (1944), Madsen (1964), Rubel (1966), and Thurston (1974).
11 See, for example, Achor (1978), Madsen (1964), Rubel (1966), Lomnitz (1977), and Ugalde (1974).
12 This approach has been manifest most commonly in work on migration to the United States, where the dominant tendency has been to challenge assumptions about full assimilation with analyses that stress the more or less gradual emergence of ethnic subcultures. See, for example, Achor (1978), Horowitz (1983), Madsen (1964), and Rubel (1966).
13 See, for example, Piore (1979).
14 A more detailed account of the *municipio* and the history of its involvement in migration can be found in Rouse (1989b). A *municipio* is a relatively small administrative unit occupying the rung immediately below the level of the state. In 1960, for example, the *municipio* of Aguililla, covering an area of roughly 630 square miles, was one of 113 such entities within the state of Michoacán. The term is difficult to gloss with any precision, however. 'Municipality' is misleading because of its urban associations, while a gloss such as 'county' runs the risk of suggesting something too large and too powerful. Given these difficulties, I use the term in its un-translated form.
15 For a fuller understanding of the broad processes affecting rural Mexico over the last 40 years, see Cockcroft (1983), Hewitt de Alcántara (1976).
16 For a fuller understanding of the changing character of the United States economy, particularly since the 1960s, see Sassen (1988) and Davis (1986: 181–230).
17 Such evidence can be found most readily in a series of studies that have appeared during the 1980s charting the emergence of what are generally described as 'binational migrant networks'. See, for example, Baca and Bryan (1983), Kearney (1986), Massey *et al.* (1987), and Mines (1981).
18 I use the term 'transnational' in preference to 'binational' partly to evoke as directly as possible the association between migrant forms of organization and transnational corporations. ('Transnational' is gradually replacing the more popular adjective 'multinational', at least in academic discourse.) I also prefer it to 'binational' because it allows for the possibility that a circuit might include sites in more than two countries. Specifically in the case of Aguilillans, there are indications that this may be coming about as migrants from particular places in Central America arrive in the Redwood City area and gradually attach themselves to the Aguilillan circuit. One of the advantages of such an attachment is that,

if they need to leave the United States, they can go to Aguililla and call on social ties established there instead of having to make the longer, more expensive, and often more dangerous journey back to their own country. I use the term 'circuit' in preference to 'network' because it more effectively evokes the circulation of people, money, goods, and information, the pseudo-institutional nature of the arrangement (over purely individual ties), and the qualified importance of place (over purely social linkages). A fine analysis, sensitive to many of these issues, can be found in Kearney and Nagengast (1989).

19 For an account of the ways in which places linked by migration can come to form a single 'field of activity', see Roberts (1974, esp. 208–9).
20 These ideas are developed more fully in Rouse (1989a and 1989b).
21 Paredes (1978: 68). See also Rosaldo (1989, esp. 196–217).
22 'En mi realidad fracturada, paro realidad al fin, cohabitan dos historias, lenguajes, cosmogonías, tradicionas artísticas y sistemas políticos drásticamante opuestos (la frontera es el enfrentamiento continuo de dos o más códigos referenciales)' Gómez-Peña (1987: 3, my translation). I do not mean to suggest by quoting Gómez-Peña that he and Aguilillans experience their particular border zones in exactly the same way. Clearly, people's experiences vary significantly according to their positions in local frameworks of power and as a function of the routes they have followed in reaching such positions.
23 See Sassen (1988, esp. 171–85).
24 Davis (1987: 71–2) and Soja (1989: 221).
25 Lockwood and Leinberger (1988: 41). According to Soja (1989: 215), more than two million Third World migrants settled in the Los Angeles area between the mid-1960s and the mid-1980s.
26 See Richman and Schwartz (quoted in Davis 1987: 77).
27 For a fuller picture of the changing political economy of Los Angeles, see Davis (1985 and 1987), Sassen (1988: 126–70), and Soja (1989: 190–248). For reflections on these trends in other parts of the United States, see Franco (1985) and Koptiuch (1989).
28 Rosaldo (1988: 85) and Sassen-Koob (1982).
29 All three quotations come from Bailey and Reza (1988).
30 See Bailey (1988).
31 See Davidson (1990) and Mydans (1990).

References

Achor, S. 1978. *Mexican Americans in a Dallas barrio.* Tucson: University of Arizona Press.
Baca, R. and Bryan, D. 1983. The 'assimilation' of unauthorized Mexican workers: another social science fiction. *Hispanic Journal of Behavioral Sciences* 5: 1–20.
Bailey, E. 1988. Tempers flare over illegals in S.D. County. *Los Angeles Times* 6 June (San Diego County edition).
Bailey, E. and Reza, H.G. 1988. Illegals, homeless clash in S.D. County. *Los Angeles Times* 5 June (San Diego County edition).
Butterworth, D.S. 1962. A study of the urbanization process among Mixtec migrants from Tilaltongo in Mexico City. *América Indígena* 22: 257–74.
Clifford, J. 1986. Introduction: partial truths, in J. Clifford and G.E. Marcus eds. *Writing culture: the poetics and politics of ethnography.* Berkeley: University of California Press, 1–26.
Cockcroft, J. 1983. *Mexico: class formation, capital accumulation, and the state.* New York: Grove.
Davidson, M. 1990. Immigrant bashing: the Mexican border war. *The Nation* 12 November, 557–60.

38   *Roger Rouse*

Davis, M. 1985. Urban renaissance and the spirit of postmodernism. *New Left Review* 151: 106–13.

Davis, M. 1986. *Prisoners of the American dream: politics and economy in the history of the U.S. working class.* London: Verso.

Davis, M. 1987. 'Chinatown', part two? The 'internationalization' of downtown Los Angeles. *New Left Review* 164: 65–86.

Franco, J. 1985. New York is a Third World city: introduction. *Tabloid* 9: 12–13.

Gómez-Peña, G. 1987. Wacha esa border, son. *La Jornada Semanal* (Mexico City) 25 October: 3–5.

Hewitt de Alcántara, C. 1976. *Modernizing Mexican agriculture: socioeconomic implications of technological change, 1940–1970.* Geneva: UN Research Institute for Social Development.

Horowitz, R. 1983. *Honor and the American dream: culture and identity in a Chicano community.* New Brunswick, NJ: Rutgers University Press.

Humphrey, N.D. 1944. The changing structure of the Detroit Mexican family: an index of acculturation. *American Sociological Review* 9: 622–6.

Jameson, F. 1984. Postmodernism, or the cultural logic of late capitalism. *New Left Review* 146: 53–92.

Kearney, M. 1986. From the invisible hand to visible feet: anthropological studies of migration and development. *Annual Review of Anthropology* 15: 331–61.

Kearney, M. and Nagengast, C. 1989. *Anthropological perspectives on transnational communities in rural California.* Working Paper 3, Working Group on Farm Labor and Rural Poverty. Davis, CA: California Institute for Rural Studies.

Kemper, R.V. 1977. *Migration and adaptation: Tzintzuntzan peasants in Mexico City.* Beverly Hills: Sage.

Koptiuch, K. 1989. Third worlding at home. Department of Anthropology, University of Texas, Austin, unpublished manuscript.

Lewis, O. 1952. Urbanization without breakdown: a case study. *Scientific Monthly* 75: 31–41.

Lipsitz, G. 1986–7. Cruising around the Hispanic bloc: postmodernism and popular music in Los Angeles. *Cultural Critique* 5: 157–77.

Lockwood, C. and Leinberger, C.B. 1988. Los Angeles comes of age. *Atlantic Monthly* 261: 31–56.

Lomnitz, L.A. 1977. *Networks and marginality: life in a Mexican shantytown.* New York: Academic (trans. C. Lomnitz).

Madsen, W. 1964. *Mexican Americans of South Texas.* New York: Holt.

Massey, D.S., Alarcón, R., Durand, J. and González, H. 1987. *Return to Aztlán: the social process of international migration from western Mexico.* Berkeley: University of California Press.

Mines, R. 1981. *Developing a community tradition of migration: a field study in rural Zacatecas, Mexico and in California settlement areas.* La Jolla, CA: Program in US–Mexican Studies.

Mydans, S. 1990. Clash of cultures grows amid American dream. *New York Times* 26 March.

Paredes, A. 1978. The problem of identity in a changing culture: popular expressions of culture conflict along the Lower Rio Grande border, in S.R. Ross ed. *Views across the border: the United States and Mexico.* Albuquerque: University of New Mexico Press, 68–94.

Piore, M.J. 1979. *Birds of passage.* Cambridge: Cambridge University Press.

Redfield, R. 1966. *The little community and peasant society and culture.* Chicago: University of Chicago Press.

Richman, N. and Schwarz, R. 1987. Housing homeless families: why L.A. lags behind. *Los Angeles Times* 24 May.

Roberts, B. 1974. The interrelationships of city and provinces in Peru and Guatemala. *Latin American Urban Research* 4: 207–35.

Rosaldo, R. 1988. Ideology, place, and people without culture. *Cultural Anthropology* 3: 77–87.

Rosaldo, R. 1989. *Culture and truth: the remaking of social analysis.* Boston: Beacon.

Rouse, R. 1989a. Men in space: power and the appropriation of urban form among Mexican migrants in the United States. Department of Anthropology, University of Michigan, Ann Arbor, unpublished manuscript.

Rouse, R. 1989b. Mexican migration to the United States: family relations in the development of a transnational migrant circuit. Stanford University, unpublished PhD dissertation.

Rubel, A.J. 1966. *Across the tracks: Mexican-Americans in a Texas city.* Austin: University of Texas Press.

Sassen, S. 1988. *The mobility of labor and capital: a study in international investment and labor flow.* Cambridge: Cambridge University Press.

Sassen-Koob, S. 1982. Recomposition and peripheralization at the core. *Contemporary Marxism* 5: 88–100.

Soja, E.W. 1989. *Postmodern geographies: the reassertion of space in critical social theory.* London: Verso.

Thurston, R.G. 1974. *Urbanization and sociocultural change in a Mexican-American enclave.* San Francisco: R & E Research Associates.

Ugalde, A. 1974. *The urbanization process of a poor Mexican neighborhood.* Austin: Institute of Latin American Studies, University of Texas.

Wallerstein, I. 1979. *The capitalist world economy.* Cambridge: Cambridge University Press.

Williams, R. 1976. *Keywords.* London: Fontana.

Wolf, E. 1955. Types of Latin American peasantry: a preliminary discussion. *American Anthropologist* 57: 452–71.

2 It's hip to be Asian

The local and global networks of Asian fashion entrepreneurs in London

Parminder Bhachu

This chapter explores diasporic cultural production in global markets through the consumer cultural products of British Asian women and the diasporean aesthetics that govern their fashion styles.[1] I examine an aspect of their consumer material culture to read their cultural maps and the diasporic materialities they stitch in global markets. I explore an economy of clothes, the designs negotiated within it, and commerce around it, to point to the new rhythms involved in the commoditization of *salwaar-kameezes*, also referred to as Punjabi suits (and henceforth as suits).[2] These suits constitute a large domain of the gift exchanges within the wedding economy. In these cultural processes, I emphasize the agency of Asian women in transnational settings in their dialectic and dynamic suturing of global cultural landscapes through their commercial and cultural agency within this highly charged consumer material culture of what were previously considered to be 'straightforward ethnic' clothes. This chapter focuses, in particular, on the commoditization processes involved in the production of the *salwaar-kameez* suits which are very semiotically charged and powerfully coded attire and a significant domain of the wedding economy (Bhachu 1994, 1996, 1997, 2004). They have become high-fashion garments globally and reflect the whole taxonomy of styles and fashion geographies – both those local to the Indian scene and those generated through the multiple diasporic consciousnesses that define and determine the styles of Asian women in the diaspora.

In the late 1990s, suits were worn by the most fashionable icons in London, and are globally available through the many distributive agencies. These include newly opened high status designer boutiques in prestigious mainstream designer locations in central London, alongside the many market stalls and ready-made clothes/designer boutiques in mainly 'ethnic' areas catering to a different clientele. The globalization of these suits through commoditization has led to the rapid increase in networks of distribution. Designer boutiques, the high status ones in Mayfair, Knightsbridge in central London and in Wembley in West London, as well as those in Southall, East Ham, Romford, and the many market stalls, have mushroomed. A whole range of women-initiated marketing niches have produced a plethora of boutiques run by women entrepreneurs who act as designers, redistributive agents, tailors, embroiderers, professional service providers and media presenters of fashion shows.[3] There are also the transnationally trained designers with global networks and the marketing power to distribute these garments in various diasporic niches, as well as making them available to trend-setting 'Sloanes' and various upper 'English' middle-class circuits.[4]

By the late 1990s, these suits had been inserted into different diaspora economies by design professionals and related distributive agencies that had emerged in the markets in the 1980s. These include glossy clothes catalogues, Asian women's magazines produced in London and the subcontinent, and many other print and globally transmitted visual media, such as Asian cable television channels and mainstream media.[5] Global markets, the related communications like faxes and courier firms, have catalysed the rapid availability of these clothes in international arenas and through travel back and forth to 'home' countries from various diaspora locations.[6] This form of consumption facilitating the international transferability of designs of this essentially 'ethnic' material culture was a new phenomenon in the 1990s. These suits are products of a 'gendered commerce' (Mort 1996), mostly controlled by Asian women entrepreneurs.[7] These currently profitable and culturally powerful 'female aesthetic communities' (Goldstein 1995) in which the circulation, production, design innovation, distribution and consumption of goods is controlled, managed and consumed by women, both within subcontinental centres and also in diaspora locations. These commercially savvy design and marketing personnel, some trained at leading design and fashion schools in India, Europe and the US, have entered this fast-growing market. They have shifted the production of these suits from essentially domestic economies, often situated within the domestic domain with highly developed diasporic sewing cultures, into highly commoditized global economies of the new millennium. These clothing economies are governed by all the codes of locality, transnationality and diasporean aesthetics which are fundamentally transforming British consumer spaces. These dialogic processes are generating new commercial and cultural spaces, which result in novel interpretations of the consumer styles of the most English and Anglo Saxon of the European circuits. In all this, the presence and influential cultural agency of these Asian women has shifted European cultural textures, to generate new cultural and consumer styles. This dynamic creation of these spaces is a facet of the common exposure of all British women to shared consumer and cultural geographies dialogically produced by these active commercial and cultural agents in these emergent new spaces and symbolic and material economies.

The *salwaar-kameez* suit encodes a multiplicity of movements and sites of production, and also a specificity of cultural identities and fashion trajectories, encoding the various dynamics of cultural production in global economies. It represents a highly inscribed and textured form of material culture, dynamically used by British Asian women as a signifier of the changing cultural textures of their location in diaspora. The Punjabi suit is intensely politically and culturally coded and a powerful consumer material culture (Mercer 1994b), the interpretation of which represents the agency of diaspora Asian women, and which has further implications for the negotiation of many versions of 'European' cultural and consumer landscapes.[8] There is nothing neutral about their cultural and consumption styles. The malleability powers of *salwaar-kameez* suits in the 1990s, in projecting a multiplicity of identities in negotiating new consumption and cultural styles and new ethnicities, are immense. Notions of the multiple 'Britishnesses' are inscribed in the interpretation of these suits, thus contesting British sartorial hegemonies through these sartorial forms. These artefacts reflect the material and symbolic economies of global, national and local class styles and constitute excellent material culture to engage in battles of semiotic warfare and sartorial terrorism, to use Angela McRobbie's terms, in the landscapes and terrains of global fashion. In many ways, they are highly localized products in their interpretation according to local sub-class and sub-cultural styles.

'Currifying Britain': 'ethnicized' consumption

Salwaar-kameez suits represent one facet of other 'ethnically driven' consumer expressions to be found in a comprehensive range of socio-economic strata in Britain. This is obvious from the many consumer goods and food products sold in British markets, which constitute 'mainstream' British consumers landscapes. A popular example of this is 'British Indian food' which has led to the 'currification of Britain' and cuisine styles.[9] A facet of this is the balti movement, of 'Indian' food cooked in balties and the easy availability of balties (cooking utensils much like Chinese woks) in most household goods shops across major British cities, and the retailing of such commodities through the cable shopping network, QVC. Similarly, the 'Indianization of royal consumption' is reported in media commentary on the Queen's taste for Indian food. The *Daily Star* (26 March 1996) headline for an article on the London Indian restaurant that 'serves' the Queen, states: 'It ain't arf hot Ma'am: Queen orders two tikkaways a week', accompanied by a computer generated image of the Queen with a turban on her head. Similarly, Prince Charles for his forty-eighth birthday party in November 1996 had Indian food served at Highgrove House, his country residence, along with sitar music by famous sitar maestro Ravi Sankar (Euro News, 15 November 1996). Indian frozen and fresh food, which is sold at all the mainstream supermarkets in major British cities, is now also available at Heathrow airport at the Noon restaurant, to eat and take away since November 1996. This is an initiative of Mr Gulam Kader Noon of Noon Products. His food company supplies over three million chilled and

frozen Indian meals per month to major British supermarkets chains like
J. Sainsbury, Waitrose and Cullens, including exclusive shops like Harrods
and Partridges.

Furthermore, there is a rapidly mushrooming market for a whole variety
of cook-in Indian sauces added to and cooked with meats and vegetables –
convenience food to create 'curried casseroles'. There have been recent TV
ads of these cook-in sauces such as, for example, Homepride, with 'British
Asian' actors with regional working-class accents from Liverpool, Glasgow
and Cockney London. The famous Indian television cook Madhur Jaffrey,
who has written the most widely read best selling Indian cook books and
has had multiple series of BBC television programmes in Britain for many
years, promotes these sauces for Tilda, the ubiquitous basmati rice
company. Tilda has recently introduced its own brand of sauces advertised
in mainstream British commercial television and newspapers. Another
example of this ethnicized consumption is that of Sharwoods, one of the
oldest established spice companies, whose television advertisements make
much of a global multiethnic world incorporating 'the hundreds of dishes
from three billion different people'. There are also various 'exotic fruits
juices' available at major high-street supermarkets which have been
'Indianized' including Marks and Spencer, J. Sainsbury etc. and the impact
of Indian restaurants on 'British' food consumption is a further example.
There are also mutually influential music, dance and language styles, labour
organizations and political styles, the proletarianization of Asian women
through their exposure to, and involvement in, British trade unions in work
places and factories (Westwood 1984, 1988).[10] These mutually influential
trends have been around for decades, in fact centuries – such as, for
example, the consumption of 'orientalist' material culture like Kashmiri
Paisley shawls, Indian cottons, indigo cloth and dyes, Chinese silks, por-
celains, etc. – though the intensity of their influence is new. These are
consequences of the changing cultural textures and demographic profiles of
Britain through migration; the commercial agency of settled British Asians,
in particular Asian women whose sartorial economies I am describing here;
the powerful presence of the ubiquitous global media; and the many
emerging markets in these consumer products in the 1990s.[11]

These nationally based British consumer trends are further reflected in
community organizations, in clothes, in the interpretation of public and
private spaces, in the interpretation of home interior decoration, etc. in
both quite simple and in very complex ways. In these mutually influential
processes of multi-faceted cultural expressions – women are central
interpreters of these cultural and consumer styles. These niches have
moved beyond 'ethnic' boundaries to the 'British mainstream' and, through
commoditization, are being interpreted in a variety of complex ways –
a facet of the 'Asianization' of the 'West' and of 'occidentalizing' forces
impacting British Asians. All this is happening at many levels of cultural production in a whole range of class arenas, consumer products and

niches, thus, transcending class and 'ethnic' boundaries. Also, these cultural dynamics are not only restricted to middle-class bourgeois consumption of women who can afford to patronize exclusive *salwaar-kameez* retail outlets like the exclusive Mayfair and Knightsbridge boutiques described below but also apply to a whole range of socio-economic groups. A point to be emphasized here about class markers and class-specificity is that Asian women in Britain come from complex and complicated class locations (Bhachu 1991) and always have been so located. I refer here not just to an exclusive elite of women who are, and have always been, transnationally located, though to assume that transnational women are elites, is an error in itself. Transnationalism is no longer an exclusive phenomenon but spreads across a range of class groups. It is not restricted to the jet-set. It is comprehensively applicable to a vast range of socio-economic groups, from blue-collar workers to corporate executives and many other multiple-migrants who regularly cross national boundaries.

Recoding the suit: 'it's hip to be Asian in Britain'

The market, the ensuing commerce and also commercialization of the *salwaar-kameez*, have resulted in their current consumption much beyond 'ethnic' markets, having been translated into a cross-section of British and other transnational economies. British royals like the international fashion icon Princess Diana, Lady Helen Windsor, daughter of the Duke and Duchess of Kent, the Queen's cousins, media stars like Academy Award winning actress Emma Thompson, photographer and former girlfriend of Prince Andrew, Koo Stark, and supremely wealthy fashionable women like Jemima Goldsmith-Khan, daughter of one of the wealthiest men in Britain and wife of the famous Pakistani cricketer Imran Khan, have all donned them in recent years.[12] These trends have recoded the *salwaar-kameez* suit from its stereotype of a dress-form of 'low status immigrant women' to that of a high fashion and couture garment. Fashion mega-stars Princess Diana and Jemima Goldsmith-Khan's donning of the suit, represent potent moments in its recoding. The suit is no longer an 'immigrant thing'. It was recontexualized in the late 1990s as a high-fashion garb, worn by the most fashionable women, indeed the fashion icons of Britain, as well as a trend-setting street-styled garb.

In September 1996, high-couture designers like Betty Jackson and street designer companies like Red or Dead demonstrated the extent of this recoding at the London Fashion Week. The *Guardian* newspaper headline ran: 'Fashion Week hails capital's many cultures' (27 September 1996). Red or Dead is an 'established mainstream white award winning' street fashion company owned by Wayne Hemingway, which received enormous media coverage in most mainstream British newspapers, including the ethnic press, and television news programmes, for their very '*salwaar-*

kameezed' interpretation of their Spring 1997 collection. The collection was described as 'a combination of street style British and Indian clothes' (Euro News, 27 September 1996). For their London Fashion Show catwalk, they used male and female Asian models picked from the streets of Southall, the British Punjabi capital in West London, alongside Black and White ones, all with Sikh headdresses and accompanied by the 'east–west' music of Kula Shaker whose album was currently in the charts. The following week in Paris, French designer Yves Saint Laurent had *salwaar-kameez*-style silhouettes in his 1997 Spring/Summer fashion collections (*Libas*, November 1996: YSL Zeroes in on the *salwaar-kameez*). 'British fashion', epitomizing London's multiracial society, was captured in the much-touted notion of 'Britfash' – the buzz word and definitive theme of one the most successful London Fashion Weeks in recent years. 'Britfash' catapulted London back onto the fashion map after decades of losing ground to Paris and Milan because 'London is where it's at', strongly influenced by the *salwaar-kameez*/sari style which 'caught fashion's new directions' (according to Rachel Royce on Cable One's 'The Catwalk Show', 29 September 1996).

These increasingly street style interpretations can also be discerned among second and third generation diaspora Asian women who are just beginning to market their own clothes companies. A new street designer label called Global Repercussions was launched in 1997. This project was hatched by a British Asian team involving a partnership between Sarb Basran, a young British-born Asian woman promoter and marketing agent, and fashion designer Bashir Ahmed, who is a product of the prestigious St Martin's School of Art and Design in London (personal communication, 4 December 1996). This label, Sarb Basran, its promoter says, is about a clothing style which emphasizes

> not where you are from but where you are at in a global world. It's a clothes label that attempts to unify cultures, races, and ideologies and attempts to harmonize the conflicts posed by a multicultural world. It reflects the choices you make in such a complex diverse setting amidst global changes.

In contemporary times, these innovative processes are re- and de-designing the *salwaar-kameez* using older designs, marketed this time by Asian retailers and designers, to a similarly wealthy clientele of both diaspora British Asians and white wealthy British women. These designs are further appropriated by second and third generation British Asian women and interpreted through their sub-class and sub-cultural contexts. This is obvious from an image of a young British Asian woman that appeared in a new newspaper called *East*, launched in November 1996. The woman is wearing an exclusive embroidered outfit similar to those found in Ritu's designer shop (discussed on p. 49). She wears a long tunic and ankle length skirt with a long waistcoat, together with Doc Marten shoes and accompanied by a bulldog covered in a Union Jack on a leash. This 'east–west' fusion style referred to in a newly launched British Asian news-paper is a much over-used and simplistic description used by practically every retailer I spoke to and by fashion media commentators, to describe and 'conceptualize' these suits. This metaphor does not, in fact, capture the complex exchanges and multiple cultural processes that are played through this 'ethnic clothing' economy in Britain. The image in the newspaper *East* is obviously influenced by the much older and innovative media-savvy image created by award winning British-Asian film director, Gurinder Chadha, who pioneered it in her film publicity blurb a decade ago. Chadha has not only a dynamic style of interpreting the image of British Asian women through the medium of film, but also presents a powerful personal image of interpreting her eye-catching fusion style 'British Punjabi East African Asian' clothes which are strongly influenced by the *salwaar-kameez*. Her publicity material shows her dressed in Union Jack socks, Doc Marten shoes, a long embroidered Indian skirt, a long *chuni* (headscarf) tied diagonally on one side, a leather jacket and leading a bulldog on a leash. Indeed, one could characterize this 'Brit-Asian-fash' as a clear and undisputed descendant of the *salwaar-kameez*, designed to counter the *salwaar-kameez*-influenced 'Britfash' appropriation, by mainstream clothes companies in the late 1990s. These various interpretative processes include exclusive clothes designed in India, now available in British and other global markets, that are further appropriated and consumed according to British sub-cultural codes in which Asian women are located. By so doing, they are de-designing strongly designed clothes according to their codes of redesigning, which are drawn as much from global cultural arenas as from the diasporean aesthetics and the fashion conventions of their local contexts.

These cultural products, including the crafting of *salwaar-kameez* suits, are governed by diasporean aesthetics and result from an incorporation or synthesis involving multiple sites of production, but which are also abso-lutely locally produced. They have a social and cultural life that emerges from specific places, migration histories, and local political and symbolic economies. For example, there is a local specificity to the consumption style of a Brummie (from Birmingham in the Midlands) Asian woman and the interpretation of her semiotically charged consumption choices/material economies, which grow out of her socialization to the codes of her locality. These specificities have widespread global currency and are locally produced (see Bhachu 1991, 1994). In the 1990s, in British public consumer spaces, there was a high level of recognition by the consuming public in the market registers generated by the commercial and cultural agency of Asian women which has led to the recoding of the suit in many 'ethnic' and 'non-ethnic' clothing economies.

Global design/retail professionals: the cultural brokers

Global markets are determining the fashion styles of these suits with multiple and simultaneous cross flows of information from the major global cities and design centres, via faxes transferring designs, cutting instructions, shapes, embroideries, *chuni/dupatta* (headscarf) styles. These styles and the fully stitched garments are inserted into global markets with great speed. Consequently, the same types of styles are retailed in the major world cities with populations of diaspora Indians. In many cases, the highly accessible clothing catalogues and the suit designs are rapidly copied for domestically stitched suits by the many women seamstresses and a few male tailors who mostly operate out of their homes in all the major British cities. Many professionally based designers will also post these garments to locations all over the world and make them available at local retailing agencies, thus increasing the market penetration of these suits in multiply-located and distributed spheres as never before. Extended kinship and friendship groups also greatly facilitate these commodity processes, sending garments to their friends and kinsmen in places where they are not easily available. Frequent travel to India and Pakistan by diaspora Asians further extends the cross flows of latest fashion designs, information about interpreting this garb and, also, an exchange of the garments themselves.

The production of these clothes has been greatly professionalized through the market, being products of multiple sites of production, and design expertise, both local and global. Although there is an exclusive market for designer suits, there is also a great deal of standardization of these clothing forms through global markets. For example, similar clothes designed and manufactured by the same wholesalers in India and Pakistan, who supply globally to major diaspora Asian markets, lead to easy availability of these clothes in all the major cities of South Asian settlement. However, their interpretation is fundamentally determined by the local context of sub-class and sub-cultural styles and the cultural baggage of migration carried by their wearers. The localization of these suits, a globally available commodity form, negates this standardization, because of the interpretation of these clothes through local and regional styles and cultural codes. Notions of multiple 'Britishnesses' are inscribed in the interpretation of these suits, thus contesting British sartorial hegemonies through these dynamically changing and potent sartorial forms. These artefacts are also strongly encoded signifiers of the material and symbolic economies of global, national and local class styles.

The processes that are commoditizing the wedding economy, of which the suits are a large component, represent a rapidly growing commercial facet of these global markets. This is obvious from the wide range of ready-made clothes boutiques catering to different class markets that mushroomed in the 1990s in all the major centres of Asian population, as well as the most upmarket mainstream high-fashion areas in London. In the late 1990s, they were to be found in exclusive central London locations such as Mayfair, Knightsbridge and Baker Street in Marylebone. The ready-made outfits sold in these shops cost anything from £30–200, up to £400–5,000 for the designer ones. These exclusive designer shops represent a retail economy run by wedding service providers – Asian women entrepreneurs who feed many other diaspora clothes markets. Some of these entrepreneurs are locally born, while others are either raised here, or are from India with excellent Indian connections and a proven record of commercial success there – such as, for example, the shop established by the renowned revivalist India-based designer Ritu (described on p. 49) in North Audley Street, Mayfair – which provides them with Indian-made goods and access to services on the subcontinent. Ritu Kumar's shop closed three years after it opened in 1996 (see Bhachu 2004 for further details).

Among the pioneers, the first to open a designer boutique was British-based Geeta Sarin. Geeta Sarin is a professionally trained designer who has worked with fashion designer Karl Lagerfeld in Paris and later worked for other leading fashion designers. She started her own label, Rivaaz (meaning 'trend'), and opened her first shop with her own label in Wembley, in the Ealing Road in West London, catering mostly to an 'ethnic' clientele. In December 1995 she opened a second shop in central London in Beauchamp Place, Knightsbridge, for a more plural customer base. She uses rapid communications networks and faxes to get garments from India into the London markets. This easy flow of information – the collapsing of space and time and the interchangeability of market sites, where her designs, patterns and stitching instructions are faxed to India and where garments are manufactured according to her very professional requirements – is a very recent market niche led by London-based Asian women designers.

Other designer boutiques include Chiffons in Green Street, East London and Soho Road, Birmingham; Yazz in Baker Street; Libas, selling exclusive Pakistani-style suits in Berkeley Street; and Ritu's shop in North Audley Street, Mayfair. The last three shops run by elite Pakistanis and Indians closed in the late 1990s (see Bhachu 2004). The Knightsbridge-based boutique Egg opened in 1994, a joint venture initiated by two influential cultural brokers, who have catalysed the insertion of *salwaar-kameez* suits beyond 'ethnic' markets, selling to upper-class British 'Sloanes' including the younger royals. Egg is a 'politically correct/ecologically friendly' and supremely upmarket enterprise, which has an art gallery on its Kinnerton Street premises and produces beautifully crafted almost 'Art-suits' in cottons and natural fabrics. It is a commercially successful joint venture of Asha Sarabhai of the Indian textile dynasty which has followed Ghandhian traditions of cloth and craft production, and Maureen Doherty, the former style supremo of the chain of trendy Joseph shops.[13] These 'female commercial spaces' constitute a gendered economy run by women entrepreneurs – mostly based in Britain, though some have partners resident in India. Another boutique, Creations in Southall, a wholesaling

and retailing outlet in West London, is the brainchild of a dynamic entrepreneur Mala Rastogi. She organized a major fashion show of *salwaar-
kameezes* called 'Threads of Fantasy' in September 1996 at Grosvenor
House Hotel, which was attended by over 2,000 people with tickets at £75
and which was widely covered in the ethnic media.

The upmarket Indian clothes chain Ritu's was opened in Mayfair in
May 1996, by the famous Indian 'revivalist' designer of beautifully embroidered and made *salwaar-kameezes*. Ritu Kumar has innovatively revived
many older embroidery and craft traditions, and also designs for Indian
celebrities, thus extending to the diaspora her chain of twelve shops already
well established in major cities in India (*Independent*, 27 July 1996). Ritu
is a very big name in India as reflected in her publicity blurb which states
that she is 'Couturier to the Stars'. Her clients include former beauty queens
Miss World and Miss Universe (both international titles were won by
Indian 'beauties' in 1995); Sonia Gandhi, the Italian widow of former Prime
Minister Rajiv Gandhi; various 'Indian royal women'; and many other
women from elite Indian circuits who appreciate her 'classically designed'
suits. Ritu Kumar was already commercially successful and renowned in
Indian markets but new to the London scene. She is considered 'a national
icon in India' who has been designing for 25 years (*East*, 29 November
1996). On the media, she sounds like 'a commercially savvy material
culture professor' as obvious from her many television interviews (Zee TV,
26 May 1996; Network East, BBC 2, 30 November 1996; Sky TV, May
1996). She is supremely articulate, speaking the language of the local and
global and the multiple contemporary domestic and 'corporate culture'
identities of Asian women as they enter the waged work place. She trained
in museology in the US and talks about the design vocabularies that she
has acquired through her research at the Victoria and Albert Museum
in London, a premier museum of decorative arts, founded in 1852, and
housing applied design and arts information and material culture. Ritu is a
conduit in translating this design syntax into the clothes made in her factories in India, which are sold at her outlets in India and London. Many of her
designs and patterns were originally taken from Indian textile and craft
economies, from where they were brought into British museums by colonial
agents in an imperial past and, also, at that time, for retail markets selling
'oriental' wares to wealthy elite white British women.

White British designers have also entered as prominent interpreters of
consumption trends among British Asians. These include designers like
Zandra Rhodes who was especially popular among Asian women in the
late 1980s. Her designer suits and saris were sold in high status Indian
clothing stores in London. A newcomer to this scene in the 1990s was
British designer Catherine Walker who designed Jemima Goldsmith-
Khan's evening wedding reception dress in June 1995. Equally, there are
locally produced *salwaar-kameezes* by young British Asian designers,
trained in Britain, mostly young women in their late twenties and early

thirties. A global cultural and consumer flow has resulted, unexpected in its impact but very important in determining wedding consumption patterns in large metropolitan centres throughout the Asian diaspora. In London, New York, Los Angeles and Sydney, Bombay-based designer clothes are readily available. These consumer flows have a strong local impact and include British-trained, Bombay- and Delhi-based Indian designers and Lahore- and Karachi-based Pakistani designers. These personnel consist mostly of women, though there are a number of important male players like Bombay-based and US-trained designer Tarun Tahiliani who designed for Jemima Goldsmith-Khan, Rohit Bahl who trained with Osca de la Renta, and the currently popular Sikh designer J. J. Valaya in Delhi, and many other young men and women who are emerging at supersonic speed from various design schools in London, New York, Delhi, Bombay, Paris and elsewhere.

Diaspora fashion globalizers

Two diasporic London-based fashion globalizers are Geeta Sarin of Rivaaz who is now in her late fifties, the first to open a designer boutique and start a mail order clothes catalogue a decade ago (described earlier), and Bubby Mahil who is 36 years old. Bubby is from the younger generation of British-raised Asian women. She is now well known as the designer of Cherie Blair, the British Prime Minister's wife's, Punjabi suits. She is owner of two innovative boutiques, Chiffons, in London and Birmingham. Both women have the same diaspora migration trajectories and ethnicities, being Punjabi Sikhs from East Africa. Both are products of elaborate diaspora sewing cultures developed over two generations in East Africa, which they have further refined on the British scene, and which they have transformed into a commodity context in the professionalized and globalized worlds of fashion in London. They are both 'time-space compressors' par excellence in transferring designs and patterns with enormous speed from London to India, where their clothes are made. These are inserted back into the London markets for local consumption within three weeks for the elaborately embroidered and bead-worked suits, and four days for the simpler non-embroidered ones in interesting rich fabrics and designs. Their clothes are circulated with great speed, facilitated by the many courier companies which have erupted to service this massive increase in clothes traffic.

Entrepreneur Geeta Sarin of Rivaaz has worked with leading Parisian designers and, via her second shop in Knightsbridge, captures a more plural customer base including American film stars and other famous media personalities. She says her white 'European/American market' constitutes 80 per cent of the clientele in her Knightsbridge shop, as well as wealthy locally born second and third generation Asians. Surprisingly, her clientele also includes transnationally based subcontinental Asians who have easy access to the best designer suit markets on the subcontinent, but who prefer to buy in high-status fashion capitals like London, befitting their positive status-reference groups. For example, in September 1996, when I interviewed Geeta Sarin, she said she was working on the wedding outfits of the current Pakistani Prime Minister (who was in the Opposition party at the time) Nawaz Sharif's son's and (at that time) future daughter-in-law's wedding clothes.

Bubby Mahil of Chiffons shares Geeta Sarin's British location and East African Asian diaspora background. These contexts are reflected in the design vocabularies they negotiate, the silhouettes they stock, and in their relatively 'egalitarian' retail interaction styles with their customers in Britain. These diaspora-driven design aesthetics and sensibilities are then transferred into the Indian scene. Their garments are stitched and embroidered, and then inserted back into British markets within three weeks. So far, neither of them is interested in, or has developed, Indian subcontinental markets, even though their clothes are produced there. Both talk of moving into North American markets: Canada – initially Toronto – in particular, in the case of Bubby, and the US – Los Angeles and New York – in the case of Geeta Sarin. To date, both are very much British-based women from East African diaspora families who are firmly located, and flourishing commercially, in Britain.

Bubby Mahil and her sister Nina are British-raised young Punjabi women. They are part of a new breed of savvy design-conscious Asian fashion entrepreneurs, who are similar to the clientele with whom they share a sub-culture and to whom they sell their clothes. They are supremely fashion and style conscious and present themselves as such in their shop. Bubby is often dressed in trendy designer track suits – Versace with swish sporty shoes – all accessorized with trendy jewellery and watches. They monitor closely 'mainstream' fashion styles, seasonal colours, fabrics and silhouettes, especially those in vogue among the young, 20–35-year-olds with money to spare. They respond rapidly to these trends and translate them in the 'British Asian style clothes'. For example, in 1996, lime was a dominant fashion colour and was reflected in the outfits Bubby designed and sold in her shop. Her shop window displays were also interpreted in different shades of lime. Some of Bubby's clothes had halter-necks and plunging back necklines, long tunics, with straight *lungi*-skirts and shawl-*chunis*, that a lot of young women were keen on wearing at the time.

A savvy diaspora design democratizer

Bubby Mahil is also a great democratizer of design in the dialogic way she produces designed suits with her customers. This dynamic formation of design through a dialogic process that she negotiates with her customers – a body dressed rather than a dress embodied – represents a different process from the design vocabularies innovated by India-based revivalist designer Ritu Kumar which cannot be negotiated by her 'everyday/ordinary'

customers. Bubby represents a British diaspora context of a young locally raised Punjabi British woman who captures the market of 'young' consumers who share her biographical trajectory, British experiences, and commodity contexts. She is also opening a floor in her shop for children and teenagers. She is quite 'egalitarian' and open to suggestions from her customers, who regularly give her suggestions and state their preferences about what she should stock in her shops. She listens with attention and often responds to their inputs which come from all age groups. Her 'British diaspora design aesthetic' is different from that of some of the other boutiques, many of which will, indeed, get outfits made for their British customers in India, on a made-to-measure basis by copying outfits already in their shops in a different size and colour. However, most shops sell the standard size merchandise already in the shop, that they had previously ordered even though they are open to suggestions and closely monitor popular trends. In contrast, Bubby facilitates a subversion of design. So 'one need not wear what is already designed and stitched for one, but one may create an individually produced suit by inputting one's own ideas by negotiating with a design/retail professional'. In so doing, Bubby makes salient diaspora voices through design, thus, valorizing Asian women's voices through a sartorial design discourse, around a material culture of clothes. All this takes place amid global commercial spaces in which these locally based fashion dynamics operate.

In engaging with a client in this fashion, Bubby is a democratic design innovator who produces a design syntax that is dynamically formed with her customer. Let me relate an incident I witnessed in her Green Street shop in East London that made this obvious. Such interactions were common and took place on a daily basis many times. A tall plump Asian woman who regularly buys from Bubby wanted an outfit to wear at a wedding. She did not choose or like a suit from the merchandise already in the shop. She and Bubby came up with a grey outfit, by going through fabric samples to choose the fabric, the neckline, the type of beadwork and area of the outfit to be embroidered, the general shape using 'a bit of this and a bit of that', from the existing outfits already in the shop alongside her own preference for 'what suited her'. Bubby did a rough basic sketch of her customer's suggestions and choices while giving her own experienced input at the same time. This basic sketch was later refined and elaborated by Bubby in her own time, with more detailed drawings of sleeves, necklines, trouser shapes, areas to be embroidered or beadworked and general pattern instructions. Later on that day she faxed these new detailed sketches to India. I saw this garment – an individually chosen outfit that was dialogically produced through many arenas of expertise – back in the shop within three weeks for the customer to wear within her London social scene. This dialogic production of design and the stitching of these clothes with global and local inputs epitomizes the suturing of cultural landscapes through clothes in global markets that I have been describing above.

This dynamic formation of design both at a highly professional level, as in the case of Bubby from Chiffons, and also at the level of domestic production among the seamstresses I have been interviewing, is representative of the stitching of cultural and consumer spaces. The latter home-sewers who represent a huge sub-rosa economy use shop-bought-globally-marketed commercial patterns and borrow from mainstream and ethnic press magazines and catalogues, to ethnicize commercially produced patterns like Vogue, Simplicity, Burda, and Buttericks, to 'Anglicize' Punjabi *salwaar* suits and to 'Punjabize' these globally available commercial patterns. These combinations and combinational freedoms constitute multiple layers of innovation representing far more complex cultural dynamics than any dialogic binary processes. There are, in fact, multiple flows of information and vocabularies embodied in this globalized fashion material culture. This is reflected in the domestic production of fashion and style, and in the professionally negotiated designs by Bubby and her British Asian women customers in dressing their bodies, and in going beyond embodying the dresses according to strict hierarchically imposed clothing codes – as do the hegemonic Parisian high couture designers. These continuously negotiated processes are products of well-established diaspora sewing cultures, and the commoditization of diasporic material cultural production in global markets.

Transformed commodity contexts

These innovative processes result in new material and symbolic economies, which are a product of the transformative agencies of ethnic and cultural entrepreneurs who are part of new forms of connectednesses and flows. None of these new cultural forms are products of static sites nor are they generated in single sites. We are dealing with more fluid patterns that emerge out of different sites of production and which are multiply produced and consumed, but which fundamentally reflect the specificities of their interpretation, according to the codes of locality and regionality. These represent dialectic and dynamic processs of the spaces created through this agency – both commercial and cultural – through clothing fashion objects. These highly charged consumer cultures which are governed by the codes of locality, transnationality and diasporean aesthetics are fundamentally transforming many British consumer and cultural spaces. These highly charged consumer and cultural dynamics represent a dialogic process that is generated through this commerce which is producing new versions of European consumer styles.

Salwaar-kameez suits constitute highly charged and powerfully coded attire representing a multiplicity of movements and sites of production, being domesticated and interpreted through the specificities of local fashion and consumer markets. These sartorial economies are reflective of the multiple sites of production and diasporic consumption. The malleability powers of the suits in the late 1990s, in projecting a multiplicity of identities and in negotiating new consumption and cultural styles and new ethnicities, are immense. A whole taxonomy of tastes of local British and international fashion trends and styles are reflected in this clothes material culture. Of course, there are many multi-directional cross flows. There are Asian women who have adopted a 'Sloaney' Lady Helen Windsor style of interpreting their Punjabi *salwaar-kameez* suits, precisely because they share a similar consumption niche or emulate the 'Sloaney' style through its popularization and commoditization through upmarket fashion magazines like *Vogue* and *Harper's Bazaar*, and by its famous 'Super Sloane' icon, the late Princess Diana. Equally, over 1994 and 1995, many metropolitan Asian women wore the full body stocking with the top half of the suit, a fusion style interpreted, with Doc Marten shoes, and with thick platform shoes which constituted the general style in vogue in the early–mid-1990s, along with many of the contemporary accessories in vogue in the different sub-classes and peer cultures. In 1997, when transparency in clothes – the see-through style using chiffons and gauze-like see-through fabric – represented the dominant fashion trend covered in every fashion magazine on the stands, Asian women in Southall immediately appropriated this by wearing transparent saris over full body-stockings, tossing aside sari blouses and petticoats. Just as in the 1980s, Mohicanized and Punkized Punjabi suits could be seen by Asian women in those sub-cultures. The whole gamut of current styles in vogue – from 'punky and funky' to grunge to baggy hip-hop etc. – can be discerned among diaspora women in their interpretation of the suits. Thus, localizing the consumption and interpretation of this garb, even though there are many standardized globally available garments in all the main diaspora markets.

The suit is also an inscription of ethnic pride. It is a highly political piece of clothing. Its politicization is obvious for the different groups who consume this garment. One example of this: after the army action at the Golden Temple in Amritsar in 1984, many Sikh women in India and in the diaspora have stopped wearing the sari, considered to be a 'Hindu' dress form, and donned the suit assertively, a gesture similar to that of Sikh men who adopted turbans, some orange coloured ones – the colour of martyrs and martyrdom. By so doing, they made a powerful political statement against the actions of the then Delhi-based Hindu government. The sari is still not worn almost 20 years after that army action and the pogroms against the Sikhs after the assassination of Prime Minister Indira Gandhi in 1985 by her two Sikh bodyguards. Their wearing of the Punjabi suit makes a semiotically powerful political statement both about their rejection of the Indian action and also as reflection of 'ethnic pride' in their British 'ethnicity'. I will not go into the many similar incidents of the assertive use of the suits by British-born Asian women in public domains to deflect British stereotypes and racist constructions of them.

Subverting sartorial landscapes: re- and de-designing Britishness

These highly politicized scenarios have different implications from the adoption of the *salwaar-kameez* suits, in the past few years by key media stars, and other wealthy and upper-middle-class women like Lady Helen Windsor, Princess Diana and Koo Stark (*Daily Mail*, 26 February 1996). Other leading ladies, including the Academy Award-winning actress Emma Thompson, Jemima Goldsmith-Khan and her sister India Goldsmith, have worn Punjabi suits at the weddings of Lady Sarah Armstrong-Jones, Princess Margaret's daughter, in July 1994, and of her best friend Arabella Cobbold, where she acted as matron of honour. This is an equally powerful semiotic act of projecting a certain type of 'ethnically plural metropolitan' image. Lady Helen Windsor's outfits were bought at the Knightsbridge boutique Egg (discussed on p. 48). These developments have created an interesting new space, reflective of an aspect of Britishness that was being negotiated in the 1990s by both British Asian women and by their many white peers in different British contexts representing a dialogic and dialectical process. British Asian women's negotiations of their Englishnesses are as potently relevant to, and determinative of, Lady Helen Windsor's negotiations of her Englishness – regardless of her location among the Anglo-Saxon (actually they are of German ancestry) aristocracy. These negotiations are facets of the 'ethnicization/Asianization' of some of the most Anglo-Saxon of upper-class British circuits, through commodity forms and consumption, and of the 'Englishization/Anglo-Saxonization' of British Asian women. Both these mutually influential and sartorial interpretations are subversive processes. British sartorial subversions are emergent forms, outcomes of the shared cultural geographies of British women, regardless of their class and ethnic locations, in British landscapes of the 1990s. These suit styles are also reflective of a shared commodity context like that generated by the Knightsbridge shop Egg. These successful commercial spaces are products of the presence of 'mainstream' media-covered cultural brokers like Maureen Doherty and Asha Sarabhai, and an increasing number of other design and retail professionals, who play a potent role as cultural brokers in producing these new spaces.

These new European spaces are not class-specific phenomena restricted to the upper classes or to a transnational elite – both Asian and European – but are processes to be found in every class and sub-cultural group. They reflect the influential cultural and commercial agency of Asian women in global markets that is generating new geographies of fashion and style that subvert mainstream and national styles of Anglo-Saxonization: the re- and de-designing of European fashion/sartorial landscapes. These new cultural textures and fashion geographies represent the diasporean aesthetics generated by Asian women. I have also referred to their transformative inputs and dynamics through design which stitch the new cultural and commercial

spaces in global arenas. Such cultural production through clothes is catalysed by the commodity contexts generated by such retailing outlets. Harjit
Samra in Southall, who has a shop and a clothes catalogue called Sheba,
says that these processes and the donning of suits 'strengthen our cultures,
make our cultures strong' – a positive reaffirmation of ethnic identities. At
the same time, there are many 'depoliticizing material cultural moments'
through such commodity dynamics in global cities like London and its markets which facilitate their appropriation – the kidnapping of the *salwaar-
kameez* suits by upper-class women, by various other white and black
groups and by powerful mainstream designers with access to enormous
'penetrating' markets, who aggressively entered these arenas in the late
1990s, to produce 'Britfash' versions of the formerly politicized ethnic
clothes. Nonetheless, these new trends and the presence and influential
cultural agency of these Asian women in various British niches remains
strong in shifting European cultural and consumer textures – to generate
new cultural and consumer styles. These transnationally located fashion
styles constitute new forms and rhythms which are as much products of the
globalization of markets as they are of the local and regional contexts. These
emergent new spaces created through the presence of Asian women's
cultural and commercial entrepreneurship, represent multiplicities of
movements, cultural and design exchanges, sites of production, and also
specificity of cultural identities and fashion trajectories, encoding the
various dynamics of cultural production in global markets.

Notes

1 My work on Punjabi *salwaar-kameez* suits constitutes research that has been
   ongoing for the last ten years. My book, *Dangerous designs: Asian women
   fashion the diaspora economies*, explores the politicized fashion and consumption styles of Asian women in Britain. In this, I detail their consumer niches, the
   role of design professionals and retail entrepreneurs who are professionalizing
   these formerly domestic economies in global markets, and the domestic seamstresses who remain vibrant in these transnational economies of clothes.
2 *Salwaar-kameez* suits are made in all kinds of fabrics, and comprise a long tunic
   with slits down both sides, loose baggy trousers, often with a cuff at the ankle,
   and a *chuni* or *duppatta* (head scarf) of between two to three metres. The length
   and width of all these components change with fashion styles as do the shape and
   silhouettes. While the basic three components remain fairly static, their interpretation varies. In the past few years, younger women have also been wearing
   the tunic with ankle-length skirts, both narrow ones and wider ones, known as
   lungi suits.
3 Cable News Channel One for London had a slot in a programme called 'Off the
   Peg' in April 1996 about how to wear *salwaar-kameezes*, demonstrated by a black
   British model. Its fashion programmes like 'The Catwalk Show' regularly
   covered *salwaar*-suit trends. In June 1995, Radio 4's 'Woman's Hour' also did
   a programme about these outfits. The Asian cable channel Zee TV covered the
   suits all the time in programmes bought from India and those produced in Britain.
   There was huge coverage of the fashion show 'Threads of Fantasy' organized by
   Mala Rastogi of Creations in which her boutique and clothes from most of the

designers described in this chapter were featured. The video of this fashion show was packaged and sold to the public by October 1996, within one month after the show.

4 'Sloane' (or 'Sloane Ranger') is a slang term which refers to young upper-class English women, typically with a public school education and connections to the aristocracy. The name refers to Sloane Square, an exclusive shopping district in London's West End.

5 The first catalogue of these 'Indian' clothes in the British market, called Rivaaz, was that of designer and entrepreneur Geeta Sarin. She published three of these catalogues in the 1980s. These designer clothes catalogues standardized the suit through the many retail outlets and distribution agencies. Some of these catalogues originate from the subcontinent and some are British produced of designers based in London with command over marketing and manufacturing centres in India and Pakistan. For example, Xerxes Bhathena is a Bombay-based designer who is aiming for the western, i.e. diaspora, Asian women market. His catalogue presented Delhi- and Bombay-designed clothes which were available through the British Indian owned Variety Silk House in Wembley and through the many mushrooming and exclusive designer-suit boutiques that sell Punjabi suits in Britain. There are very many Bombay and Delhi catalogues that advertise for both internal and external/export markets. These catalogues are very easily available in ethnic magazine/newspaper and record shops that are to be found in most of the major Asian shopping areas all over Britain. Some of these magazines are transnationally available through subscriptions via the post.

6 The Pakistani market (with its distinctively Punjabi version, versus Delhi/Bombay's less Punjabi interpretations of *salwaar-kameezes*), is obvious from *Libas* magazine produced by Pakistanis based in London. The Punjabi suits displayed in Libas represent the Pakistani high-status market and are aimed at the up-market retail niches in Mayfair (Libas) to tap wealthy Asians and Whites. Libas has been available since December 1995 in the US, as is obvious from recent advertisements in the *India Abroad* newspaper, a US-based Indian newspaper also distributed in Europe.

7 See Frank Mort's (1996) analysis of the transformations in, and the politics of, masculinities as produced through consumption and fashion styles in 'gendered commerce' driven by innovative style entrepreneurs and design professionals.

8 I find Kobena Mercer's work on 'Black hair/style politics' (see Mercer 1994a) very stimulating in thinking through some of these politically charged cultural and consumer processes. The same applies to Angela McRobbie's work (see McRobbie 1989, 1996 and Cosgrove 1989).

9 A report broadcast on its main news programme, Euro News, on the Asian cable channel Zee TV (26 June 1996), stated that 15 per cent of the British population chose curries as their favourite meal, surpassing roast beef at 12 per cent and Chinese food at 11 per cent. The 'average British person' ate curry once a week.

10 For example, the music of Apache Indian in Britain has specific origins in the work of a young Punjabi man raised in multi-ethnic working-class Birmingham in the English Midlands. His music topped both the reggae and bhangra charts in 1991, a year in which he was also voted Best Newcomer at the British Reggae Industry Awards. He has played to packed stadia in India and is famous and controversial in the international South Asian diaspora while at the same time being authenticated by African Caribbean diasporic communities. Apache, himself, is Steven Kapur, whose Hindu Punjabi parents migrated from Jalandhar district of Punjab, which has produced the majority of Punjabi migrants internationally since the late twentieth century. Anthropologist Les Back (1995) who has known and written about Apache Indian's music states:

Apache's music is a cultural crossroads, a meeting place where the languages and rhythms of four continents intermingle producing a culture that cannot be reduced to its component parts. Rather, it needs to be understood in the context of the global passage of linguistic and cultural forms and the localities where they converge; the culture is simultaneously both local and global . . . The new form was dubbed bhangramuffin . . . The types of 'fusion' that Apache's music personifies is not arbitrary. What his music demonstrates is a series of departures, identifications which traverse a number of continents then return, and pause in Birmingham's cultural crossroads only to re-depart again.

11   Similar cultural products include the books of British Indian writer Salman Rushdie, products of his 'mongrel self' (he states) and a hybrid space in the diaspora which are potently produced in his literature as a British Indian writer. He characterizes his recent book *The moor's last sigh* as centred on the 'image of miscegenation of cultural hybridity' (Florence Nolville, writing in *Le Monde* 17 February 1995). Similarly, the music of PBN (Punjabi By Nature) – a Toronto-based group of Canadian-born South Asians – has been influenced by Apache Indian's innovative and path-breaking combination of Rap and Bhangra (Britishified Punjabi harvest music). PBN produces these sounds through their socialization to the Toronto scene. This new music is as much a reflection of their diasporic Punjabiness as it is of their Canadianness, as it is of their location in the subcultures of Toronto, as it is of the trends of global music!

12   Princess Diana's visit to Pakistan and her Punjabi *salwaar-kameez* outfits – three of them: pink, light turquoise blue and creamy pink – were widely covered in just about every British newspaper and other mass media. The *Daily Express* (23 February 1996) headline ran: 'A touch of Eastern cool: How to follow Diana's example and spice your summer wardrobe'. She wore Catherine Walker's version of the traditional Punjabi *salwaar-kameez* 'in the palest pink', reputed to have cost around £2,000. This article also had Koo Stark's choices and advice about these Punjabi clothes and information about some of the up-market retail outlets which sell them (some of which are discussed in this chapter).

13   Asha Sarabhai states: 'We talked about the idea of a shop for a long time because we were both tired of the way that the whole point of retailing seemed to persuade people to buy things they didn't really want' (*Sunday Times*, 27 February 1994). According to this same report, Sarabhai, a Girton graduate, has dedicated her career to the protection of crafts and skills that are under threat from high-tech mass-production. Quality is the essence of Egg, and Sarabhai's clothes and fabrics succinctly embody its philosophy. They are seasonless and labour-intensive, made to last and even improve with age. The labour, of course, is relatively cheap. A full length evening coat, cut like a kimono and finished to couture standard, is £700, a natural indigo cotton tunic £40:

In terms of fame, Doherty's partner Sarabhai has a head start as an established designer of textiles and clothes. She has a one-man exhibition at the V&A to her credit and a cult following that includes serious aesthetes such as the painters Frank Stella and Robert Rauschenberg, the writer Gaudy Mehta and Issey Miyake. Sarabhai's career in textiles began in 1975 when she married a man from a respected and wealthy Indian textile dynasty. Its headquarters [is] at Ahmedabad. It was at Ahmedabad that the plan for Egg was hatched. As the frantic consumerism of the 1980s gives way to a new appreciation of lasting quality, Doherty and Sarabhai appear to have captured this new spirit.

(*Sunday Times*, 27 February 1994: 35)

References

Back, L. 1995. 'X amount of Sat Siri Akal': Apache Indian, reggae music and inter-mezzo culture, in R. Sunquist ed. *Cultural studies and the discourses of ethnicity.* Amsterdam: Rodopi, 139–66.

Bhachu, P. 1991. Culture, ethnicity and class among Punjabi Sikh women in 1990s Britain. *New Community* 17: 401–12.

Bhachu, P. 1994. New cultural formations and transnational South Asian women: culture, class and consumption among British Asian women in the diaspora, in P. Van Der Veer ed. *Nation and migration: the politics of space in the South Asian diaspora.* Philadelphia: University of Pennsylvania Press, 222–44.

Bhachu, P. 1996. The multiple landscapes of transnational Asian women in the diaspora, in V. Amit-Talai and C. Knowles eds. *Re-situating identities: the politics of race, ethnicity, and culture.* Peterborough, Ontario: Broadview Press, 283–303.

Bhachu, P. 1997. Dangerous designs: Asian women and the new landscapes of fashion, in A. Oakley and J. Mitchell eds. *Who's afraid of feminism? Seeing through the backlash.* London: Hamish Hamilton, 187–99.

Bhachu, P. 2004. *Dangerous designs: Asian women fashion the diaspora economies.* London and New York: Routledge.

Cosgrove, S. 1989. The zoot suit and style warfare, in A. McRobbie ed. *Zoot suits and second-hand dresses.* London: Macmillan, 3–22.

Goldstein, J. 1995. The female aesthetic community, in G.E. Marcus and F.R. Meyers eds. *The traffic in culture: refiguring art and anthropology.* Los Angeles and Berkeley, CA: University of California Press, 310–29.

McRobbie, A. ed. 1989. *Zoot suits and second-hand dresses: an anthology of fashion and music.* London: Macmillan.

McRobbie, A. 1996. Looking back at New Times and its critics, in D. Morley and Kuan-Hsing Chen eds. *Stuart Hall: critical dialogues in cultural studies.* London: Routledge, 238–61.

Mercer, K. 1994a. Black hair/style politics, in *Welcome to the jungle.* London: Routledge, 97–128.

Mercer, K. 1994b. *Welcome to the jungle: new positions in Black cultural studies.* London: Routledge.

Mort, F. 1996. *Cultures of consumption: masculinities and social space in late twentieth-century Britain.* London: Routledge.

Rushdie, S. 1995. *The moor's last sigh.* London: Cape.

Westwood, S. 1984. *All day every day: working class women in factories.* London: Pluto Press.

Westwood, S. 1988. Workers and wives: continuities and discontinuities in the lives of Gujarati women, in S. Westwood and P. Bhachu eds. *Enterprising women: ethnicity, economy and gender relations.* London: Routledge, 103–31.

3 Tracing transnationalities through commodity culture

A case study of British-South Asian fashion

Claire Dwyer

This chapter uses a case study of the transnationalities associated with British-Asian fashion to broaden the conceptualization of transnational space.[1] The Introduction to this volume highlighted some of our concerns about continuing to define transnationalism as a social formation, identity or cultural process that is only experienced by immigrant groups (Portes 1997: 16; Portes *et al.* 1999: 219). While we are sensitive to concerns about the lack of specificity or uncritical celebration in the ever-broadening conceptualization of transnational identities, interactions or experiences (Mitchell 1997), our work has sought to open up an alternative approach to thinking about transnational spaces. This approach is indebted in the first instance to the anthropologist Roger Rouse (1991), whose classic essay is reprinted in Chapter 1. Rouse's ethnography of Aguilillan 'transmigrants' whose lives are lived not simply between two locations in Mexico and the US, but instead within 'transnational circuits' of people, money, goods and information, was one of the earliest exemplars of transnational geographies. Most interesting, for us, was Rouse's suggestion that it was not only the Aguilillan transmigrants that were affected by these processes. As he suggests: 'the comfortable modern imagery of nation-states and national languages, of coherent communities and consistent subjectivities . . . no longer seems adequate . . . [D]uring the last 20 years we have *all* moved irrevocably into a new kind of social space' (Rouse 1991: 8, emphasis added).

Rouse's evocation resonates with Massey's discussion of 'extroverted' geographies (Massey 1994) through which oppositions between 'local' and 'global' are unsettled. It also signals a challenge to the narrow specification of 'transnational' groups, which, we fear, is in danger of being recuperated into discourses of 'ethnic minoritization' (Crang *et al.* 2003). Instead, Rouse's evocation of transnational social space parallels the way in which Avtar Brah (1996) conceptualizes 'diaspora space' as a related, but also distinctive, project to the tracing of the trajectories and spatialities of different diasporas. Brah argues that 'diaspora space' is space inhabited not only by those who might belong to identifiable diasporas, but is a space of (national) re-configuration which involves both those represented as (national) majorities and minorities. As she explains:

My argument is that diaspora space as a conceptual category is 'inhabited' not only by those who have migrated and their descendants, but equally by those who are constructed and represented as indigenous. In other words, the concept of diaspora space (as opposed to that of diaspora) includes the entanglement, the intertwining of the genealogies of dispersion with those of 'staying put'. The diaspora space is the site where the native is as much a diasporian as the diasporian is the native.

(1996: 209)

What Brah suggests, is that diaspora space is both multiply and differently inhabited. Her framing of diaspora space alludes to the possibility of transnational geographies which are not simply grounded in identifiable diasporic communities. Our approach to unravelling the multiple and different inhabitations of these transnational geographies is through the analysis of commodity culture.

Transnationalism and the spaces of commodity culture

Our focus upon the transnational spaces of commodity culture draws inspiration from Leontis' discussion of a (Mediterranean in this case) topography produced through the notion of *emporium* – or commerce – which creates 'not a world of boundaries that separate but of routes that connect' (Leontis 1997: 189). It is also inspired by Appadurai's injunction 'to follow things themselves, for their meanings are inscribed in their forms, their uses, their trajectories . . . it is the things in motion that illuminate their human and social context' (1986: 5). To trace the 'traffic in things' (Jackson 1999) is to seek to explore both the physical movement of people and goods across different geographical spaces, but also to trace the processes of commodification which accompany this circuitry. As Cook and Crang (1996) argue in relation to food, we need to view commodities not as having a fixed cultural meaning or identity, but as artefacts which acquire cultural meaning within the complex circuits of commodity culture. Tracing these flows for different British-South Asian commodities (namely food and fashion) allows us to explore a transnational space which operates beyond the confines of specific ethnically defined communities – while also recognizing that we are not all equally or similarly transnational. Second, it allows us to explore the commodification of ethnic difference without re-inscribing simple dichotomies between minoritized transnationals and ethnically unmarked members of a nationalized 'mainstream' majority.

Undertaking research on the transnationalities of commodity culture involves multi-sited ethnographic work such as that advocated by Marcus, 'tracing a cultural formation across and within multiple sites of activity' (1995: 96; see also the work of Appadurai (1998) and Breckenridge (1995) on South Asian public culture). To trace the transnational spaces of British-South Asian commodity culture we need an approach which follows people and things, but also metaphors (signs, symbols and images), stories, allegories or narratives, lives or biographies and conflicts. Our understanding of transnational commodity culture emphasizes that this is a space which is inhabited by a whole range of differently positioned actors including producers (labour and capital), wholesalers, buyers and retailers (in a range of different outlets), cultural intermediaries (including advertisers, journalists and other expert writers) as well as a wide array of consumers in a wide range of places. Those who occupy different positions are likely to have different investments in, experiences of, and expressions of, transnationality. It is also true that transnationalism can take a variety of forms in contemporary commodity culture. Thus, one can explore transnationalism in terms of the personal biographies of particular entrepreneurs involved in specific commodity cultures, or focus on the personal or corporate histories of particular firms. Or, we can also think of transnationalism in terms of the practices involved in the operation of the business including networks of suppliers, sourcing practices and distribution. Finally, we can discuss transnationalism in terms of the stylization and marketing of a company's products. For example, when are goods marketed as 'authentic', 'traditional' or 'exotic'? How is the signifier of 'Indianness', itself constructed and contested, whose meaning varies according to context (Gillespie 1995; Dwyer 1999), used and with what effect? Our task in tracing the 'social life of things' in the commercial work of British-South Asian transnationality is to explore both the operation of, and process of, transnational geographies, and how these geographies were deployed and understood by a range of different actors including producers and consumers in Britain and India.

The transnational geographies of British-South Asian fashion

Our research on the transnationalities of British-South Asian commodity culture began by considering a sector overview derived from secondary sources such as trade publications. We then conducted interviews with a wide range of companies. From these interviews we selected a smaller number of case-study firms with whom we worked more intensively over a two-year period, which involved in-depth interviewing, work shadowing and more ethnographic styles of research. We also conducted focus groups with consumers in both London and Mumbai.

Our conceptualization of the transnational commodity space of British-Asian fashion is broad. It includes the specialized market of clothes sold to British-Asian consumers which is, itself, a dynamic and highly differentiated market which reflects changes both in the Indian fashion industry and its transnational trajectories (Tarlo 1996) and in Britain (Khan 1992; Bhachu 1998; Bhachu this volume). Our case studies include companies such as Banwait Brothers, who cater for an established British-Asian market by providing both fabric to be made up into 'Asian'-style clothing favoured by older women and ready-made clothes. It also includes companies such as Damini's, Raishma and Afreen which are at the forefront of the new boom in British-Asian designer fashion, supported through fashion shows and glossy magazines such as *Asian Woman and Bride*, aimed at young, affluent British-Asian women. Our slice of transnational commodity culture also encompasses companies that do not specifically target a British-Asian market, although their clothes have a South-Asian stylization. These include designers producing clothes for street or club wear which celebrate variously understood 'fusions' between Eastern and Western influences – such as the Nottingham-based designers OneBC or the trendy leather *salwaar-kameez* produced by London-based Scream Clothing. These garments inhabit and, in part, emerge from, the commercial space of so-called 'Asian cool'.[2] Yet, the space of British-South Asian commodity culture also includes high-street retailers such as Monsoon and EAST both of which produce clothes which are designed with an 'ethnic' inflection, sourced in some cases from the Indian sub-continent (see Dwyer and Jackson 2003). These latter companies are, perhaps, the most obvious examples of a more general 'Indian' aesthetic that has re-emerged to influence high street fashion particularly since 1998 (see Garratt 1998; Blanchard 2002).

In the sections that follow we draw on five case studies from our own research in order to illustrate the different ways in which the transnational geographies of commodity culture might be traced. In writing through each case study we emphasize four different dimensions of transnationality highlighting how each of these dimensions are articulated rather differently in each case and how these different dimensions are enacted within commodity culture. First, we engage with transnationality as *biography*, tracing the ways in which personal and corporate identities are intertwined. Second, we emphasize the role of transnationality as *business practice*, focusing on the role of supply networks and asking how such transnational networks are incorporated into the presentations of the products themselves. Third, we consider transnationality as *stylization*, focusing on how the clothes are situated within discourses about transnationality. Finally, we explore transnationality in relation to *consumers*, emphasizing that these garments are bought by a range of different consumers who are inserted into transnational spaces in different ways and with varying degrees of investment.

Banwait Brothers[3]

Banwait Bros & Co. was established as a fabric wholesale business in 1967 by three brothers who emigrated to London from the Punjab region of India. The business expanded to include additional shops in Southall and

Birmingham before two of the brothers emigrated to Canada in the 1980s where they opened businesses in Vancouver and Toronto. The London part of the business is now run by the two sons, Raj and Jags, although Mr Banwait senior is still involved, as well as his wife and daughters-in-law. Banwait Bros & Co. sell both ready-made clothes and fabrics. While fabrics were originally sourced from India and India remains an important market for particular kinds of fabrics – including specially commissioned hand-embroidered organza – China, Korea and Japan are now important sources for fabrics like chiffons and silks. Although they had sold ready-made clothes since the mid-1980s the expansion of this section of the business into a separate label and retail space called 'Sequinze' has been spearheaded by Jasleen, who came to London from India on her marriage to Raj in 1993. The designer clothes collection is sold within a separate upstairs gallery of the shop which is styled through references to an Indian heritage – carved wooden chests and vases are displayed. As Raj explained to us, the name 'Sequinze' was chosen to sound modern and 'not too Asian' and this upper gallery is intended to entice a particular kind of customer – younger Asian women seeking ready-made designer clothes – and is thus separate from the ground floor salesroom of the shop which caters for older women seeking fabrics rather than ready-made clothes.

In January 1999 Jasleen launched her own designer collection. This is a collection inspired by new fabrics designed for Sequinze and imported from China which are silk brocades with 'Chinese style' printed designs – dragons and willow patterns. Jasleen's designs (see Figure 3.1) are a fusion of Asian styles that incorporate Chinese style collars and fastenings. This collection has been advertised in Asian style magazines[4] and fashion shows. Although originally made in India this designer collection is now made-to-measure in London.

From this brief account it is possible to trace a number of different dimensions of transnational space. One starting point is to trace the transnational geographies inherent within individual biographies and company history. When interviewed, Raj at Sequinze rejected the characterization of Sequinze as a 'family business' – perhaps because of its association with the perceived narrow niche market of ethnic enterprise. Instead, in their corporate brochure, Sequinze describe themselves as 'multinational', emphasizing their branches in Canada, drawing self-consciously on a transnational family history whose links have shaped the growth and focus of the business. Second, the company is transnational in terms of how its sourcing and production is organized. For Sequinze, transnational production extends both to India – where the company deals with fabric suppliers and designers in Mumbai and Delhi whose associations with the family go back 20 years – and to newer associations in China and Korea reflecting shifts in the global fabric market. The production process requires frequent visits to both places to ensure that production standards are met. Third, the company exemplifies transnationality in terms of stylization. Sequinze

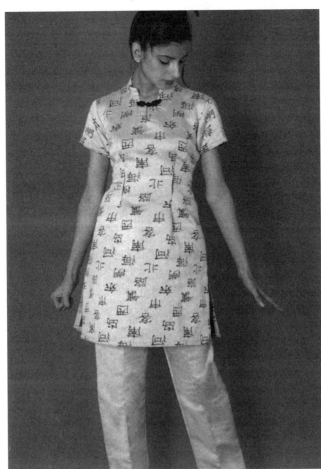

Figure 3.1
Advertisement
for Sequinze
collection

(Photograph:
Vincent Dolman,
*Eastern Eye
Magazine*, 3 March
2000. Used with
permission)

situate their designer collection within a transnational stylization. In their
promotional brochure, Sequinze emphasize that their collection 'has
captured and combined the Traditional and Modern look. A Collection that
uses types of embroideries that are hundreds of years old to create outfits
that have a cut and design of the 90s.' As Jasleen explained: 'our clothes
are East–West, the cuts and designs are Western even if the fabrics are seen
as Asian'. The new 'Chinese style' collection suggests a different kind of
transnationality as the caption on their advertisment reads: 'Southall
Broadway meets Chinatown as Asian Fashion goes Oriental'. Finally, we
can trace transnational geographies in relation to Banwait/Sequinze's clientele which, while embedded within the local Asian population within
Southall (seen as an 'Asian retail centre') also extends beyond this.
Customers include non-Asians seeking specialist fabrics (the shop has been
included in specialist 'ethnic' features in design magazines such as *Elle*) as

well as Indian visitors from the sub-continent seeking fabrics from China or Japan which, until recently, were not available in India because of trade protection.

Damini's

Damini's is a retailer of ready-made Asian clothes, specializing in suits and *lenghae*. The company is run by Deepack Mohindra in London with a business partner Dax Govind in Leicester. Like Banwait Bros, Damini's has its origins in a fabric shop that was started by Deepack's mother (called Damini) in London in 1970 after her arrival as a refugee from Iraq in 1968.[5] However, the trajectory of the business has been different. Deepack joined the business in the early 1980s after training as an accountant and sought to change the direction of the company away from wholesale fabric towards more ready-made clothes with their greater profit margins. At the same time he met Dax, who was a business graduate working in Leicester but also running a small retro clothes business. Dax came from an African-Asian migrant background whose family business had been in grocery retailing. She was introduced to Deepack by another shop owner when she was looking for shoes to sell in her shop. Dax and Deepack saw an opening for shops selling ready-made Asian clothes aimed at younger Asian women who were seeking fashionable Asian clothes that were 'East–West' in their design. They opened their first shop in Belgrave Road in Leicester in 1989, a second shop in Green Street (East London) in 1995 followed by a third shop in Southall Broadway in 1999 – all shops sited within areas recognized as distinctive Asian retail areas. A new store was opened in the West End of London (Edgeware Road) in 2001.

Damini's have sought to make their shops highly distinctive from existing Asian shops that they describe as lacking light and being over-crowded and cluttered. Instead, their shops are light and airy with large plate-glass windows and stylish window and store displays.[6] As Deepack explained to us, the aim was to create an environment which would be comparable to shops like Next or Oasis in order to attract both young Asian women customers and what was perceived as a growing non-Asian market. Damini's describe their clothes as 'East-meets-West'. They specialize in suits and argue that their designs are mainly driven by trends in the Western fashion market rather than from the sub-continent. They have also been pioneers in selling men's tailored suits (which they see as a growing market) and a wide range of children's clothing. Clothes are mostly made in the Mumbai area in small workshops and factories although there are designers based in Jaipur, Rajasthan. Deepack travels regularly to India and works closely with his local agent Viki who runs a clothing manufacturing company, Vanshik, which also produces clothes for the Mumbai market. This close relationship ensures that trends within the British shops can be quickly matched by production in Mumbai. In contrast to some of the Asian designer boutiques, Damini's do not sell only 'one-off' pieces but will have a range of styles in contrasting colours. Their shops are distinctive in the ways in which such clothes are arranged by colour in the store reflecting high-street retailing practice.

Recognizing the current interest in 'Asian' fashion Damini's has sought to extend their non-Asian market through a catalogue marketed through the celebrity glossy *OK! Magazine* and by opening their first 'West-End' store (on Edgeware Road) in 2001. They are also interested in selling in the US and are developing their e-commerce as well as exploring retail opportunities in New York and California as well as Morocco. Such expansion is aimed not only at a market within the Indian diaspora but more broadly. They have also sought to move into the non-Asian wedding market. After attending the Wedding Fair at the NEC in 1998 Damini's have worked with the company Russell and Haslam – mainly by providing Zardosi embroidery through their workers in India.

Discourses and practices of transnationality work rather differently for the Damini's case study. Clearly both Deepack and Dax have transnational biographies but mobilize them in particular ways. While Damini Mohindra established the original fabric business, drawing upon her familial links with India after the death of her husband and her flight from the Middle East, her son sees the current enterprise as very different from a family business. He sees his own business training as being crucial in identifying new opportunities for the business and has established new business partnerships with up-and-coming businesses in Mumbai such as Vanshik. Dax, too, brings a business background to the organization although she also has a postgraduate qualification in fashion. Dax suggests that her own family business did not draw upon any ethnic links – she had never been to the 'Asian area' of Leicester, Belgrave Road, until she began to look for stock for her shop. The sourcing of clothes for Damini's continues to depend upon transnational links with companies in Mumbai (and in other parts of India). Production and design is also organized transnationally – ideas and sketches are taken from the UK to India and then developed by designers and manufacturers. As Dax explains, 'it is not simply a two-way process, lots of different people are involved'. Designers in the workshops in Mumbai also develop ideas through watching what is popular in Bollywood movies and in fashionable Mumbai shops as well as on Western catwalks. The stylization of Damini's collection reflects this intersection as they describe their clothes as 'a fusion between East and West' – clothes which are aimed at modern, young British Asian women as well as non-Asian women seeking, as their catalogue puts it, 'fashion from the East' (see Figure 3.2). This fusion is achieved by the use of light-skinned or non-Asian models in their advertising and the use of modern rather than traditional Asian backdrops. Interestingly, Damini's stylization of their shops which reflects this 'East-meets-West' theme is achieved through the decor which includes an 'ethnic' feel but is not necessarily concerned about

Figure 3.2
Damini's mail-order catalogue, 1999
(Copyright: Damini's. Used with
permission)

being 'authentic'.[7] In terms of their clientele Damini's is at the forefront of a move to broaden the appeal of the Asian aesthetic beyond a British-Asian population which might include both white-British customers as well as other ethnic groups such as the Arab population targeted by their new West End store.

Afreen[8]

Naella Ahmad, who sells her clothes under the name Afreen, works from home in Northwest London and represents a significant but rather different element of the British-Asian fashion market. The business in London was established in 1998 and grew out of the family business in Karachi, a shop in the city's up-market boutique and restaurant area, run by Naella's sister-in-law. Naella, whose husband is a student, designs garments individually for clients and faxes or emails these designs to Karachi where her sister-in-law organizes production through her own tailoring contacts. Family visits are combined with fabric buying and research on current design trends as well as specific tasks such as printing brochures to advertise the collection. Naella's client base is built up through word of mouth (friends and relatives) and through her participation in specialist Asian wedding fairs such as *Asia Live* held annually at Wembly Exhibition Centre in London. Naella's designs are defined as 'classic' and she seeks to emphasize traditional Pakistani hand-work such as embroidery while also using 'English cuts'.

Naella's enterprise is closely related to the 'suitcase collections' described by Khan (1992). Yet, while earlier female entrepreneurs brought clothes back from the sub-continent to sell in Britain, Naella's business is a rather different transnational enterprise although still essentially small-scale and home-based. Naella is able to mobilize fax and email to carry out a transnational 'family' business linking Britain and Pakistan. Like the other companies, she also mobilizes a discourse about transnational stylizations seeking to incorporate 'English' cuts with 'traditional Pakistani embroidery'. Naella's clientele is a small but diverse group which includes both Asian friends and relatives as well as non-Asian customers, including a woman who owns a boutique who is interested in 'ethnic' clothing.

Ghulam Sakina

Ghulam Sakina is a new designer label, set up by Liaqat al Rasul, and sold for the first time in Liberty of London in the summer of 2000. Liaqat, a fashion graduate from the University of Derby, was born and grew up in Wrexham, Wales, although he describes his 'country of origin' as Pakistan. Liaqat's father ran a business as a clothing retailer, selling Western-style clothes which he bought from Asian wholesalers in Manchester. Liaqat describes accompanying his father on buying trips as a child, seeing this as one of the ways he became interested in fashion. At Derby University, Liaqat spent a sandwich year studying in India, including periods at the prestigious National Institute of Fashion Design (NIFT) in New Delhi and working with Indian fashion designer Ritu Kumar. Kumar is well known as a key figure in the revival of the Indian handicraft tradition and the emergence of 'ethnic chic' – Indian designer fashion drawing on indigenous embroideries and block printing (Kumar 1999). Liaqat's graduate degree show was entitled 'Multicultural Mind Mayhem' which he describes as 'a collection which combines Eastern heritage with modern fashion concepts, expressing the shift towards global awareness that permeates music, art, communications and industry, as well as fashion'. More generally, he talks about his aesthetic and his clothes as a critical engagement with multiculturalism (see Dwyer and Crang 2002). Through sewing together many different culturally inflected pieces (in the garment in Figure 3.3 these include recycled paisley prints and bed sheets, printed packaging material,

Figure 3.3
Liaqat al Rasul
graduate
collection, 1999
'Observational
Composite'

(Photograph:
Masoud Golsorkhi.
Used with
permission)

traditional Bengali embroidery) or by putting different fabrics alongside each other, he tries to produce an impact which is 'jarring', or mixed up, reflecting his understanding of the nature of contemporary multiculturalism. At the same time, Liaqat wants to tell the story of each of these cultural elements – he rejects a 'cut 'n' mix' approach to 'ethnic' products which dislocates them from any sense of their material origins, something he attributes to some 'Western designers'. His publicity materials emphasize, instead, his use of traditional production techniques and his work in partnership with 'the craftsmen and women of New Delhi'. His collection also uses recycled fabrics and industrial materials such as packaging 'to create clothes that have longevity and a sense of nostalgia'.

His first collection of garments for Ghulam Sakina (the name combines the first names of Liaqat's parents meaning 'servant' and 'beauty') were produced in Delhi in a workshop he secured through local contacts. The clothes were made under Liaqat's close supervision over a ten-month period. He found that he had to closely supervise the sewing of the designs which were unfamiliar to the Indian workers schooled in more traditional embroidery and design and unused to working with some of the recycled materials. Once completed, the collection was sold in Liberty in the section designated for 'contemporary new designers', and thus orientated not to a particular ethnicized market but rather a broader affluent, although often international, elite. Liaqat describes himself as a designer working 'from two cultures via the fusion of each country's style, tradition, innovation and craft', aspiring to create something new, 'the multicultural'. While his own cultural heritage is a crucial influence he is also very wary of being pigeonholed as an 'Asian' designer, and ambivalent about the promotional possibilities and professional limitations of such an ascription.

Like the other case studies it is possible to trace through the transnational geographies of Ghulam Sakina. One way of thinking about its transnationality is in terms of biography. Clearly, Liaqat has a transnational personal biography and this has been an important resource in, and influence upon, his work as a designer. However, this is not a straightforward trajectory. He chose to work in India rather than Pakistan because of its professional opportunities and it is, arguably, the work of Ritu Kumar which has been most influential in his choice to work with traditional Indian embroideries and techniques. Liaqat also prefers to engage with his biography by tracing a 'multicultural' identity. Another transnational geography here is sketched out by Ghulam Sakina's business practices. Liaqat's clothes are made in India and his business depends on transnational production and sourcing. In establishing these networks, Liaqat has spent increasing amounts of time in India – both in Delhi and, more recently, in collaboration with the company Anokhi, based in Jaipur (see next section). Finally, this case study suggests an understanding of transnationality as stylization. Liaqat's clothes embody a particular transnational aesethic – 'a fusion of two cultures' that tries to take seriously the aesthetic traditions and practical skills of both. He describes his collection as designed with a 'Western silhouette' but drawing upon an Indian aesthetic. As we suggested above, he prefers to situate his clothes within a discourse of 'multiculturalism' – see Dwyer and Crang (2002) for further discussion. In terms of clientele Liaqat's customers, particularly through Liberty, span an international elite, particularly from the Middle East.

EAST and Anokhi

Our final examples are the British company EAST, a woman's wear chain with over 40 stores concentrated particularly in Southern England and the

India-based company Anokhi – see Dwyer and Jackson (2003) for further discussion. Anokhi was founded in 1967 by Faith Singh, who had been born in India of missionary parents and returned there in the 1960s, and her husband John Singh, a member of the Rajasthani elite. Anokhi, which means 'unique', was set up to develop the commercial potential of traditional Rajasthani handicrafts such as hand-block printing and emphasizes its commitment to retaining traditional crafts and social development. Anokhi's clothes and textiles first sold in Britain in Liberty of London in 1967 before becoming the founding brand of the British high-street chain Monsoon in the early 1970s. In the mid-1970s, as Monsoon began to expand and diversify, they parted company with Anokhi and Anokhi struggled to gain an independent presence in the British market. In 1986 three former employees (Clive Pettigrew, Penny Oliver, Jonathan Keating) from Monsoon approached Anokhi to sell their products in the UK and founded a new company Anokhi Wholesale Limited which opened its first shop in London in 1986.

As this new company grew, it sought to diversify its range and in 1994 the first EAST collection was launched. This was an attempt to expand the business to attract a younger market, in the words of several interviewees within the company, to move beyond an association with a 'hippie' image.[9] According to their corporate publicity the intention was to 'extend the range of fabrics and design . . . whilst still retaining some of the ethnic roots, colour and fashion quirkiness that originally drew the Anokhi fans'. EAST emphasize their use of natural fabrics and hand techniques such as embroidery, describing their clothes as 'designed to be individual' for 'women who want something a little exotic but also wearable'. By the late 1990s EAST had re-branded its stores although they continued to sell Anokhi prints alongside the EAST collection in some of their stores and had a wholesale warehouse selling Anokhi-print home furnishings. Anokhi continues to sell through its own shops in Delhi, Mumbai and Jaipur in India as well as through three shops in the US in San Francisco, Boston and Concord, Massachussetts, and shops in Paris and Marbella.

Anokhi's clothes are all designed and made in India in their own factory and workshops and through partnerships with locally based block printing workshops and embroiderers. EAST's clothes are made both in India (where they deal with about a dozen factories in Delhi and Jaipur, including Anokhi, as well as with outworkers such as embroiderers and weavers) and in China and the Far East, which is particularly important for winter fabrics such as knitwear and velvets. While fabric patterns are designed, or commissioned, in Britain they are sent out to be printed in India or the Far East and then sample designs are sent out for manufacture. EAST's designer and product director will visit suppliers about three times a year and their associations with some factories and workers go back many years. EAST's designer stresses the significance of India as an inspiration for her designs and explains that 'the ethnic look is EAST's handwriting as a label'.

This is characterized by their use of natural fibres and hand techniques as well as the styling of the garments themselves. This 'ethnic' styling of the collection is complemented by the organization of fashion shoots in 'exotic' settings such as Morocco or Barbados (see Figure 3.4) and the styling of the shops themselves which use Eastern images such as Mughal windows and tropical plants. In contrast to the Anokhi collection, less emphasis is placed upon the origins of EAST's collection as the company strives to establish 'a *brand* rather than clothes which are made in India or China'. However, EAST maintains its customers' interest in India through a charity fundraising scheme that supports a school for disabled children in Rajasthan. EAST targets mid-range customers and the company advertises in 'mainstream' fashion glossies and women's magazines such as *Red* and *Good Housekeeping*.

The case study of EAST and Anokhi once more illustrates the multi-dimensional quality of transnationality which we have outlined above. Again, it is possible to trace, through this example, the notion of trans-nationality as biography, although this is a rather different trajectory from the previous case studies described above. The founders of Anokhi and EAST have familial connections with India through the transnational biographies of John and Faith Singh which open up an alternative (colonial but anti-imperialist) trajectory to the post-colonial migration history of the founders of many British-Asian companies. Anokhi is now run by the Singhs' son and daughter-in-law who see themselves as 'living between Britain and India' reflecting their own transnational biographies. The other founders of EAST include one who had a colonial childhood in India while others have developed a longstanding relationship with India through their working lives which began as buyers for Monsoon in the late 1960s.

Transnational business practices are organized differently in Anokhi and EAST. While Anokhi is an Indian company which seeks to develop 'partnerships' with international buyers, EAST is a growing British high-street name that works with supply networks and factories across India, China and Korea. For both companies clothes are styled through trans-national discourse, but these differ in important respects and, at times, are in tension with each other. For Anokhi, their emphasis is on Western fashion styling which used traditional block printed Indian cottons and silks. In the case of EAST, their brand is built upon a more generalized, less specific, reference to the 'exotic' and the 'ethnic' through a discourse of 'difference'.

What EAST and Anokhi also clearly illustrate is the multiple inhabita-tion of the transnational field of British-Asian commodity culture. It is clear that this field cannot be imagined as occupied solely by those who have a connection with a designated British-Asian 'ethnic' community. While the case study suggests the complexity of belonging and affiliation which such a bounded notion of community entails, the discussion of the various biographies of those who run Anokhi and EAST demonstrate other kinds

Figure 3.4
'Shekhavati', EAST
spring/summer catalogue 2000
(Copyright: EAST. Used with permission)

of belongings within this transnational social field. This case study, in particular, also emphasizes that the market across which their garments are sold is not simply confined to one group of consumers but is multiply inhabited by differently placed consumers with different levels of investment in a British-South Asian transnational style or aesthetic.

Conclusion

Our aim in this chapter has been to respond to calls for the 'grounding' of transnational studies in empirical research (Mitchell 1997), through an examination of the specific movements of particular people, things and goods associated with transnational commodity culture, examining both their material and symbolic geographies. Our argument is that the study of the transnational geographies of commodity culture may offer a productive means through which to re-figure the study of transnationalism.

There are a number of reasons for this. First, through our emphasis on the circuits of commodity culture we are seeking to extend the social space of British-Asian transnationality beyond the confines of specific, ethnically defined, communities. While it is important to recognize the diverse connections British-Asian communities have with their places of residence in the UK, with their real and imagined homelands in South Asia, and with fellow South Asian transnationals elsewhere in the diaspora, it is also important to extend the boundaries of transnationality to include differently located groups and individuals who may, or may not, be members of these specific 'ethnic' communities. The case study firms discussed here suggest a wider transnational field that is *multiply inhabited* by a range of actors, including differently positioned producers, cultural intermediaries and consumers with different degrees of 'investment' in British-Asian commodity culture. Such a view expands the notion of transnationality beyond specific 'ethnic' groups and actively de-stabilizes traditional views of 'Britishness' by refusing to restrict the transnational to members of specific ethnically defined minority groups. This suggests a notion of trans-national space which is multiply and differently inhabited and transnational cultural geographies which are more fluid and multi-dimensional.

This sense of transnational space as not only multiply inhabited but also *multi-dimensional* is the second point which can be made by focusing on the transnational spaces of commodity culture. It can be argued that commodity culture has this multi-dimensionality at its heart in so far as a commodity is inherently many things: the product and embodiment of social relations of production; a form of aesthetics; a means of realizing an exchange value; the product of particular businesses and organiza-tional geographies; and a resource allowing the objectification of social relations for consumers. We wish to suggest that commodity culture is a particularly powerful lens through which to see the many dimensions of transnationality, and the disjunctures between them, whether in terms of transnational biographies, transnational modes of business organization and practice, or transnational stylizations that characterize contemporary commodity culture.

Third, we would argue that commodity culture is a valuable way of bridging the unhelpful separations of transnationality as an abstract cultural discourse and transnationality as a *lived social field*. Rather than insist-ing that the 'hype of hybridity' should be grounded in concrete analyses of real lives and political economies, commodity culture brings political and symbolic economies together. Cultural discourses and stylizations of identity are a central part of what is being produced, circulated and con-sumed, but always through specific material forms and through variable, economically motivated, social practices.

This chapter opens up the definition of transnationalism, moving beyond specific ethnically defined or spatially dispersed 'transnational commun-ities' to a more encompassing notion of transnational space. This is a space characterized by multiple strands involved in transnational networks with complex circuits of meaning fabricated from a range of social practices by differently positioned actors. The case studies examined here also offer the possibility for a deeper understanding of commodity culture – particularly the commodification of 'ethnic' difference (Hutnyk 2000; Dwyer and Jackson 2003) as well as providing material for more specific studies of the fashion industry and the role of ethnic entrepreneurship.

Notes

1   This chapter draws on a research project entitled 'Commodity culture and South Asian transnationality', funded by the Economic and Social Research Council as part of the 'Transnational Communities' programme (award no. L214252031). The research was undertaken in collaboration with Philip Crang and Peter Jackson, with research assistance from Suman Prinjha and Nicola Thomas.

2   The notion of Asian Cool is both promoted and undercut in Pratibha Parmar's film *A Brimful of Asia* (Channel Four, 14 February 1999) which features fashion designer Bashir Ahmed alongside musicans such as Talvin Singh. The title of her film, of course, refers to Cornershop's chart-topping album, *Brimful of Asha* (1998). See also Hutnyk (2000).

3   All case studies are referenced by name reflecting the considerable support we have been given by the companies involved. Quotes in the text that are not otherwise acknowledged come from interviews conducted with these companies in 2000 and 2001.

4   *Eastern Eye* and *Asian Woman and Bride.*

5   For an alternative account of the history of Damini's, see Bhachu (2004).

6   Having designed their own refurbished shop in Green Street (at a cost of £800,000), Damini's used design consultants Redjackets, who had previously worked on store designs for retail chain Oasis, to design their new shop in Southall.

7   For example, the earthenware pots in the newly refurbished Leicester shop were sourced locally rather than from India.

8   We gratefully acknowledge the help of Suman Prinjha, a research assistant on this project between 1999–2000, in the compiling of this case study material.

9   Quotes are taken from interviews with the fashion designer, retail director and other key members of staff at EAST conducted between February and August 2000, Press releases provided by EAST and an interview with the founding director of Anokhi in August 2000.

References

Appadurai, A. ed. 1986. *The social life of things.* Cambridge: University of Cambridge Press.

Appadurai, A. 1998. *Modernity at large: cultural dimensions of globalization.* Minneapolis: University of Minnesota Press.

Bhachu, P. 1998. Dangerous designs: Asian women and the new landscapes of fashion, in A. Oakley and J. Mitchell eds. *Who's afraid of feminism?* London: Penguin, 187–99.

Bhachu, P. 2004. *Dangerous designs: Asian women fashion the diaspora economies.* London: Routledge.

Blanchard, T. 2002. 'Who's sari now?' The *Observer Magazine*, 7 April 2002, 24–6.

Brah, A. 1996. *Cartographies of diaspora: contesting identities.* London: Routledge.

Breckenridge, C.A. ed. 1995. *Consuming modernity: public culture in a South Asian world.* Minneapolis: University of Minnesota Press.

Cook, I. and Crang, P. 1996. The world on a plate: culinary culture, displacement and geographical knowledges. *Journal of Material Culture* 1: 131–53.

Crang, P., Dwyer, C. and Jackson, P. 2003. Transnational communities and the spaces of commodity culture. *Progress in Human Geography* 27: 438–56.

Dwyer, C. 1999. Contradictions of community: questions of identity for young British Muslim women. *Environment and Planning A* 31: 53–68.

Dwyer. C. and Crang, P. 2002. Fashioning identities: the commercial spaces of multi-culture. *Ethnicities* 2: 410–30.

Dwyer, C. and Jackson, P. 2003. Commodifying difference: selling EASTern fashion. *Environment and Planning D: Society and Space* 21: 269–91.

Garratt, S. 1998. 'Who's sari now?' *Sunday Times* (Style section), 23 August, 4.

Gillespie, M. 1995. *Television, ethnicity and cultural change*. London: Routledge.

Hutnyk, J. 2000. *Critique of exotica: music, politics and the culture industry*. London: Pluto.

Jackson, P. 1999. Commodity cultures: the traffic in things. *Transactions, Institute of British Geographers* 24: 95–108.

Khan, N. 1992. Asian women's dress: from burqah to Bloggs, in J. Ash and E. Wilson eds. *Chic thrills: a fashion reader*. Berkeley: University of California Press, 61–74.

Kumar, R. 1999. *Costumes and textiles of Royal India*. London: Christies Books.

Leontis, A. 1997. Mediterranean topographies before Balkanization: on Greek diaspora, emporium and revolution. *Diaspora: A Journal of Transnational Studies* 6: 179–94.

Marcus, G.E. 1995. Ethnography in/of the world system: the emergence of multi-sited ethnography. *Annual Review of Anthropology* 24: 95–117.

Massey, D. 1994 (original 1991) A global sense of place, in *Space, place and gender*. Cambridge: Polity, 146–56.

Mitchell, K. 1997. Transnational discourse: bringing geography back in. *Antipode* 29: 101–14.

Portes, A. 1997. Globalization from below: the rise of transnational communities. ESRC Transnational Communities Programme Working Paper No. 1 (available at http://www.transcomm.ox.ac.uk).

Portes, A., Guarnizo, L.E. and Landolt, P. 1999. Introduction: pitfalls and promise of an emergent research field. *Ethnic and Racial Studies* 22: 217–37.

Rouse, R. 1991. Mexican migration and the social space of postmodernism. *Diaspora: A Journal of Transnational Studies* 1: 8–23.

Tarlo, E. 1996. *Clothing matters: dress and identity in India*. Chicago: University of Chicago Press.

4 Returning, remitting, reshaping

Non-Resident Indians and the transformation of society and space in Punjab, India[1]

Margaret Walton-Roberts

Introduction: transnational spaces

Since Glick Schiller *et al.* (1992) introduced their analytical framework for transnational understandings of immigrant communities, studies of transnational spaces or transnational social fields have produced rich illustrations of the ways in which space and social relations are being shaped by migrant networks that operate across the boundaries of multiple nation states. Much of this work has been driven by investigations focusing on the US and Central and South America (Goldring 1998; Kearney 1995; Mountz and Wright 1996; Rouse 1991). In this chapter, I turn my attention away from Latin America and the US to India, Canada and Britain – three nations joined through shared, but unequal, colonial experiences and linked in the present through a post-colonial transnational space built primarily around Indian immigration. Within India, I focus on the Doaba region of Punjab (the districts of Hoshiarpur, Kapurthala, Jalandar and Nawanshahr), in northwest India (see Figure 4.1), the site from which millions of Indian immigrants have dispersed to numerous places of settlement and resettlement to form extensive global networks.

Researchers such as Ballard (1990), Helweg (1984), Johnston (1984), La Brack (1989) and, more recently, Tatla (1999), have focused on Punjab specifically through diasporic migrant links, but the density and continued development of Indian transnationalism merits further attention. In this chapter I will review these distinctly transnational connections by considering Canadian NRI (Non-Resident Indian) fundraising for community development projects in Punjab.

Indians overseas

The number of Indians overseas is estimated by the magazine *India Today* at around 15 million with approximately 3 million each in Europe and

Figure 4.1 Map of Punjab

North America.[2] Within India the regional sources of migration have been highly concentrated in a few states, namely Punjab, Gujarat, Kerala, Andhra Pradesh, Tamil Nadu and Goa. Particular migration patterns have also been linked to particular regions; for example, there are strong migratory networks connecting Punjab, Kerala, Andhra Pradesh, Gujarat, Goa, Maharasta and Tamil Nadu with Middle East countries. Similarly, migrants to the UK and Canada tend to come from Punjab and Gujarat; while all of the above states have contributed to migration to the US, Australia and West European countries (Madhavan 1985). Although definitive numbers are impossible to secure, the state of Punjab is thought to be one of India's most significant out-migration regions and exhibits very close links to several countries of Punjabi settlement overseas. During discussions in 1999 with NRI Sabha officials in Jalandhar, Punjab, I was told that possibly five million Punjabis, documented and undocumented, were currently overseas.[3] This represents almost one third of the total estimated number of Indians overseas, for a state with less than two percent of the total Indian population. This over-representation of Punjabis overseas becomes evident when traveling through the state, where one is struck by not only the intimate geographical knowledge many locals have with the sites of Punjabi settlement overseas, such as Vancouver in Canada, Southall and Wolverhampton in the UK, and Yuba City in California, but also, especially in the winter months, the number of British, Canadian and US citizens of Punjabi origin visiting family and friends in the region.[4]

Such concentration results from sustained and long-term migration networks between Punjab and multiple sites of settlement (Jensen 1988; Ballard 2000; Walton-Roberts 1998). The on-going resilience of these networks is confirmed by current immigration application data; for example, 80 percent of applications for family class immigration visas through the Canadian Embassy in Delhi emanate from Punjab and Haryana, and British and Canadian immigration officials in Delhi commented that they cooperate closely on immigration matters because of the similar regional immigration patterns the two countries have experienced.[5] Punjab certainly qualifies as a transnational space, one that has, over at least a century, been subjected to intense international migration, creating a territory that continues to be at the center of multiple transnational networks linking migrants and their relatives back in Punjab.

The history and significance of international migration for India

The notion of communities having global links that form a kind of transnational space, social field or linkages of multiple 'translocalities' (Appadurai 1996) may be a relatively new idea, but in the case of Punjab the actual links and processes are not new. Punjab, especially the Doaba region, has been a traditional site of international out-migration for over a century. Initiated during the colonial period, a combination of declining land holdings and increasing options through military and other paid employment, encouraged families to support the movement overseas of a large number of young single men, with the initial intention of sojourning (Kessinger 1974; Fox 1985). The networks resulting from these movements enabled information, people and money to circulate between Punjab and overseas Punjabi settlements with significant consequences. For example, Punjabis on the west coast of North America played an important role in advancing the Indian independence struggle through the Gadar party (Juergensmeyer 1982) and, as a result, were subject to intense surveillance from British and Canadian Colonial forces (Johnston 1988). In the post-independence era, especially in the 1960s and 1970s, the contribution remittances made to Punjab assisted in the agro-technological advances of the Green Revolution through the purchase of tractors and the construction of tube wells, with significant, though not always positive, results (Shiva 1991). There have also been challenges to the central Indian state through the role Sikhs overseas played in the rise of the Khalistan movement through the 1980s and 1990s (Tatla 1999).

In searching for more politically stable influences, the states and central government in India have been encouraging all overseas Indians, referred to as Non-Resident Indians (NRIs),[6] to play a greater role in India's economic development through various investment initiatives, for example the India Resurgent Bonds launched in 1998, and well-established NRI investment accounts held in hard currency with favourable rates of return. These investment initiatives serve to satisfy India's desire to develop along with the global economy, but also to retain important cultural, economic and political control (Lessinger 1992). Such investment is in addition to the significant transmission of worker remittances that overseas individuals send to family members in India. The current rate of these transfers places India as the single largest remittance receiving country with close to US$10 billion received in 1998.[7]

Grounding transnational research

While it is important to place immigration from India within a wider political-economic context, my purpose in this chapter is to reveal the circulations and transformations transnational linkages entail at the village level by focusing on two villages, both in the Doaba region of Punjab: Palahi, near Phagwara in District Kapurthala, and Dhesian Kahna, in District Jalandhar.

Methodology

A brief review of the methodological framework of my study is important to contextualize these examples. My research into immigrant networks initially focused on Vancouver, Canada and Punjab, India. In Vancouver, using a qualitative, open-ended interview structure, I interviewed several Punjabi immigrants who maintained strong commercial and cultural links back to Punjab. Following these networks, I spent four months in India with the majority of my time in the Doaba region of Punjab. In total I conducted 76 interviews of varying length and intensity with transnational actors both in Vancouver and Punjab. In this chapter I review two of those networks with particular reference to the transformations caused at the village level through overseas migrant fundraising and subsequent development initiatives. I was introduced to each of these villages through initial Vancouver contacts and toured each village with members of the community on various occasions.

Palahi: the global village

Palahi is located on a link road between Phagwara on the main GT road and the Hoshiarpur road. It has a population of 3,800, with an equal number of former residents settled abroad. Of the village's working population, 70 percent are agriculturalists, and the village has 548 hectares of irrigated arable land. The village is home to a successful rural polytechnic, which since 1984 has trained over 12,000 technical and computer students. The majority of students are rural, unemployed, male youth, but women are trained in computer and stenography courses. The polytechnic also has seven extension centers around Punjab where young women complete embroidery and sewing classes. Palahi has become something of a model village boasting a library, post office, two banks, a community park, three schools, solar street lighting, a community hall and a community bio-gas project[8] and, as a result, has been profiled in the television and print media as a local, as well as national, success story (Hartosh 1999; Vinayak 1997).

Palahi benefits from a number of committed individuals on the village council or *panchayat*, but the large communities of Palahi people abroad have been central in funding the major village improvement projects. There are important precedents to these overseas contributions. Early migrants who settled along the North American Pacific west coast in the early twentieth century were active in raising funds for the needs of several villages and educational institutes back in Doaba. Palahi set up its own educational society as early as 1922, and village elders believe that US$17,000 was donated by Palahi men working in North America at this time. More recent fundraising has been channeled through the village NGO, the National Rural Development Society Palahi (NRDSP), which was set up in 1983 and was responsible for establishing Palahi's polytechnic. Collecting money through an NGO rather than the village council or *panchaya* has the advantage of allowing funding decisions to be made independently of the local block development officer. The head of the society is Jagait Singh Palahi, who for many years was village head or *Sarpanch*. Mr Palahi is now a permanent Canadian resident, and spends his time visiting his family in Victoria, Canada, touring throughout North America collecting money for village projects, and returning to Palahi to oversee developments. His global mobility is central to his fundraising effectiveness.

The most recent project to be completed in Palahi was the Miri Piri community hall (see Figure 4.2). This sound-proofed hall with a capacity for 1,100 people cost 35 lakh (over US$83,000) to construct, and was financed with US$80,000 contributions from Palahi people overseas. The hall also has a clock tower and solar powered clock that cost 5 lakh (US$11,900), which was fully financed by one man from Slough in Britain.[9] Currently, the society is raising funds for an underground sewage system, which has been denied a matching grant from Punjab's rural development program because officials argued that many larger towns in the region have no underground sewage system.

Beside contributions to community projects, a significant amount of personal capital flows into the village from abroad. At the Punjab and Sind Bank, Palahi, the manager told me that 20–30 percent of the money handled by his bank came from NRIs. The manager of the Cooperative Bank told me that since 1996, when the bank came into operation, they have taken in 4 crore rupees (roughly US $900,000).[10] A significant amount of this, he felt, came from NRIs and was most commonly used for the purchase of land, building houses, financing weddings and donations to the village, especially the religious temple or Gurdwara.[11] Most villages in Punjab have at least one Gurdwara, which acts as a central gathering point and spiritual focus for the community. As a measure of the transnational networks Palahi is embedded within, three of the five-person Gurdwara management committee are Canadian residents who meet annually during the Gurdwara's main festival, the birthday of the sixth Guru, Guru Hargobind.

It is difficult to get any figures on the number of people who have left this village (or indeed Punjab for that matter), but a few examples show how extensive the global migrations have been. My host, the principal of the village polytechnic, guided me through a survey of 60 houses in the central part of the village where Jat and other higher caste families reside.[12] Residents had moved abroad in forty of the houses, mostly leaving them to

Figure 4.2 The Miri Piri community hall in Palahi

be inhabited by other family members. But ten of these houses were empty and locked, and eleven were rented or had a caretaker (see Figure 4.3). The destination of migrants from the 40 households is indicated in Figure 4.4 and reveals the diversity of settlement sites.

Despite the significant out-migration – two-thirds of households are affected by international migration – Palahi does not represent a landscape of decline. In most cases those overseas were still maintaining their properties for occasional annual or biannual visits, and I was told that it was very rare for migrants to sell the family home. In this sample only one house had been sold, and that belonged to one of the first people to leave Palahi. Despite what seems like a massive exodus, there was a very regular movement back to Punjab, especially during November to March when the best weather brings people back for family visits, wedding arrangements and tending to family property. To facilitate this movement coach companies – some run by NRIs – transport people directly from Delhi airport to the major out-migrant areas like Phagwara, Jallandhar and Ludiahana. This allows returning migrants to go directly to their towns and villages without having to negotiate Delhi, and contributes to maintaining the perception of proximity between distant overseas sites of migrant settlement, and the home village in Punjab.

Figure 4.3 Tenant-occupied houses belonging to NRIs

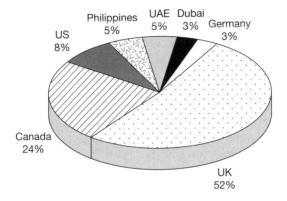

Figure 4.4 Overseas location of residents from 40 Palahi households affected by international migration

Increasingly, these regular networks are enhanced by the effects of communication technologies, allowing the villagers greater and more regular contact with their relatives. The village has about 270 phone connections for 500 houses and 5 Public Communications Offices offering the ability both to make and receive international telephone calls. This is relatively high for a village of this size, which might normally have only 25 or so home phone connections for 500 houses. Other forms of communication are shaped by very intimate personalized connections; the principal of the rural polytechnic, for example, acted as a type of local correspondent for an international Punjabi language newspaper based in Vancouver. Most evenings he would scan the local newspapers and select stories he thought people overseas might be interested in. Late in the evening he would then fax the stories to the newspaper and for this he received a small payment. One communications resource the people of Palahi particularly prided themselves on was the polytechnic internet connection. All villagers and visiting NRIs can send and receive emails through the college, and it also enables the principal of the polytechnic to maintain contact with Jagait Singh Palahi, the chairman of the village development society, as he tours North America gathering funds. This situation, a village with an internet connection, was seen as rather unique in India, and in one local television story Palahi was termed a 'Cyber village'. The report's story-line reveals how processes of time-space compression have introduced spatial complexity to this village through its contradictory relations with 'nearby local' government officials and 'distant global' migrants overseas:

> The state officials in Phagwara, a three-kilometer drive away, remain as inaccessible as ever to the villagers here. But their NRI relatives are only a click away. Step aside Mr. Postman; Palahi is zooming ahead on the info-highway.[13]

This type of communications technology has enabled Palahi to promote itself through a monthly internet newsletter sent to Palahi people overseas and others who have a connection to the village (such as myself, development agencies and environmental NGOs in Europe). This newsletter is, increasingly, becoming a central means through which villagers connect themselves more closely to a globally dispersed community, and is certainly an example of how new globalizing technologies are intensifying, extending and transforming traditional immigrant networks. It also presents an example of Latour's (1999) ideas of how space becomes folded and creased as networks transform physical distance through the circulation of information.

Transnationalism and immigrant settlement

Transformations at the level of the village are also accompanied by transformations at the site of overseas settlement. As Appadurai (1996) argues, we need to see how immigrant communities and networks are often formed across nation-states in very personal and intimate ways, revealing the highly emotional connections immigrants maintain with their home villages. My link into Palahi was Ajit Singh,[14] a man who emigrated to Vancouver in 1974 with a degree in economics. By 1982 he became a real estate agent, but prior to that he held several jobs as a cleaner, glass-cutter and taxi-driver. Despite, or perhaps because of, the hard times he faced in achieving a successful life in Canada for himself and his family, he always felt extremely attached to his village. Soon after Palahi's National Rural Society was set up in 1983, Ajit felt he was in a financial position to contribute, so in 1985 he assisted in collecting over Cdn$30,000 for Palahi from Canadians connected to the village. About 10 years later he helped coordinate a similar collection, gathering Cdn$32,000. Such fundraising was facilitated in part by the spatially concentrated geographical settlement pattern of Indo-Canadians. Of the 126 donors in 1995, all were in British Columbia, and three-quarters lived in the Lower Mainland region of the province, with over one-third from just one municipality, Surrey, in the south-east of Greater Vancouver. Palahi village became an important symbol of success both in India and for immigrant communities abroad, and Ajit explains why the collection was so successful:

> [This] is an exemplary thing, because most villages they don't have electricity, and here we are talking about Internet web site. So I think the main inspiration was since I spent my time, I have studied there; I was totally involved with the commitment to my village. But here, when I came here, I could not forget it, I even thought I was more in a position to do something . . . Why we did it? It was needed, how we did it? Because we were able to do that, and people were cooperative.[15]

The impact of such actions is important not only for the positive material transformations of place in the receiving locality – Palahi – but also because of the ways they allow for the maintenance of important emotional attachments for immigrants as they negotiate their position both within and between multiple sites of home:

Ajit: Like for me, this is my community now, Canada is my community. If I am thinking about my village . . . I think how I can contribute to a fund for Surrey Memorial Hospital, because when a patient is turned down there, my pain is equally, same or more, than for people suffering in India. Plus, I can make a contribution if we are here, because, there [in India] it is a very hard task to make enough money . . . Whereby here, we can make, I mean if we don't go to McDonalds one time, that is worth 236 rupees, and one can teach their child for 236 rupees for a whole year!

MW: So your contribution is much bigger if you are earning in Canada?

Ajit: Definitely, definitely. But my psychological problem is I am a Canadian, but I am Punjabi and Indian and living psychologically in Punjab all the time.

The actions of maintaining these linkages across 'source and destination' countries, therefore, are not merely a matter of economic development, measuring the impact of remittances and the pace of development and change in the source region, but of negotiating and maintaining positive forms of transnational identity and attachment to place, which can also contribute to successful settlement overseas.

Honouring parents and luring children: Dhesian Kahna

While Palahi represents the successful mobilization of a significant overseas community, Dhesian Kahna represents a much smaller project, but nevertheless still draws upon transnational networks in order to effect change at the level of the home village. Dhesian Kahna is a small village in District Jalandhar, roughly one hour's drive from Palahi. The village has about 800 houses, 4 Gurdwaras, some successful light industry, and 6 banks. There is also a very large Gurdwara complex built around Sant Gurmail Singh, attracting many devotees and funds from abroad. One similarity between Palahi and Dhesian Kahna, which indicates the lack of formal development assistance from the state, is the condition of the roads connecting the village to external routes. Although in 1996 state officials made political gestures by unveiling two foundation stones to mark road improvement schemes, by 2000 there was no evidence of any progress.

I had been introduced to this village by my Vancouver contact, Mr Dhesi, to study a development project he was funding to drain a large pond of stagnant water in order to convert it into a village park. Mr Dhesi had set up the Mehroki Patti Development Fund, which, according to receipts, was financed by Non-Residents, but in reality had overwhelmingly been financed by Mr Dhesi, whose sole financial contribution up to 1999 was 705,608 rupees, or around Cdn $25,000.[16]

As with Palahi, the village had been a site of out-migration for several decades, and Mr Dhesi estimated that between 50 to 80 percent of his generation had left the village. Many of the houses were empty, locked and in poor repair. Contact appeared to be on-going however, with several new houses being built by NRIs from Britain and Canada, and communication facilitated through about 50 phone connections, as well as 5 PCOs. Most of the international calls placed through the PCOs were to the UK.

Immigrant communities, despite the different areas of settlement overseas, can still effectively operate as a network across these different sites. In the case of Dhesian Kahna, though Mr Dhesi in Vancouver provides much of the finance, his cousin from Bradford, England oversees and manages the actual project during his annual visits to Punjab. Each of these individuals represents different processes of migration and settlement overseas. Both are financially secure and well established, and both maintain important links to their original migratory site.

Mr Dhesi, an Indian-trained engineer, came to Canada in 1969 assisted by his uncle, an early migrant to Canada, and found work with BC Rail. In 1979 the Chief Engineer, who had promoted and mentored Mr Dhesi, died and was replaced by a man from Saskatchewan. Under this new manager Mr Dhesi was made to feel like an outsider:

> As soon as he became in charge of our engineering services department, I start feeling same thing that I did when I came to this country ... What he did, he start bringing all his close friends ... I was in charge of department, then he put me aside, then he put another person beside me. Then he says, now, 'you teach him what you are doing.' Of course I train him a full year, then the fellow is fully acquainted with what I am doing, then he again sub-divide our sections. Then he put me on the corner, and for about one year and a half, I was going back to the office, eight o'clock, come 4 o'clock, for a full year I never touched one thing, and I was being fully paid and I was getting frustrated, and junior people than me become my boss. They were promoted; I was sort of demoted, you know because I didn't get my promotions.[17]

Mr Dhesi left BC Rail in 1982 and opened his own business importing and exporting goods from India. He developed a business partnership with a London-based company importing and manufacturing fruit juices, initially for the Indo-Canadian community. Over time the business became so successful he set up alone and now runs a fruit juice production plant as well as having an interest in an engineering consultancy. His work with his fruit juice company requires him to visit India regularly, where he usually stays with relatives in Delhi. In 1996 he took a day out from the Team Canada Trade Mission he was involved in to visit his home village, and what he found disturbed him:

> I was going in the winter time . . . still January it start getting hot there. So I say I can't stand it I have to go back, people say . . . how come you are not going to live with us anymore? . . . Then I say, why is it such a smell? This smell comes from this pond . . . I could not sleep, the wind was blowing and smelling this, you know . . . You were born here, you played here, you played with the dirt you know, you lived here, you jump in the pond, swim in the pond. Those days there was no sewage water, nothing like that it was just simply rain water, it was clear water! And the animal was drinking water there because there was no sewage there.

The presence of the large drainage pond filled with stagnant water and sewage was a shock to his nostalgic childhood memories. Perceiving his shock, the older local men asked him to do something to help them, telling him; 'Son, if you can do something for your own village, if you can afford to do, look that you have everything, all these things, we heard about you.' Having 'heard about you', they were implying that they knew he was a successful man in Canada, and that meant he had the funds to help the village improve. In response Mr Dhesi paid Cdn$10,000 towards having a park built in his father's name in place of the stagnant pond, and eventually his contributions rose to Cdn$25,000. His main motivation came from the desire to honor his father, but also, as is common in Punjab, to compete with other villages to create something unique:

> There is no village in Punjab, I search all over [where] there is a park, where the kids can play, have a good health, and in the evening, after the sun, after the hot day, go in the cool air, sprinkling water, all these things, sit there, talk, exchange ideas, look after it . . . We have a school, dispensary, banking, you name it, but there was no park.[18]

Due to Mr Dhesi's business concerns, he rarely had time to visit his village, so in his place, his cousin, Mr Singh, agreed to manage the project during his annual visits. Initially Mr Singh felt there was little interest in the project, and the responsibility to motivate the community and oversee construction work became excessive for him. A letter he wrote to his cousin in Vancouver in December of 1998 hints at the frustration he was experiencing with the project: 'As you know I have been tied down to this responsibility for last 2/3 years. Nobody co-operated or given any help to me. This job was too demanding and pressurous [*sic*]. Now, somebody else should take responsibility.' But by February 1999 things appeared to have improved as other village improvement projects received funding and there was increased interest from both village officials and NRIs: 'New *Sarpanch* . . . is taking keen interest in improvement work. But, still, nothing is being done to the drains that lead to the big pond . . . people hope that this *Sarpanch* would do something to rectify.'[19] Though there appeared to be more support from the *Sarpanch* for improvement schemes, the designation of the land as a *park* strictly for recreational purposes in a village where function and utility – whether material or spiritual – are paramount, was creating some tension:

> [E]ntrance gate must be finished soon, so that misusing of park could be stopped. People graze cattle sometime we have to quarrel with them to stop. Sometime farmers park agricultural machinery in the park. So once gate is fixed we can control the entrance.

By late 1999 the progress made on the park had impressed some other NRIs who maintained houses in the village, about ten of whom had contributed funds, giving the project a further 300,000 rupees. Despite these gestures, during my visit to the village, Mr Singh indicated to me the frustration he felt that the older generation of immigrants were the only ones with any emotional attachments to the village. With nothing motivating their well-settled children overseas to develop any attachment to their parents' home village, he was concerned about the long-term viability of the project. Though Mr Singh's children did occasionally visit the village, he commented that his son had advised him not to assume he would visit regularly, and therefore he should not spend too much money on improving his house there. To compound this detachment, despite Mr Dhesi's attempts to convince state officials of the importance of this project, the Punjab State government offered no matching grant for the development project, and Mr Singh was unable to gain information on those projects that were funded.

The park development offers an interesting reading of the desires of NRIs to improve the status of their village. In part, the motivation is clearly a feeling of emotional responsibility to honor their family name, but it is also in response to their own desire to spend more time in the village as they approach retirement. To fully enjoy their regular annual trips back to Punjab, it was important that children and grandchildren felt comfortable with the idea of spending time in the village. While improvements could be made to individual homes – and they certainly were in Dhesian Kahna – the surrounding environment would continue to intrude unless action was taken. In Mr Dhesi's case it was the smell that first offended him, but in other cases the potential for disease, especially malaria, was of major concern to NRIs. Ranjit Kaur Singh[20] and her husband, who had been living near Bradford in the UK for almost 20 years, were building a large house with six bedrooms and bathrooms close to the park. In discussions with Ranjit it became clear that she was excited at the prospects of her children and young grandchildren visiting them in their new house while they stayed in Punjab for extended periods. This was complicated, however, by the fact that her young granddaughter was terrified of mosquitoes after her grandmother contracted malaria while in India. The illness the child witnessed her grandmother endure once she was back in the UK had sensitized her to the possibilities of disease from mosquitoes. Ranjit felt something had to be done about the standing water in order that the family would feel comfortable enough to visit. In this way the transformations occurring in Dhesian Kahna result from a series of complex interactions between generations, as well across a landscape shaped by uneven development and international flows of capital.

General processes

These two examples are obviously selective, but after four months of fieldwork, seventy interviews and thirty-nine field visits throughout Punjab viewing NRI-funded community development schemes, they do highlight a series of processes common to several of the projects I viewed. I will review these processes under the following headings: spatial and temporal linkages, the myth of return, demographic markers, on-going circulation, inter-generational issues and community conflict, in order to demonstrate the wider importance of transnational migrant activities across both source and settlement regions.

Spatial and temporal linkages

Most of the NRIs I interviewed had migrated from *rural* villages in Doaba to *urban* regions in the west, and their lasting attachment to their village – a socio-spatial merging of family and place – sustained their desire to return. Even when NRIs buy houses in towns away from their villages of origin, they often retain ownership of their village family property, and contribute to village fundraising projects. In this way the territorial link to a specific place is retained despite the reality of a long-term movement away from the village.

It is also important to understand that Punjab, and Doaba in particular, is a region fundamentally shaped by long-term and sustained global out-migrations. The intensity and scale of these movements has changed as opportunities fluctuate globally in line with changing immigration policies. As immigration regimes have changed so has the nature and magnitude of flows out of this region, but it needs to be stressed that any human migration must not be interpreted as a one-time event. The whole point of using a transnational approach to understanding migration is to emphasize the long-term effects of such movement, which, in conjunction with new technologies, accelerate and sustain the creation and recreation of multiple social and spatial outcomes over time. The examples of transformation within Palahi and Dhesian Kahna offer one attempt to chart these outcomes.

The myth of return

Linkages between the source region and multiple sites of Punjabi settlement overseas must also be emphasized within a transnational approach. Punjab is a central symbolic anchor for many migrants who are well settled overseas, and understanding the strength of this connection is central to why linkages are so resilient over time and across space. This anchoring has been referred to in numerous studies of Indians overseas through consideration of the 'myth of return'. In Britain, Harlan (1991) suggests that despite the fact that only 5 to 15 percent of Punjabis in Southall actually do return to India, the myth of return functions to provide important mechanisms for social control and psychological security, as Robinson (1986) and Helweg (1979) have also argued. Indeed, Helweg, throughout his extensive research on Indians overseas, has continually highlighted how individuals balance the desire to return with the reality of their settled life overseas, arguing that the plan to retire in India 'is a dream held by many Indians in the States' (Helweg 1987: 169). In a Canadian example, Helweg found that one immigrant's decision to buy a house was accompanied by regret: 'I procrastinated on buying this house because it symbolized permanency in Canada. I did not want to face the fact that I would not be returning to India' (Helweg 1985: 69). In Australia, Helweg found the initial intention of returning to India was present for both the 'new' and 'old' immigrant groups (Helweg 1991). The intention to return is also recorded by Rangaswamy (2000) in a survey of 574 Indian immigrants in the Chicago area. Rangaswamy found that though 51 percent of respondents stated that they had initially intended to return to India, only five percent had actually made this a reality. She also reports that men exhibited a greater desire than women to return to India.

In the two examples I have highlighted above, both male Vancouver contacts indicated their desire to return to India on at least a semi-permanent basis, and their socio-economic position allowed for such possibilities. It is important to stress, however, that many immigrants, young and old, are unable to exercise their desire for return due to a lack of financial resources. In addition to financial concerns, permanent return is also made difficult for the older generation once their children become successfully established in the country of settlement. The idea of permanent separation from sons, daughters and grandchildren becomes too distressing, especially for women.

In place of permanent return it is more likely that the current trend of visiting India for extended trips will increase. In the case of Vancouver, such transnational flows are evidenced by the fact that scheduled flights from Vancouver to Delhi (both via London and Singapore) are often fully booked in the winter months.[21] Additionally, the Indian Consul issues 30,000 visas annually to Canadians of Indian origin across Western Canada, and a Vancouver survey of 3,500 South Asians puts this estimate higher, suggesting that approximately one-third of those sampled reported traveling to India in the previous year (Ethnimark 1997). I offer these figures to suggest that, though the idea of return may well remain a myth for many Indian immigrants, the desire to return is a potent force that may be satisfied though regular trips to India. Such movement has the potential for a variety of outcomes, including development projects funded and/or directed by NRIs.

Demographic markers

Who are the people organizing these transnational networks and linkages? My field visits to NRI-led community development projects were overwhelmingly directed by men. This is the result of a number of factors: my limited language ability, which curtailed my ability to confer with many women at the village level, the patriarchal nature of Punjabi society, and the cultural norms of interacting with 'honored' guests – as I was often deemed to be. I tried to rectify the absence of women from much of my fieldwork through specific visits to women's schools and colleges, and through secondary sources and expert interviews. However, it is clear to me that older men control most of the fundraising and community development projects funded by NRI money. This reflects normal Indian cultural patterns, since in most Indian families authority is determined by gender and seniority (Sharma 1993). Elder males are seen to deserve the most respect, and those who have attained significant reputation and success overseas are often treated with special deference, especially in villages. Most of the projects I visited were explained to me as the direct outcome of the 'vision and sacrifice' of certain male individuals, with little comment on similar sacrifices made by their spouse and/or children. The customary importance of honoring and deferring to such individuals needs to be understood as an important aspect of Punjabi, indeed Indian, cultural relations. Most of these men were retired, and at a point in their life where they could afford a significant amount of time to be either in Punjab overseeing developments, or traveling to overseas sites of Punjabi settlement in order to raise more funds. It was particularly striking that British citizens of Indian origin were involved with many of the projects I visited. In many interviews with British and Canadian NRIs, it struck me how similar their life-cycle patterns were: emigrating in the late 1950s and 1960s, employed in a semi-skilled occupation or running their own business, and working through to retirement to enjoy considerable financial savings and success (at the time of my research the value of a British sterling state and private pension alone was financially significant in Indian rupees). Most respondents had grown children who were successfully established in the country of settlement, often pursuing professional and managerial careers with the support of their extended family, especially older females who provided child-care services. Seeing their families well settled seemed to reassure many of the men I met, freeing them to pursue regular contact with their remaining Indian relatives, and deal with any outstanding Indian property or business interests.

The demographic profile of Indian immigrants in both Britain and Canada, as shown in Table 4.1, provides an indicator of the population under discussion. The age profile of older Indian immigrants is fairly similar across Canada and Britain, but the Indian-origin population over 45 years old in Britain is larger in absolute numbers than Canada's. The larger percentage of Indian-origin population in Britain over 45 compared to South Asian Canadians reflects the nature and timing of significant migrations, with Britain's most active Indian immigration occurring a decade before Canada's. Assuming the continued desire for some form of return or connection for this group, increased transnational activity may become more evident between India and Canada as this age group of Indo-Canadians finds both the time and the finances to satisfy their desire for regular and longer trips to India. This suggests that the type of connections already present in the form of transportation networks, financial transfers and cultural interactions and exchange will intensify.

On-going circulation

As with other transnational communities, status plays an important role in transnational social fields (Goldring 1998). The ability of NRIs to display wealth and power through their material investments in the village indicates success and increased status. Many of those who left in the 1960s and 1970s were relatively uneducated men and their success abroad proves an immense incentive for young men and women in the villages of Doaba, despite the fact that the economic conditions and labor market demands overseas have changed since the 1960s. The fact that many recent migrants face great hardship, especially if they are undocumented, does not seem to deter young men and women inspired by the NRI wealth they observe directly in their village. Young people find ways to go overseas by utilizing different migration options that are highly gendered and carry with them a number of potential negative effects for the individuals concerned. For men, a common option is to use an agent who, for upwards of 1 lakh (approximately US$2,500), can provide a fake visa.[22] I heard many reports of men who found themselves stranded in Eastern Europe for up to two years waiting for a chance to enter the European Union. For women, most cases I came across involved marriage to an NRI which, in itself, can present great difficulties depending upon the intentions of the receiving family overseas.[23] While many middle-class urban families I spoke to held more ambivalent attitudes regarding overseas migration, marriage was

Table 4.1 Indian/South Asian-origin population in Canada and Britain over 45 years old

Britain: Indian origin[a] (years)	No.	%	Britain: total population[b]	%	Canada: South Asian[c] (years)	No.	%	Canada: total population[d]	%
>75	18,840	2.0	4,266,000	7.4	>75	10,505	1.5	1,465,905	5.1
60–74	84,780	9.0	7,593,000	13.1	65–74	26,425	3.9	2,668,815	9.2
45–59	150,720	16.0	10,669,000	18.5	45–64	127,355	18.9	5,592,975	19.4
Total >45	254,340	27.0	22,528,000	39.0	Total >45	164,285	24.3	9,727,695	33.7

Notes
a Indian origin 1999 population 942,000. Annual Abstract of Statistics (Wisniewski 2000).
b Great Britain 1999 population 57,804,000 www.gad.gov.uk/population/.
c South Asian population, Census, Statistics Canada, 1996, total 1996 South Asian visible minority population 670,590.
d Canada Census 1996 total population profile tables, total 1996 population 28,846,765.

often a time when families would seriously consider the possibility of selecting an NRI partner, attested to in the matrimonial pages of Indian and overseas newspapers which often include detailed information on immigrant or foreign citizenship status.

Attitudes to work are also influenced by the possibility of working overseas. Many respondents referred to young men who refused to work on their family farms because they saw it as demeaning, preferring instead to hire in-migrants from Bihar and Uttar Pradesh. These same men, however, would willingly work overseas in the most menial janitorial and laboring jobs because of the potential to earn foreign currency. In conversations justifying the reinterpretation of status across transnational labor markets, it struck me that people always referred to foreign earnings in terms of Indian rupees, another sign that the intention to return to India to display this foreign wealth was central to their actions. The display of wealth NRIs exhibit through land investment, property improvement, lavish weddings, etc., and the increased status performed through charitable giving and preferential choice in the selection of a match for their sons and daughters, all contribute to perpetuating the desire for overseas migration within rural Doaba. This desire is served via several mechanisms, including the extensive range of services provided for fake document production and migrant smuggling, and the cultural norms and mechanisms for increasingly globalized marriage networks. These influences are important to highlight, albeit briefly, because they reveal how transnational networks contribute to the *continuous* nature of migration across an extended spatial and social field, a point that both academics and policy makers should recognize.

Inter-generational issues

For Mr Singh, the long-term viability of improvement projects in Dhesian Kahna depends upon the interest and contribution of the second generation. Concern about the second generation's interest in its cultural roots and attachments to Punjab have been displayed in a number of ways. In a report on a group of Punjabi writers settled in the UK visiting Punjab, the impression was that the second generation was detached and selfish: 'Where the older generation, which once migrated to the west from here, desperately pines for the motherland, the new generation is only concerned about their growing individual interests' (Tribune News Service 2000).

Concern over this detachment was given official recognition at the Fourth Annual NRI Sabha Punjab convention in January 2000, where government officials, NRIs and Sabha officials dedicated one day of the conference to discuss 'Dilemma of Punjabi Disapora'. Part of the program read as follows:

> The first generation of NRIs has the anchorage of their memories but the new generation which was born and brought-up in foreign lands

does not have any moorings in the motherland of their parents. Elders want to mould their children according to the Punjabi culture and they expect from them adherence to age-old values and obedience to social norms which appear ridiculous to the younger generation. Both live in a state of dilemma – the old ones live in nostalgia, the younger ones in the new world.

(NRI Sabha 2000)

The NRI Sabha, responding to the general concerns of NRIs, also lists one of its main objectives as to: 'Maintain cultural and ethnic bonds of Punjab with the NRIs especially with the new generation of the NRIs' (NRI Sabha 2000: 1). The intention of the NRI Sabha merges with so many of the concerns academics have pinpointed in work that focuses on second-generation youth and identity formation (Gillespie 1995). But building second-generation interest in the home village in order to sustain its viability and vitality needs to be critically evaluated. Palahi manages to maintain its vitality not just through the active overseas fundraising, but because it has a rural polytechnic which attracts hundreds of local young people into the village every year, as well as an active involvement in a number of sustainable development initiatives coordinated at the national and state level. These interests extend to involvement in bio-gas projects, ferro-cement technology and advocating environmentally sustainable agricultural methods. Without involvement in local and national projects directed by local residents, a village will not be able to prosper. In this way, NRI fundraising needs to be included in an overall development scheme, mediated by locals who are residents and can confer with those still resident in the village. Though many NRIs may worry that their children are losing interest in their cultural roots, the actual improvement of their home village needs to be seen as something more locally rooted that will not be improved through migrant transnational actions alone.

Community conflict

Transnational movement and the social influences exercised in the source region do not necessarily result in wholly positive processes. Kearney (1995) for one has indicated how flows of capital and development processes within Mexico can contribute to furthering the uneven nature of development within and between villages and regions. Punjab also exhibits this trend. At the level of the village, Helweg (1983) has considered this process of NRI-led development, detailing how the allegiances formed between emigrant families and trusted 'managers' who remain in the village, alter power dynamics, displacing traditional structures of control and social norms. In both Palahi and Dhesian Kahna, investment and change depend upon having people in place at the village level in order to control project development. How villagers accept the project is also open to various interpretations. In the case of Palahi, the respect shown to both Mr Jagait Singh Palahi and the polytechnic principal are certainly due to their long-term presence and activity in the village – Jagait Singh Palahi only recently emigrated to Canada. In the case of Dhesian Kahna however, Mr Dhesi, though respected, cannot be present in the village, and his cousin, though present part of the year, has to work with other people in the village to get cooperation and support from the wider community in order to sustain the project.

Across the whole of Punjab, and Doaba in particular, the injection of significant overseas funds has transformed villages economically, socially and culturally (Shiva 1991; Mehta 1990), but such transformations have not occurred equally across the landscape. Regionally, Punjab is seen as one of the more prosperous states in India due to its agricultural production,[24] but in recent years agricultural productivity has declined with very little replacement manufacturing and hi-tech diversification (Singh 2000a). While many village families and properties in Doaba receive remittances and investment through NRI channels, other parts of Punjab are not so fortunate. Across the whole of Punjab it is widely acknowledged that the local state has failed to invest in rural areas to provide basic civic ameni-ties such as adequate water, lighting, roads, sewage systems and schools, and only half of the funds budgeted for rural development actually reached villages (Thukral 1999). In the financial vacuum left by the state's failure, villages with no alternative sources of revenue are left to flounder. This is particularly evident in those districts south of the Sutlej River, which are not traditional sites of out-migration and do not have extensive overseas resources to call upon. Three such districts, Mansa, Sangrur and Bhatinda in the Malwa region, have been reported in the media as the sites of a number of farmer suicides prompted by massive debt, and the lack of state concern has prompted widespread criticism (Shiva 2000; Gill 2000). Many villages in this region are also cited as suffering from the lack of state investment in basic amenities such as schools (Singh 2000b). In periods of economic decline and transition coupled with local state withdrawal, the insertion of external capital such as NRI remittances and investment exaggerates and perpetuates uneven development, protecting some while others are impoverished.

While NRI development funds can often be deployed far more efficiently than those from the local and central government, associated problems of community tension, unplanned and uneven development are present at all levels. At a time when Punjab faces a number of domestic challenges, espe-cially the limited ability of the state to mold and implement policies that advance some kind of overall development throughout the region, these migrant contributions are examples of development almost entirely out of the hands of the local state. Driven by deep cultural attachment to specific *people* and *places*, the positive impacts of such investments, though undoubtedly evident, are highly fragmented both spatially and socially.

Conclusion

The interpretation of a transnational space implies a spatially extended field. As a result of this extension, multiple sources of information from several locations need to be integrated in order to illustrate how networks operate, and the role of the various actors involved. In this chapter I have attempted to follow through two specific networks from Vancouver to Punjab but, as this chapter has illustrated, the material consequences of actions transmitted through these transnational networks contribute to wider processes of change in both the source and destination regions. In both of the examples I have traced, though the intentions and aims of those involved have material effects, they are highly motivated by *cultural* meanings and desires. This cultural contextualization of capital and information flows repositions such actions outside the typical model of capitalist expansion from the west into less-developed zones, as well as challenging the ideas of assimilation in the destination country.

This chapter has also contributed to the field of transnational literature by moving away from the dominant US–Mexico continuous land border focus, to a more spatially dispersed context. Also, unlike previous anthropological studies which considered migrant fundraising and impacts on the home village by tracing links from the rural village to the urban site of migration settlement (Kearney 1986), this chapter has traced networks in the opposite direction, from the urban site of settled 'home' to the rural village 'home', several decades after the initial, now permanent, migration was undertaken. This indicates the long-term resilience of transnational attachment and the material consequences such attachments have on the landscape of the sending region.

In this chapter I have made connections to South Asian-origin settlement experiences such as the myth of return, demographic and generational patterns of change. In the source region I have highlighted the links to factors of local state involvement and the grounded realities of village development through external funding. The combination of the Punjab state's failure to advance development and the insertion of outside capital from NRIs has led to a patchwork landscape of success and decline, and though a forceful participant in the development of Doaba's rural villages, the NRI is not a panacea for the problems faced by many Punjabi villages. Recognizing this unevenness, and the on-going place of international migration within it, highlights that fact that these processes are no longer separated as distinct fields of enquiry – immigrant settlement on the one hand and 'third world' rural development on the other – but brought together into one field of interpretation as a transnational space.

Notes

1 A version of this paper was originally presented at the Annual Association of Geographers meeting in Pittsburgh, 2000. The author wishes to thank respondents

both in Vancouver and Punjab, and David Ley and Daniel Hiebert for comments on an earlier draft. Funding for this research was provided by the Indo-Canadian Shastri Institute, Vancouver Centre of Excellence for Research on Immigration and Integration in the Metropolis (RIIM) and the Social Sciences and Humanities Research Council Canada.

2 Plus 5 million in South Asia (Nepal and Sri Lanka), 3 million in Mauritius, Fiji, South Africa, Trinidad, Guyana and Surinam, 2.5 million in the Middle East and 1.5 million in east Asia (Kautilya 1998).

3 The NRI Sabha is an organization representing the interests of NRIs, especially with reference to property related matters.

4 Throughout this chapter I will refer to 'Punjabis' overseas rather than Sikhs. While Sikhism is strongly associated with Punjab, and the majority of Punjabis overseas would define themselves in some way as influenced by Sikhism, it is not necessarily the case that all Punjabis are Sikhs. To refer to a person as a 'Punjabi' does imply certain shared cultural understandings, which may or may not include religious influences emanating from Sikhism which is, in itself, also a highly *cultural* as well as religious marker. For a discussion of the complexities of 'Punjabi' self-identity in London see (Raj 1997).

5 Personal interviews with Canadian and British immigration officials, conducted in Delhi, India in December 1999 and February 2000.

6 The NRI Sabha (organization) of Punjab defines an NRI as 'an Indian citizen who stays abroad for employment, carrying on business or vocation outside India or stays abroad under circumstances indicating an intention for an uncertain duration of stay abroad as a non-resident. It will also include non-resident foreign citizens of Indian Origin and Indian citizens having green card or otherwise the right of residence in a foreign country' (NRI Sabha 2000: 5).

7 The Reserve Bank of India collects remittance data from banks and authorized currency exchangers, and quarterly surveys are conducted to ascertain unclassified receipts (IMF *Balance of payments statistics yearbook*, 1999, methodology section, p. 210). Of course this official data, it is widely agreed, tends to under-represent the true magnitude of remittance flows (Choucri 1986).

8 This involves capturing methane from human waste and using it as an energy source.

9 One lakh is 100,000 rupees. One US dollar is equal to approximately 42 rupees.

10 One crore is 100 lakh.

11 He estimated that 50 percent of the NRIs he dealt with came from Canada, 45 percent from the UK, 1 percent from the US, and 4 percent were in the Middle East.

12 Most villages in the Doaba region are set out in a particular pattern, with the central houses inhabited by the Jat Sikh landowners and other higher castes, with the 'untouchable' sweeper and tanner castes experiencing the most residential isolation on the periphery. Hershman (1981) argues that the presence of caste as an organizing system within Sikh villages is still important despite the religious teachings of Sikhism, which shun caste-based practices. The fact that this survey was carried out in the central part where higher caste families live probably causes an over-representation of certain settlement locations. Even with lower caste village members, however, migration is common, but there would probably be greater emphasis placed on temporary or undocumented migration to the Middle East and Europe.

13 'Cyber village on self-help mission', Gajinder Singh, January 5, 2000, TV Today.

14 Pseudonym.

15 Personal interview, Vancouver, November 1998.

16 The fund was established in Canada and had secured charitable status.

17 Interview July 13, 1999.
18 During my fieldwork I did visit other villages that had parks, but generally the presence of a park was not common.
19 Letter February 3, 1999.
20 Pseudonym.
21 Interview with Air Canada official, October 1998.
22 I heard many different reports about the cost of fake documents and assistance to go overseas – some were as high as 9 lakh (over US$20,000) for a genuine visa. Other newspaper reports indicated that agents were selling fake visas for 1 lakh, and for cases where assistance to the destination was provided – in one case to Korea – over 2.5 lakh.
23 I heard of several cases where the NRI deliberately deceived the family in Punjab regarding his educational and class status. Details of such events have become common throughout Doaba, and though many people are more cautious about going through with such unions, the demand for NRI matches, especially grooms, is still high (see Walton-Roberts 2004).
24 Though only 1.5 percent of the area of India, in 1998 Punjab produced 21 percent of Indian wheat, 9 percent of the rice and 15 percent of cotton.

References

Appadurai, A. 1996. *Modernity at large: cultural dimensions of globalization.* Minneapolis: University of Minnesota Press.
Ballard, R. 1990. Migration and kinship: the differential effect of marriage rules on the processes of Punjabi migration to Britain, in C. Peach, C.G. Clarke and S. Vertovec eds. *South Asians overseas.* Cambridge: Cambridge University Press, 219–249.
Ballard, R. 2000. The growth and changing character of the Sikh presence in Britain, in H. Coward, J. Hinnells and R. Williams eds. *The South Asian religious diaspora in Britain, Canada and the United States.* New York: State University of New York Press, 127–144.
Choucri, N. 1986. The hidden economy: a new view of remittances in the Arab world. *World Development* 14: 697–712.
Ethnimark 1997. Ethnic marketing and advertising. *South Asian Lifestyles.* Vancouver.
Fox, R. 1985. *Lions of the Punjab: culture in the making.* Berkeley: University of California Press.
Gill, P.P.S. 2000. Poverty, indebtedness behind farmer's suicides. *Punjab Tribune*, 2 December.
Gillespie, M. 1995. *Television, ethnicity and cultural change.* London: Routledge.
Glick Schiller, N., Basch, L. and Blanc-Szanton, C. 1992. Transnationalism: a new analytical framework for understanding migration, in N. Basch, L. Glick Schiller and C. Blanc-Szanton eds. *Towards a transnational perspective on migration: race, class, ethnicity and nationalism reconsidered.* New York: New York Academy of Sciences, 1–24.
Goldring, L. 1998. The power of status in transnational social spaces, in L. Guarnizo and M.P. Smith eds. *Transnationalism from below: communities/identities unbound.* Rutgers: Transaction Press, 165–198.
Harlan, W. 1991. Changes in the Sikh community of Southall, London 1963–1985. Paper delivered at the Punjabi Perspectives: Proceedings.

Hartosh, S.B. 1999. Government help be damned, residents of a village in Doaba use funds by NRI relatives to make it a life worth living. *Indian Express,* 22 November, 3.

Helweg, A. 1979. *Sikhs in England: the development of a migrant community.* Delhi: Oxford University Press.

Helweg, A. 1983. Emigrant remittances: their nature and impact on a Punjabi village. *New Community* 10: 435–443.

Helweg, A. 1984. Emigration and return: ramifications for India. *Population Review* 28: 45–57.

Helweg, A. 1985. India's immigrant professionals in Toronto, Canada: the study of a social network. *Population Review* 29: 67–79.

Helweg, A. 1987. Why leave for America? A case study approach to understanding migrant behaviour. *International Migration-Migrations Internationales* 25: 165–176.

Helweg, A. 1991. Indians of the professions in Australia: some theoretical and methodological considerations. *Population Review* 35: 75–89.

Hershman, P. 1981. *Punjab kinship and marriage* (ed., Hilary Standing). Delhi: Hindustan Publishing Corporation.

IMF 1999. *Balance of payments statistics yearbook.* Washington, DC: International Monetary Fund.

Jensen, J.M. 1988. *Passage from India: Asian Indian immigrants in North America.* New Haven: Yale University Press.

Johnston, H. 1984. *The East Indians in Canada.* Ottowa: Canadian Historical Association.

Johnston, H. 1988. Surveillance of Indian Nationalists in North America 1908–1918. *B.C. Studies* 78: 3–27.

Juergensmeyerr, M. 1982. The Gadar syndrome: ethnic anger and nationalist pride, in S. Chandrasekhar ed. *From India to America: a brief history of immigration: problems of discrimination, admission and assimilation.* La Jolla, CA: A Popular Review Book, 48–58.

Kautilya, J.R. 1998. Woo brains not only bucks: India's NRI policy is economically and socially skewed. *India Today,* 9 November.

Kearney, M. 1986. From the invisible hand to visible feet: anthropological studies of migration and development. *Annual Review of Anthropology* 15: 331–361.

Kearney, M. 1995. The effects of transnational culture, economy, and migration on Mixtec identity in Oaxa California, in M.P. Smith and J. Feagin eds. *The bubbling cauldron: race, ethnicity and the urban crisis.* Minneapolis: University of Minnesota, 226–243.

Kessinger, T.G. 1974. *Vilyatpur, 1848–1968: social and economic change in a north Indian village.* Berkeley: University of California Press.

La Brack, B. 1989. The new patrons: Sikhs overseas, in N.G. Barrier and V. Dusenbery eds. *The Sikh diaspora: migration and experience beyond the Punja.* Delhi: Chanakya Publications, 305–336.

Latour, B. 1999. On recalling ANT, in J. Law ed. *Actor network theory and after.* Oxford: Blackwell.

Lessinger, J. 1992. Investing or going home? A transnational strategy among Indian immigrants in the United States, in L. Basch, N. Glick Schiller and C. Blanc-Szanton eds. *Towards a transnational perspective on migration: race, class, ethnicity and nationalism reconsidered.* New York: New York Academy of Sciences, 53–80.

Madhavan, M.C. 1985. Indian emigrants: numbers, characteristics, and economic impact. *Population and Development Review* 11: 457–481.

Mehta, S. 1990. *Migration, a spatial perspective: a case study of Bist Doab-Punjab.* Jaipur: Rawat Publications.

Mountz, A. and Wright, R. 1996. Daily life in the transnational migrant community of San Agustin, Oaxaca and Poughkeepsie, New York, *Diaspora* 5: 403–428.

NRI Sabha, Punjab. 2000. Dilemma of Punjabi diaspora. Conference publication.

Raj, D.S. 1997. Partition and diaspora: memories and identities of Punjabi Hindus in London. *International Journal of Punjab Studies* 4: 101–127.

Rangaswamy, P. 2000. *Namasté America: Indian immigrants in an American metropolis.* Pennsylvania: Pennsylvania State University Press.

Robinson, V. 1986. *Transients, settlers and refugees: Asians in Britain.* Oxford: Clarendon Press.

Rouse, R. 1991. Mexican migration and the social spaces of postmodernity. *Diaspora* 2: 8–23.

Sharma, U. 1993. Dowry in North India: its consequences for women, in P. Uberoi ed. *Family, kinship and marriage in India.* Delhi: Oxford University Press.

Shiva, V. 1991. *The violence of the Green Revolution.* London: Zed Books.

Shiva, V. 2000. Poverty and globalisation. Paper delivered at the BBC Reith Lecture, Delhi.

Singh, P. 2000a. Punjab: sans direction. *Hindustan Times*, 15 February, 13.

Singh, S. 2000b. No teacher, no doctor, no grant: plight of villages in Punjab, *Sunday Tribune*, 20 February, 1.

Tatla, D.S. 1999. *The Sikh diaspora: the search for statehood.* London: UCL Press.

Thukral, G. 1999. Punjab villages starved of funds. The *Tribune*, 27 November, 3.

Tribune News Service 2000. New generation selfish, regret UK-based Indian writers. *Chandigarh Tribune*, 13 February.

Vinayak, R. 1997. Palahi, a rural showcase. *India Today*, 31 March, 120.

Walton-Roberts, M. 1998. Three readings of the turban: Sikh identity in Greater Vancouverr. *Urban Geography* 19: 311–331.

Walton-Roberts, M. 2004. Rescaling citizenship: gendering Canadian immigration policy. *Political Geography* 23: 265–282.

Wisniewski, D. 2000. *Annual abstract of statistics: Office for National Statistics.* London: Stationery Office.

5　Transnational migration and the geographical imperative

David Ley and Johanna Waters

We are told that with the rise of globalization we live in an era when boundaries are transcended, when borders are transgressed. A putative global space of flows has carried Von Thunen's isolated state to a further level of abstraction, for, if on the land surface of the isolated state everything was held constant except transportation costs, we are informed that the tyranny of distance itself has now largely been dismissed by the electronic transmission of information and capital. It was, of course, transportation costs that brought geographical differentiation to the Von Thunen land surface, so now with their transcendence, pure isotropic space awaits the decisive arrival of flows through a supercharged global network. The globalization of space suggests that the isolated state, now minus its sticky friction of distance, has been reconfigured to the world itself.

In this context the status of the nation state is politically and theoretically compromised. The creation of trading and geopolitical blocs in Europe, Asia and the Americas promises to attenuate the state's boundary-maintenance efforts. Ken'ichi Ohmae's much-debated ode to 'a borderless world' was followed logically enough by his declaration of 'the end of the nation state' (Ohmae 1990, 1995). The influential work of Manuel Castells and other globalization theorists has moved in a similar direction, where 'globalization limits the sovereignty of the state' and even in such domestic spheres as the organization of the labour force and educational policy 'the relative autonomy of the state is fading away' (Carnoy and Castells 2001). There is some truth to these assertions, not least when we consider the international movement of labour, a key constituent of the space of flows. The ever more elaborate fortifications along the Mexico–US border still leave it more permeable than the Berlin Wall, and both barriers highlight the hard-pressed efforts of the state to protect its own borders.

Human smuggling and undocumented arrival are significant aggravations to national jurisdictions, but they are not the only cases of subversion of the state's intent to gather in its citizens. Transnational migrants, who arrive at their destination without ever fully leaving their origin, represent another manifestation of the space of flows, for such sojourners have converted the linearity of migration into the circularity of transnational movement and, in so doing, seek to renegotiate the state's desire to reproduce national citizens. While much of the literature on the transnational migrant emphasizes movement of poorer households between the Caribbean islands or Central America and the US (Basch *et al.* 1994; Leavitt 2001), a rather different account applies to expatriates rich in human capital, whether Japanese business people in Europe (White 1998) or European managers and financiers in Hong Kong or Singapore (Beaverstock 2002). Related to the expatriates are the middle-class and wealthy sojourners among the Chinese diaspora who engage in global scanning as they seek to optimize economic prospects around the Pacific Rim and beyond, while approaching the issue of residential selection and national citizenship strategically and flexibly (Mitchell 1993; Ong 1999). Expatriates and sojourners are a very particular type of transnational migrant, part of an emerging cosmopolitan class who seem to be the natural denizens of a 'borderless world' (Appadurai 1996; Sklair 2001). Their incorporation in transnational capitalism, their hyper-mobility – conjured up most evocatively by the Hong Kong or Taipei 'astronaut household' – and their strategic approach to the containment of national borders encourage a representation as *Homo economicus* incarnate (Ong 1999; Ley 2003).

What we are suggesting is that the discourse of globalization has moved to a new scale the idealizations of an earlier economic geography that traded in the simplifications of an isotropic plain and economic rationality. The erosion of distance and national borders has, it seems, aided the substitutability of location; moreover, neo-liberal economic policy has drawn attention to the figure of the cosmopolitan entrepreneur, 'at home' in any setting. As an overseas Chinese businessman told Aihwa Ong in northern California, 'I can live anywhere in the world but it must be near an airport' (Ong 1999: 135). We do not necessarily subscribe to the generality of this condition, but we would argue that it is a part of the rhetoric of globalization that has been absorbed, sometimes too uncritically, by governments and policy-makers.

In the discussion that follows we outline briefly the attempt by the Canadian State to recruit just such cosmopolitan entrepreneurs to contribute to economic development in Canada – a policy pursued with similar presuppositions and expectations by governments in Australia and New Zealand. We will see the underlying assumptions of the globalization thesis that skills can be transferred and locations substituted unproblematically across the Pacific Ocean. But, in practice, these outcomes did not eventuate. The variable cultures of regulation between Canada and East Asia limited the transferability of successful economic development, while entrepreneurs themselves sometimes changed their stripes when they landed in Canada. Not least, the long-range transnational commuters found that frictions of distance remained in unanticipated ways; patriarchal control of the Chinese family, for example, underwent a subtle subversion with the extended absence of the household head. The appearance of the footloose entrepreneur with portable skills conceals the broader play of a geographical imperative that continues to assert regional difference over sameness, and rewards spatial proximity over separation.

Canada's Business Immigration Programme

The category of business immigrant was developed from the pre-existing class of economic migrants who qualified for landing in Canada through the points system on the basis of their human capital. In 1978 the entrepreneur stream was introduced, conferring enhanced points to applicants with significant business skills planning to develop a business in Canada; in 1986 a second stream was added, with immigration fast-tracking permitted for investors prepared to invest several hundred thousand dollars in venture capital funds in Canada. While the first initiative was developed with an eye to European entrepreneurs, its initial take-up was limited, and the investor category was launched with a clearer sense of the opportunities in East Asia, and notably Hong Kong, where discussions between Britain and China concerning the 1997 expiry of the colonial lease had created considerable instability, particularly among wealthier entrepreneurs, many of whose families had stayed one step ahead of communist rule in fleeing to Hong Kong a generation earlier.

In the peak years of the early 1990s, the business programme accounted for over 10 per cent of all landings in Canada, reaching a peak of 32,000 migrants in 1993. As it turned out, Hong Kong and Taiwanese residents have been dominant among the more than 300,000 people who landed in Canada through the business programmes.[1] From 1984 to 1998, Hong Kong was the principal source region, amounting to between a third and a half of the annual total, with Taiwan adding another 15–20 per cent of arrivals by the 1990s. With its proximity to Asia, British Columbia, on the Pacific Coast, was the most popular destination for business landings, with a third or more of the annual totals, and of this group, some 90 per cent chose a residence in Greater Vancouver. Their recruitment was regarded as a considerable prize, for competition existed among business programmes in Australia, New Zealand, Canada and, to a lesser extent, the US and Singapore to attract these capital-rich immigrants. In the 1990s, entrepreneurs declared a self-worth in excess of a million dollars to Canadian officials, investors in excess of two million dollars. In Greater Vancouver their net worth represented an influx of some $20 billion in household wealth between 1990 and 1996 alone (Ley 1999). Effects on housing and consumer expenditures were pronounced, and Vancouver overtook Toronto as the nation's most expensive housing market; between 1977 and 1996 there was a remarkable correlation of 0.96 between house prices in Greater Vancouver and levels of immigration (Ley and Tutchener 2001).

Some 60 per cent of household heads specified self-employment as their intended occupation on their landing cards. The response of local government was very positive: 'These new immigrants tend to be very entre-preneurial, and provide much of Vancouver's contemporary economic dynamism' (City of Vancouver, 1988, cited in James 1999). Not surprisingly, perhaps, the senior Canadian immigration officer in Hong Kong was no less enthusiastic about this new stream of entrepreneurs: 'They are one of our best immigrant groups. They are used to standing on their own feet. They bring education, language skills, a good attitude and enough finances. They hit the ground running' (Brian Davis, in Mickleburgh 1996). Here, then, was the model immigrant, essentialized, as Aihwa Ong (1999) noted in California, with the ascribed, but also self-ascribed, identity of *Homo economicus.*

An isotropic world . . . or national differentiation?

The Business Immigration Programme assumed the portability of entre-preneurial skills across the Pacific. The economic and human capital of the business immigrant was expected to prime economic development at the landfall in an unproblematic transfer across the surface of a de-territorialized world. But, in fact, the partitions of space still matter. Zhou and Tseng (2001), for example, have shown how the 'astronaut households' of the San Gabriel Valley in Los Angeles are dependent on a spatially concentrated enclave of co-ethnic professional and personal services that facilitate their own footloose (but highly channelled) movement. To this, we will now add another set of sticky local circumstances that shape the entrepreneurial success of business immigrants in Vancouver.

We completed more than 120 ethnographic interviews in Vancouver with economic migrants from Hong Kong and Taiwan (Waters 2000; Ley 2002). Although a large majority had landed in Canada through the guidelines of the Business Immigration Programme we discovered, to our surprise, that only a minority were involved in economic activity in Canada. Some were engaged in passive investment in real estate or the stock exchange, while many (particularly the investors) had taken early retirement in Canada. Others were 'astronauts', commuting to East Asia where they maintained professions and companies and spent the majority of the year, while leaving their family members in Vancouver. Others again, particularly those with younger children, had rejected the astronaut lifestyle, and were hunkering down, putting in time until they had their three year qualification for citizenship. At that stage, return migration would be a likely action. Constant interaction with Hong Kong and Taiwan was ubiquitous among respondents, via personal and family travel as well as through television, radio, newspaper, telephone, e-mail and Internet connections.

The entrepreneur class of migrants was obligated to sustain a business for two years that hired at least one Canadian outside family members. The aim of government was to enlist a cadre of value-added manufacturers from these entrepreneurs, but very few migrants moved into this sector.

Alien labour and environmental regulations, high taxes and labour costs, and unfamiliar backward and forward linkages all made manufacturing an unpopular option. For example, Mr So had been in the dyeing and finishing sector of the textile industry in Hong Kong with a factory that employed 100 workers. However, he had concluded that anti-pollution laws, labour legislation and start-up costs made the business unfeasible in Canada and, upon arrival in Vancouver, he took early retirement.

Most respondents who were employed had become small business owners as retailers or restaurateurs, though this selection often represented considerable downward mobility from positions in larger enterprises prior to migration. The common experience was to buy or open a business in the Chinese enclave economy. But although the Chinese-origin population in Vancouver is around 300,000 it is also heavily overcrowded with small businesses. Mrs Chi opened a health food store but is finding the competition from within the enclave economy crippling: 'Here people have to steal customers from each other. We are not able to make a reasonable profit.' Business failure is a common and demoralizing experience. Mrs Lam had a disappointing story to tell about her family's entry into retailing:

> We started the business. We thought it was like Hong Kong. There we had a retail shop. If you start a business [there] people will come and we will have business. But no, here it's completely different. So we lost quite a big sum. From that time on, we are very cautious, very careful with what we have left. We dare not venture into another business. We try to keep our savings as much as possible.

In this family dilemma, transnationalism emerges as a problem-solving solution. Mrs Lam's husband has a senior professional position in Hong Kong and this is the source of the family's income. For now the family lives on both sides of the Pacific while their daughter completes her education in Vancouver, but their long-term plans are uncertain. In terms of Canadian immigration policy, their story underscores the palpable differences between Hong Kong and Vancouver. Business skills and experiences were *not* transferable across the Pacific.

More generally, the economic cultures of Canada and Hong Kong/ Taiwan have proven far too divergent for many business immigrants. There is the flat income tax of 15 per cent in Hong Kong that is no preparation for marginal rates that quickly reached 50 per cent in Canada. There were many complaints about Canada's tax structure; our respondents found it to be a major disincentive to economic activity. A prominent professional in Hong Kong has moved into voluntary service in Vancouver. For him economic activity is not worthwhile under a tax regime viewed as punitive: 'What really surprised me and is still surprising me is the tax situation. Not surprising, it's shocking compared with Hong Kong.' Many immigrant entrepreneurs simply do not consider that economic returns could offset business risks, and abundant business failures only reinforce these anxieties. Then there is the culture of regulation – permissions, licences, monitoring, inspection, accounting, not to mention labour, environmental and consumer legislation, articulated by a mostly neutral civil service. Navigating through these regulatory shoals is difficult enough without the added limitations of language and social networks that rarely leave the enclave economy. National borders matter profoundly; the isotropic world remains what it always has been: an abstraction. Precisely *because* of the distinctive geographies contained within state boundaries, transnationalism has emerged to maximize access to the advantages of national differences.

Homo economicus? contra essentialized identities

Various post-colonial writings have referred to a decentred identity among former colonial subjects that partake of more than one national culture. Decomposition may then lead to recomposition of a hybrid identity that integrates aspects of different cultures. Katharyne Mitchell (1997) has properly challenged this frequently indeterminate and obscure 'hype of hybridity' as unrecognizable among the Hong Kong families she has interviewed who have members dispersed in different national jurisdictions. In such interviews she has encountered, in contrast, strongly centred and focused individuals who have taken up a coherent family strategy for maximizing accumulation.

But there is also a danger in buying too completely into the perspective of Hong Kong as compromising only 'cosmopolitan capitalists' (Hamilton 1999). It is this view, of course, that has informed the outreach of business immigration policy into East Asia. The extraordinary growth of the economies of the Asian tigers has conferred the title of *Homo economicus* upon the region's entrepreneurs. Their identity has too readily become essentialized around not only business acumen, but beyond this, around a shared cultural obsession with economic maximization that pervades all corners of the life-world. It is no longer the Manchester mill-owner but now the Chinese trader who seems to qualify for Engels' depiction as 'a walking political economy'.

But our interviews with economic migrants from Hong Kong and Taiwan indicated that *none of them* had moved to Canada for primarily economic motives. Indeed, economic opportunities in Canada were not on their horizon. There were two major reasons nominated for movement. The first was geopolitical anxiety in Hong Kong and Taiwan from the expansionary ambitions of the communist regime on the mainland. The second was an often-expressed desire to advance opportunities for one's children through a western education and, more broadly, to advance family goals in the superior quality of life offered by leisure, a cleaner environment and the welfare state in Canada. But there was a downside, for it was widely known that entrepreneurship in Canada offered much slighter rewards and much more irksome risks. One solution was the transnational strategy to partition the family's life-world.

A widely shared axiom among the Chinese community in Vancouver is 'Hong Kong for making money, Vancouver for quality of life'. This rule to live by has savagely undercut the presuppositions of the Business Immigration Programme that *Homo economicus* simply could not help but make money wherever he was domiciled. It did not occur to policy-makers that to contain the immigrant family within the nation state was not to contain their economic activity. The 1996 Census saw the genius of trans-nationalism in subverting the expectations of the state. Self-described Chinese immigrants who entered Canada during the 1986–1996 period claimed very high levels of home-ownership in the expensive Vancouver housing market on their census forms. But half of the same families declared that their incomes *fell below the poverty level*. Tax consultants have advised us that declared income normally represents Canadian income. For a number of households cash flows were coming from income-generating activities on the other side of the Pacific. In many cases, businesses in East Asia continued to be run directly by fathers who comprised one portion of the separated astronaut household and whose family members were based in Canada; in other cases, passive absentee ownership or partnerships maintained income levels; in still others, firms in East Asia gave their favoured managers and professionals a three-year leave of absence, time enough to acquire a foreign passport, and then return to employment back home (Mak 2001).

But shuffling around the location of economic effort by no means exhausted the subversive agency of business immigrants. A number of migrants from the East Asian economies have proven that, contrary to expectations, the offspring of tigers can change their stripes. For a number, the move to Canada has been intentionally undertaken as a status passage to escape from the frenetic economic activity they had willingly pursued before. The very basis of their high evaluation by the Canadian State was now exactly the life they wished to leave behind. Immigrants often use metaphors of slow and fast to differentiate Vancouver from Hong Kong, Taipei or Seoul; one male teenager told us that whereas 'Vancouver was a Pentium I, Hong Kong was like a Pentium III'. These terms are used eval-uatively and inform geographical strategies; those seeking a 'fast' life are drawn back to the opportunities of East Asia as astronauts or return migrants. Among those who stay, 'slowness' has its own charms.

As we have seen, early retirement was a common strategy, especially for those who had entered Canada as investors. At the age of 52, Mr Leung, a senior manager in a multinational corporation in Hong Kong, moved to Vancouver through the investor stream and began his retirement.

> Frankly, you can't earn any money here. [If] you have your own money you can come. Just stay here and relax. You cannot earn good money

here because the tax here is so high . . . Those who come recently, they, were, are all retired people.

But some other business immigrants, too young and insufficiently wealthy to retire, willingly undertook downward mobility in order to spend more time with their families, to pursue leisure activities, and to explore spirituality – all dimensions of life that had been squelched by the demands of their business activities in Hong Kong and Taiwan. A lifestyle in Canada that offers a range of leisure and personal development options is highly valued: the menu we heard commonly included gardening, tennis, golf, swimming, language courses and further education, arts and other therapeutic activities, all pursued with friends and family members. Former business-women come to appreciate closer contact with their children in Canada, though it removed them from the labour market; conviction about the advantages of closer parenting seems to be prevalent (Waters 2000). Volunteering and community activities are pursued by some, especially in association with a desire for spiritual formation. In this latter context we should note the explosive growth of the Chinese-Canadian church in Vancouver, now numbering in excess of one hundred congregations.

A number of these themes are evident in the following extended dialogue from a husband and wife who had both held responsible management positions prior to migration, but had intentionally acquired a much less demanding fast food franchise in Vancouver in order to open up space for other family priorities.

Mr Yee: When we were in Hong Kong, we both felt very busy for life, and we both wanted some life changes. And so we travelled a lot around the world to Australia, States, Canada. We went to Toronto, and Vancouver. One morning in the summer in Vancouver, I stepped out the door of the house of my distant relative's house. I felt the air so fresh, and the sun so bright and everything so beautiful. And then I said to my wife that's the place that we want to go. So when after travelling we went back to Hong Kong and then we made application to immigrate to Canada, Vancouver is the place that we chose.

Mrs Yee: [In Hong Kong] it's the pressure you can hardly face because the whole society is so rushed, you know, and life is so busy that you can hardly slow down a little bit to enjoy life . . . It's both too busy for adults and the kids. So we want to slow down our pace a little bit so we came . . . the first year we came here we just enjoy life. We didn't bother to find job for at least one year. That's what we decided. We'd been working for twenty years so busy . . . And we actually had one year to do nothing, just travelling in this country. After one year we felt that we had to find a job.

Mr Yee: Yes, so we decided to change our lifestyle, to do some business of our own. We'd get a business and we'd provide some jobs for people. So we have a better lifestyle and we can take care of the house and the kids. And we can go to church, worship our Lord. We were not, like, having any religion when we were in Hong Kong . . . We say if there's a Lord we're grateful to you because we don't know who you are.

Mrs Yee: And when we were leaving Hong Kong we were in the peak of our profession or business at that time. That's why we were too busy and we find too little time giving to the family and the kids at that time. So when we came over to Canada, and we first get away from that fast living we still maintain the family life. This is the first priority, we need to have otherwise it ruins the meaning of coming to Canada if we put all the time into working and still neglecting our kids. We find we can adjust so well here. This is what I think because God changed my point of value. Like we are not looking at money so important as we were in Hong Kong.

Like when we were in Hong Kong, you know, everything is, was, so pinpointed on money. Once you get the money you get everything in the world. But life is not like that as we now know. But it takes time for people to change their mind. Like they have to . . . to adjust themselves. I find it may be difficult if people, like, still are the same, not like us who have the religion. And have a change in mind what is the priority in life. If they once know this, then they can adjust much better. Otherwise they still keeping the mind like what they do in Hong Kong, like making money easier and so on. Then they will find it very difficult here and they just can't enjoy the good things here like the good environment, the nice people here and so many different places, like you can go golfing, paying just a few dollars here.

There were a number of variations upon this theme in other interviews but the general points remained constant. Hong Kong (and Taipei) were fast, too fast, and after a number of years of relentless long hours and successful money-making, families longed for a status passage, from the quintessentially fast to the comfortably slow, from single-minded economism to a more rounded life of work, family, leisure and self-realization, for a number of households through new-found Christian beliefs and practices. This new subjectivity, a reconstituted consciousness, was necessary for successful adjustment in Canada. Fast expectations were out of place in Canada. A different place permitted, and rewarded, a different subjectivity. 'Chineseness' was redefined.

There is, of course, a profound irony to all of this. Canada's Business Immigration Programme was designed to effect a transfer of the single-minded entrepreneurial lifestyle from East Asia to Canada. But, instead, it has provided an opportunity to redefine life's priorities away from economic activity as an obsession to a more rounded model of citizenship that grants appropriate attention to family and community life. The Business Immigration Programme has permitted this family to escape the prison of *Homo economicus*. Those for whom such an identity remains powerful will not make an easy adjustment in Canada, and are likely to select astronaut status or return migration to a region where such subjectivity is rewarded. Identity, too, is subject to a geographical imperative.

Transnational separation and family relations

This final section considers the effects of migration on the business immigrant household through a closer examination of the astronaut family. In these circumstances, the choice has been made for one family member to return to East Asia to earn the household income, while the spouse and children remain in Vancouver. The experiences of the astronaut arrangement, however, do not support the contention that spatial separation is irrelevant; rather, the separation of husband and wife has fundamental implications for the identities and aspirations of individual family members.

Within many recent accounts of the mobile Chinese capitalist an equally essentialized notion of 'the Chinese family' can be found. 'Traditional' cultural elements such as filial piety, patriarchy, familism, and Confucian ethics are frequently invoked in explanation of the successful financial strategies of contemporary Chinese entrepreneurs (e.g. Tai 1989; Mitchell 1993; Nonini and Ong 1997), ensuring the efficient operation of the household as a 'unit of accumulation' 'whose members work in concert for the benefit of all' (Greenhalgh 1994: 748–9). Like depictions of *Homo economicus* that disregard the importance of space and place, so too the 'Chinese family' is expected to function effectively irrespective of the spatial separation and social experiences of individual members. The astronaut arrangement could be conceived as the most complete household strategy to maximize financial, social and cultural capital (Ong 1999).

Once again, however, this essentialized portrait subsumes and disregards the individual experiences of family members amid assumptions about collective goals and unified perspectives. Moreover, the geographical imperative impinges on family relations. Interviews with family members testified to the fundamental significance of spatial separation and rootedness in place upon identities and relations *within* the astronaut household. The efficient 'operation' of the apparently flexible Chinese family was clearly challenged in these circumstances, as the following examples testify.

As a member of an astronaut family, Cheryl's husband spends three months at a time in Taiwan, returning to Vancouver for a few weeks in between to visit his wife and two young children. She described her experience of this family arrangement:

When my husband is here I don't have my freedom . . . First time he go back to Taiwan I think that I miss him. I think, if he were here he could do many things – many fixing things [for example] if the car has some problems . . . But now . . . anything I want to do . . . it's okay with anything. I don't need him . . . My husband, he don't like that I can do many things . . . I think he don't like I go anywhere. He likes I stay at home. But I don't think so. I think, 'you not here. I'm free. I can go anywhere' *(laughs)*.

Cheryl captures some of the unexpected outcomes of this family strategy for individual household members and for family relations. At first, women miss their husbands, and face practical as well as emotional difficulties in the new environment of Vancouver (Waters 2002). The contrast with pre-migration circumstances is striking – the majority of women interviewed had had full-time careers and described daily lives dominated by constant, frantic activity. Cheryl was used to the fast pace of Taiwan ('very busy, every day very busy'). In migration, all of the women had relinquished their employment. As noted, the slow pace of Vancouver came as a particular shock:

Fiona: At the beginning I feel, sometimes I just feel bored and I feel like . . . loneliness and emptiness.

Cheryl: When I first came to Canada I'm really sad. Everyday I sit in that chair and look outside. I think, why in Canada nobody walks [by]? Nobody, nobody . . . You don't see any people . . . In Taiwan, many, many people . . . Here, nobody. Like just me in the world . . . Very sad'.

Loneliness and feelings of isolation, resulting from the loss of support networks and some language difficulties, were common initial problems. For most women, however, such experiences were only a temporary adjustment and a year of the astronaut arrangement proved sufficient to transform an uncertain and difficult circumstance into one of considerable independence and freedom. Interestingly, the majority of women interviewed did not, in fact, seek employment in Vancouver, nor entertain the prospect in the foreseeable future. With the passage from East Asia to Canada, their priorities had shifted. Immigration to Vancouver had provided a crucial distance from their former lives, giving women the time and the space to reflect deeply on their personal goals. When making money and seeking success through their careers had been a priority, little time was available to spend with their children. This was one issue that was frequently discussed:

Nancy: We were having a very busy life in Hong Kong, particularly my husband. At that time he worked five days but he had a lot of parties, meetings going on, and also he had to travel a lot during weekends to Southeast Asia. The only thing I could wish was I have to put more attention onto my kids. And this life in Hong Kong would not allow me to do so.

Sylvie: When I talk to my friends they have the same idea that when we are in Hong Kong we really neglected our kids . . . But when we are here, because I have more time to be with them, they talk more . . . In Hong Kong they have a more luxurious life: many toys and whatever they want. But maybe the concern is less. Actually I prefer this way, to look after them closely.

It transpired that far from finding independence and freedom in their financially independent situation, prior to emigration women had often experienced significant stress.

Sarah: You know, in Hong Kong I have pressure. Yes, everything has pressure. Whenever I am walking, shopping . . . a lot of pressure for me . . . I always work very late . . . When I go home my kids are also working – doing their homework – until they sleep.

As a consequence of the social pressures exerted through the expectations of friends and family members, women felt obligated to behave as the 'superwoman'. It was common for women, prior to migration, to sustain a full time career at the same time as caring for the husband and family, organizing the care of the children and the running of the household, in addition to keeping up with the latest East Asian fashions. In contrast, the informality of life in Vancouver was perceived as a very welcome relief. Several women commented on the execution of household tasks. Contrary to expectations,[2] the 'burden' of housework in these new circumstances seemed like no burden at all:

Sylvie: [As] for the cleaning, I think it depends . . . It is how often you like to do it . . . the only problem is if you want to do it or not.

Sarah: I have more freedom . . . I can do it by myself, whatever I like to do, because no one asks me to do that. Yeah, I like to clean up now and then I will clean up.

Jen: No person pushes me to do that [domestic tasks]. That is the point. I can do those things as I planned.

Another woman remarked that she and her children had lived off fast food ('McDonalds') for 18 months, until a friend taught her how to cook. The freedom to wear t-shirts and jeans was an unanticipated pleasure. Said Laura: 'When I come here I feel very relaxed . . . It's good for me.'

Moving to Vancouver gave these women the opportunities to focus on *personal* development, beyond a concern with the success of the family. Women found significant joy in a diverse number of hobbies, unthinkable in the context of their career-orientated lives in Hong Kong and Taiwan. Spending leisure time with friends was highly valued, and speaking English and learning to drive were especially important in providing a strong sense of independence. They also demonstrated a creative ability to integrate childcare and their own newly acquired personal activities, as Lisa here demonstrates:

Lisa: About 8.45 I pick up my son to go to school and . . . I have English classes at 9 o'clock everyday: Monday to Friday, 9 to 11 o'clock. After 11 sometimes I go to the library to study my English. I learn painting now, one time a week.

Claire came to Vancouver in 1992 with her husband and two daughters. When her husband returned to Taiwan to work, she made it her goal to master English:

Claire: I read, basically, every day. For the first two or three years I still read Chinese book, but after that I throw all the[m] aside and I think I should read some English books . . . I start on the children's book . . . three or four hours when the kids go to school I am just sitting here after breakfast [reading].

The absence of constant mobility was undoubtedly crucial to the kinds of transformation the women experienced. Settlement *in a place* continued to provide security against the free-flow of a borderless world: anchoring social networks, acquiring resources and establishing routines.

The disruption of patriarchal relations resulting from these periods of spousal separation became particularly stark when the husband would return from overseas, to rejoin his family for a short time in Vancouver. As a former 'astronaut' himself observed: 'Each time I was absent for about three weeks . . . Every time I came back I disturbed my wife's schedule. She did complain – she told me to stay longer in Hong Kong.'

Sylvie explains her sense of the way in which family separation results in the development of separate lives and divergent aspirations:

Sylvie: For the first year . . . we talk to each other for about thirty minutes when we are separate. We long for the time when he come back. And then when he came back, for the first week, I found that there were many things I needed to encounter. It's different, in that my emotions is not peaceful . . . Many things make me feel a bit frustrated or not feeling comfortable, so . . . I had a lot of quarrels with him.

JW: *Can you explain what types of problems?*

Sylvie: Because he had been away for six months and everything, I became more independent, actually. And then I had to do many adjustments to cope with him. For example, the taste of food, how many dishes for each day . . . Actually this is minor. But it accumulates . . . because I used to be free when he's away – I'm in charge of everything – and then when he came back I seem to step back and he's in charge . . . I feel rather frustrated.

Several participants echoed these sentiments, reflecting upon the ways in which their husbands attempted to reassert dominance on their return – often regarding the woman's new activities as evidence that she is neglecting the family. Consequently, it was common for women to drastically change their daily routine when their husbands visited:

Emma: Because you can manage your own time you can have your own social life. But when my husband is settled down all my attention had to go back to the family. I had to cut out some of the activities because of my husband. I have to consider his feelings.

Barbara: When he's not here, I used to go to school, after that lunch with my friends, and then maybe play tennis. When he's back I have to cancel the lunch appointment . . . because I have to keep him company . . . So the only thing I keep is to go to school. Other than that . . . all cancelled until he left.

Nowhere, however, is the transformation of social roles more starkly observed than in the few cases of astronaut husbands – business immigrants to Vancouver whose *wives* had returned to Taiwan to work and provide the family income. While clearly an unusual case, these examples provide a striking demonstration of the impact of immigration on gendered subjectivities, a sense of self, and a sense of life goals, in a powerful challenge to the existence of *Homo economicus*.

Like the experience of the women, the loss of a career and relocation to a new environment transformed the daily lives of these male business immigrants. The initial shock was substantial: moving from a situation of high-flying entrepreneur to being economically dependent – from a situation of having very little contact with their children to daily, sustained interaction. At first, life had lost its meaning. Over time, however, a new sense of priorities began to emerge and *new personal roles* were constructed. Simon, for example, described the major changes he faced in his first few months as a lone father and unemployed businessman in Canada:

Simon: I didn't make any money. This is a very big change for a man. And I thought, 'I am nobody'. When I make money I think I am somebody . . . I lost my self-esteem . . . I have no job so my daily life is empty ... But after six months I go to school. Every morning, every afternoon and I study every evening because we have a test every morning ... Learning took the place of my job in my daily life.

In addition to seeking the expansion of personal horizons beyond their business concerns, these men experienced a dramatic shift in the relationship they held with their children. Not only were they now forced to spend more time together, but their children also exerted pressure to conform to a different 'Canadian' parenting style:

Simon: In Taiwan the father has got very good authority. [He] is powerful within his family. But not here! So I change a lot – I improve myself to be low profile, to be very communicative with them [the children].

Taking care of the family became part of the daily routine. Gary described a typical day in Vancouver, comparing this to his previous life in Taiwan:

Gary: I get up ... very early. Because my wife [is] not here I have to take breakfast and make the lunch for the two kids ... and then take them to school. And in the morning I then go to take the English class ... Afternoon, between two and three go ... swimming ... And 3.30 to pick them up ... Saturday my daughter learns the flute, so I take [her] ... and then I use Saturday and Sunday to do shopping.
        In Taiwan [I went] to work always very early – about 6.30am go to the office and I leave about 8.30pm [to] get back. So I don't have any time to do the ... work in the family and have no time to talk with my kids.

JW: *So when you came here you had to change ...?*

Gary: Change [my] whole life.

Of course, as has been mentioned already, the astronaut arrangement is often a temporary strategy, until citizenship has been attained and the family can return to the more financially prosperous environments of Hong Kong and Taiwan. However, as has also been suggested, a high-flying business-man can change his stripes. Simon explains his decision to remain in Canada:

Simon: Originally I intended to go back to Taiwan [when the children] enter to the university. But after I start English here – for three years – I feel very comfortable here. So I intend to stay here.

JW: Would you not make more money if . . . you went back to Taiwan to start a business?

Simon: Get more money? Of course!

JW: Why [do] you want to stay?

Simon: Good question . . . What is your definition of success? . . . Most of the men would say 'reputation, wealth and power'. Those three things were my objects that I am looking for in Taiwan. I already achieved very good of that. [Then] when I was immersed in the study of English literature [in Canada] I found a lot of positive concepts . . . One day I asked my tennis friend . . . 'what is your definition of success?' and he said 'happily playing tennis' . . . Everybody likes him. So my values are changing in these three years. I almost lost my health three years ago because I was looking for wealth, reputation and power very, very hard . . . I work[ed] almost twelve hours every day . . . [Finding] a valuable life is probably the key factor to many changes.

In another example, Frank made explicit reference to his sense of his own transformation. He has a daughter and a son, in grade 7 and grade 12, living with him in Vancouver. His wife works in Taiwan, providing the family income.

Frank (Interpreter): In Taiwan he (Frank) never think about change, but now he knows how to change very well . . . Adapt, adjust . . . Because in Taiwan we always think about office or business things, we don't think about the life or think about the valuable things.

In these men, we can observe a fundamental shift away from a concern with profit and family success towards a concern with quality of life and an enriched relationship with the children. Their sense of what constitutes 'value' in life has been challenged through their immigration and subsequent settlement experiences. Crossing the Pacific Ocean coincides with working out new subjectivities.

Conclusion

In this chapter we have re-examined some of the pre-suppositions of those who see globalization as establishing a space of flows that includes migration, a space that transcends the nation state and incorporates actors with essentialized identities. Our suggestion has been that business immigration programmes have been predicated on such assumptions – that economic agents can move across a homogeneous global space and act out an essentialized entrepreneurial identity among divergent national spaces unproblematically. Business immigration policy then has been one attempt by the state to play the globalization game. But we have seen that these assumptions are severely flawed. Space does matter, and in several ways. First, the regulatory and cultural characteristics of regions, and entrepreneurs' embeddedness within them, introduce significant barriers to the portability of entrepreneurship. Second, subjectivities are not fixed and eternal, and the act of migration between nation states can, itself, be an intentionally sought status passage to a new identity. Ironically, as we saw, those immigrants who make the clearest commitment to Canadian residency are also those who seek to escape from the economic hot-house of East Asia for a 'slower' lifestyle. Third, among astronaut households, the purest case of transnational behaviour, where the prerequisites of a space of flows seem most fully met, spatial stickiness remains. The spatial fragmentation of the astronaut family on both sides of the Pacific Ocean introduces its own tensions, in terms of challenges by women and children of classical role models in 'the Chinese family'. Patriarchy, in particular, is eroded by frequent absences and spatial separation. Among even the well-greased movements of overseas Chinese entrepreneurs we continue to see clear evidence of a geographical imperative.

Notes

1   For more information on the Business Immigration Programme in Canada, see Nash (1996) and Ley (2003).
2   Guida Man (1997) identifies negative effects of immigration for middle-class women from Hong Kong to Toronto in terms of increased domestic responsibilities through the 'loss' of paid help in the home.

References

Appadurai, A. 1996. *Modernity at large: cultural dimensions of globalization.* Minneapolis: University of Minnesota Press.
Basch, L., Glick Schiller, N. and Szanton-Blanc, C. 1994. *Nations unbound: transnational projects, postcolonial predicaments and deterritorialized nation states.* Amsterdam: Gordon and Breach.
Beaverstock, J. 2002. Transnational elites in global cities: British expatriates in Singapore's Financial District. *Geoforum* 33: 525–38.
Carnoy, M. and Castells, M. 2001. Globalization, the knowledge society, and the network state. *Global Networks* 1: 1–18.
City of Vancouver 1988. *Vancouver: an analysis of economic structures, growth and change.* Vancouver: City of Vancouver, Office of Economic Development.
Greenhalgh, S. 1994. De-orientalizing the Chinese family firm. *American Ethnologist* 21: 746–75.
Hamilton, G. ed. 1999. *Cosmopolitan capitalists: Hong Kong and the Chinese diaspora at the end of the twentieth century.* Seattle: University of Washington Press.
James, A. 1999. Class, race and ethnicity: Chinese Canadian entrepreneurs in Vancouver. Vancouver: University of British Columbia, unpublished MA thesis.

Leavitt, P. 2001. Transnational migration: taking stock and future directions. *Global Networks* 1: 195–216.

Ley, D. 1999. Myths and meanings of immigration and the metropolis. *The Canadian Geographer* 43; 2–19.

Ley, D. 2002. Immigrant entrepreneurs: indicators of success. Report for the Department of Community, Aboriginal and Women's Services, Province of British Columbia, Victoria.

Ley, D. 2003. Seeking *homo economicus*: the Canadian state and the strange story of the Business Immigration Programme. *Annals of the Association of American Geographers* 93: 426–41.

Ley, D. and Tutchener, J. 2001. Immigration, globalisation and house prices in Canada's gateway cities. *Housing Studies* 16: 199–223.

Mak, A. 2001. *Relocating careers: Hong Kong professionals and managers in Australia.* Hong Kong: University of Hong Kong, Centre of Asian Studies, Occasional Papers and Monographs No. 142.

Man, G. 1997. Women's work is never done: social organisation of work and the experience of women in middle-class Hong Kong Chinese immigrant families in Canada. *Advances in Gender Research* 2: 183–226.

Mickleburgh, R. 1996. Quality of life is driving influx from Hong Kong. *Globe and Mail*, 24 June, A1.

Mitchell, K. 1993. Multiculturalism, or the united colors of capitalism? *Antipode* 25: 263–94.

Mitchell, K. 1997. Different diasporas and the hype of hybridity. *Environment and Planning D: Society and Space* 15: 533–53.

Nash, A. 1996. The economic impact of Canada's Business Immigration Program: a critical reappraisal of theory and practice. Paper presented at the symposium on Immigration and Integration, University of Manitoba, October.

Nonini, D. and Ong, A. 1997. Chinese transnationalism as an alternative modernity, in A. Ong and D. Nonini eds. *Ungrounded empires: the cultural politics of modern Chinese transnationalism.* New York: Routledge, 228–56.

Ohmae, K. 1990. *The borderless world.* New York: Harper Business.

Ohmae, K. 1995. *The end of the nation state.* New York: Free Press.

Ong, A. 1999. *Flexible citizenship: the cultural logics of transnationality.* Durham, NC: Duke University Press.

Sklair, L. 2001. *The transnational capitalist class.* Oxford: Blackwell.

Tai, H. ed. 1989. *Confucianism and economic development: an Oriental alternative?* Washington, DC: The Washington Institute Press.

Waters, J. 2000. *Flexible families? The experiences of astronaut and satellite households among recent Chinese immigrants to Vancouver, British Columbia.* Vancouver: University of British Columbia, unpublished MA thesis.

Waters, J. 2002. Flexible families? 'Astronaut' households and the experiences of lone mothers in Vancouver, British Columbia. *Social and Cultural Geography* 3: 117–34.

White, P. 1998. The settlement patterns of developed world migrants in London. *Urban Studies* 35: 1725–44.

Zhou, Y. and Tseng, Y.-F. 2001. Regrounding the 'ungrounded empires': localization as the geographical catalyst for transnationalism. *Global Networks* 1: 131–54.

6 Transnationalism in the margins

Hegemony and the shadow state[1]

Katharyne Mitchell

Many scholars interested in the intersections of economy and society take the profound, widespread, and startlingly rapid growth of the philosophy and economic practices of neo-liberalism over the past two decades as the starting point of their socio-economic analyses. They link the growth of neo-liberal rhetoric and policy worldwide with macro shifts in the nature of capitalism, especially the global restructuring of production systems, deterritorialization of finance, and general flexibility of new systems of accumulation. But how exactly does the process of neo-liberal expansion *actually work*? How does neo-liberalism as material practice and ideological discourse snowball, and begin to occupy greater and greater space? How is it economically and socially entrenched in the minds of citizens and the capillaries of society to the point where, even with a change of government, the practices and ideology remain?

In this chapter I examine the process of neo-liberal expansion in Canada, focusing, in particular, on the ways in which a relatively minor federal immigration programme of the 1980s operated recursively to reinforce the ideology and material effects of a much broader social and political agenda of neo-liberalism in Canada during that same time period. I make two main claims: the first is that although neo-liberalism is generally framed in terms of its economic components and effects, its actual institutional entrenchment as a broad system is deeply bound up with the socio-cultural norms and taken-for-granted assumptions of any given society. In order to understand how and why neo-liberal rhetoric and policy is able to expand, especially in what might be considered the 'hostile' territory of a long-standing welfarist community such as Canada, it is thus necessary to examine hegemonic formation at the micro level, the level at which cultural expectations and understandings are in a constant state of flux. Here I show how micro economic practices, such as a new immigration policy for 'business' migrants, is one component of a myriad of small, incremental policy shifts in the 1980s that led, not just to economic transformation, but also to social and cultural re-workings which affected the hegemonic norms of the society and ultimately altered state–society relations on a fundamental level.

The second claim I make is that one of the major changes in state–society relations occurring in Canada over the past decade has been the increasing scope and power of interstitial voluntary organizations located in the margins *between* the state and society. These organizations, which have been termed 'shadow state' institutions because of their close, yet often obfuscated relationship to the state, are growing in both numbers and in their degree of control over functions formerly handled exclusively by the state. Wolch (1989: 201) writes of the rise of these types of voluntary institutions in the United States: 'The voluntary sector has in effect become a *shadow state*: that is, a para-state apparatus with collective service responsibilities previously shouldered by the public sector, administered outside traditional democratic politics, but yet controlled in both formal and informal ways by the state.' The growth of this type of 'para-state apparatus' in Canada from the mid-1980s through the 1990s occurred alongside the redefinition of the state vis-à-vis its 'proper' role in providing collective welfare, and paralleled and facilitated the general restructuring of public service provisioning in the provinces.

As I will show through a case study of one of these types of institutions in Vancouver, British Columbia, a primary effect of the rise of these in-between voluntary organizations, was a corresponding decline of *direct* social service provisioning from the government sector. As shadow state organizations grew in prestige, power and number, the state was able to either contract out services and supplies to these institutions, or to delimit or discontinue direct social service provisioning now covered under the auspices of the new organizations. This substitutive phenomenon allowed Prime Minister Brian Mulroney's government to roll back the Canadian welfare state, but without suffering a significant loss of legitimacy related to an immediate decline in service provisioning. In an effort to promote their conservative agenda, Canadian politicians such as Mulroney, of the Progressive Conservative Party, and BC Premier William Vander Zalm, of the Social Credit Party, effectively borrowed from the rhetoric of freedom and individual choice espoused in the early 1980s by US President Ronald Reagan. In Reagan's words: 'We've let Government take away many things we once considered were really ours to do voluntarily out of the goodness of our hearts and a sense of community pride and neighborliness.'[2] This ideology was, in turn, borrowed directly from the British Conservative Party Manifesto of 1979, which claimed, 'In the community, we must do more to help people to help themselves and the family to look after their own. We must also encourage the voluntary movement and self-help groups acting in partnership with statutory services.'[3] As I will argue throughout the paper, the general effect of the rise of these shadow state voluntary institutions was to help entrench the original economic policies of neo-liberalism in a hegemonic and recursive process.

How then does transnationalism play into this scenario? In Canada, the federal immigration policy known as the Business Immigration Programme, which was initiated in 1978 and greatly expanded in the mid-1980s, attracted a large number of wealthy capitalists from Hong Kong. As a result of the programme's stipulations, discussed below, many of these immigrants maintained strong social and economic connections to Hong Kong and lived essentially in a social field that stretched across national borders. In order to establish local ties, deflect allegations of 'sojourner' status, and smooth racial frictions in a rapidly changing urban environment, many of these Hong Kong immigrants donated time and money to one of the rising 'shadow state' organizations in Vancouver known as SUCCESS (United Chinese Community Enrichment Services Society). In this paper I examine the ways in which these philanthropic and volunteerist activities dovetailed with the neo-liberal project of deregulation, privatization and the decrease of direct social service provisioning that was heavily promulgated in the 1980s by conservative Canadian politicians at all three levels of government. I demonstrate how a particular immigration policy, that might be considered a minor piece of economic legislation, quickly became imbricated in a much broader set of socio-cultural and political processes, and operated recursively to reinforce and promote a neo-liberal agenda that included the devolution of state control and the attrition of the Canadian welfare state.

The aim here is not to focus on the impact of a particular set of relations of migration or of transnationalism per se, but rather to examine it as *one example* of the multiple ways that neo-liberal policies such as the Business Immigration Programme can have much broader, often unanticipated effects. In this case, what is interesting is the manner in which the policy itself developed a type of feedback loop owing to the timing and stipulations of the policy, the people that it attracted, and to the agency of the immigrants after their arrival. In the next section I discuss the context of the immigration policy, then examine some of the many repercussions caused by the rapid influx of both capital and capitalists into the society. As I will argue throughout the chapter, the repercussions were social and cultural as well as economic, and ultimately led to actions by the migrants themselves, which aided in the entrenchment of Canadian neo-liberalism during that time.

Transnationalism: the Hong Kong–Vancouver connection

Migration

Over the last decade and a half there has been a large-scale exodus of wealthy emigrants from Hong Kong into several urban areas around the world. This new Chinese diaspora constituted a major migration process that had important repercussions for both the sending society and destination areas. Statistics show not only vast increases in the emigration of the best educated and highly skilled from Hong Kong, but also flows of capital from Hong Kong to several urban sites worldwide, reckoned in the tens of billions of dollars. For Canada in general, and for Vancouver in particular, the Hong Kong influx of both capital and people has been absolutely colossal, with immense economic, political and social repercussions for the society.[4]

One of the key distinguishing features of this migrant group is its essential transnationalism. Transnationalism is defined as 'the processes by which immigrants forge and sustain multi-stranded social relations that link together their societies of origin and settlement' (Glick Schiller *et al.* 1995: 7). It differs from the standard conceptualization of international migration primarily in the emphasis on the simultaneity of economic, social and political connections that bind immigrants to two or more nation-states. Rather than a movement 'from' a society of origin 'to' a country of settlement, the migrants operate in a social field of networks and obligations that extend across international borders (Mitchell 1997; Smith and Guarnizo 1997; Rouse 1995). The number of Hong Kong Chinese people living and working across borders, with families and businesses in two or more nation-states, has been so great that new terms in Cantonese have been coined to depict this phenomenon. *Tai hong yan* (astronaut or 'empty wife'), for example, is a commonly used description of the Hong Kong or Taiwanese businessman who flies between his 'new' home in Canada and his place of business in East Asia (Ong 1993; Mitchell 1993).

Since the end of the Canadian Exclusion Act in 1947, there has been a significant influx of immigrants from Hong Kong into Vancouver. The two most important post-war periods of migration from Hong Kong to Canada included the era following the transition to a 'points' system in 1967, and the period after the expansion of the Business Immigration Programme in 1984.[5] The major force for change to the points system was related to the perceived economic advantages accruing from a system based on achievement and education rather than on national origin, race or colour. The points system privileged those with the education, skills and training that were presumed to be beneficial to the growth and well-being of Canada. In contrast with policies of the past, which encouraged the entry of unskilled rural labourers, and then the sponsorship of their relatives, the new system favoured urban, middle class applicants with a particular trade or professional skill. With the economic and social liberalizations instituted by the government of Prime Minister Pierre Trudeau in the early 1970s, the opportunities for people with the types of skills and background held by many of these new, 'unsponsored' Hong Kong immigrants, were vastly increased.

The second major migration from Hong Kong to Canada was also related to economic and political factors in both countries. In Hong Kong, the primary consideration for emigration in the 1980s was the pending transition to control by the People's Republic of China in July 1997. The signing of the Sino-British Joint Declaration by Prime Minister Margaret Thatcher in 1984 was the first clear indication that the transfer of power between Britain and China would take place as originally planned. Following this, and especially after the massacre in Tiananmen Square in 1989, there was a major increase in Hong Kong emigration worldwide (Skeldon 1994). Although the type of migrant leaving Hong Kong during this period varied, and included many in the 'retired' and 'family' classes, there was a particularly large increase in the movement of business entrepreneurs and professionals.

Much of the movement of this upper strata group to Canada in the late 1980s can be attributed to the refinement and extension of a new federal immigration policy informally entitled the 'Business Immigration Programme'. This programme, which was created in 1978, redesigned in 1984 and augmented in 1986, was designed to facilitate the immigration of business-people who could 'make a positive contribution to the country's economic development by applying their risk capital and know-how to Canadian business ventures which create jobs for Canadians' (Employment and Immigration Canada 1985: 1). In 1986, entry into the programme was divided into two categories, 'investor' and 'entrepreneur'. As a condition of entry, investors were required to have a minimum personal net-worth of Cdn$500,000 obtained by their own efforts, and to invest at least half that amount in a business or privately administered investment fund in a Canadian province for at least five years.[6] Entrepreneurs were required to have a strong business 'track record', and to buy or establish a business in Canada that employed at least one Canadian and made a significant contribution to the economy (Young 1992; Smart 1994; Nash 1987, 1993).

The desire to stimulate business and expand trade was an important impetus for Prime Minister Mulroney and other politicians of the Progressive Conservative government following a severe recession in Canada in the early 1980s. In the context of the rapid economic growth of the Newly Industrializing Economies (NIEs) in the 1970s, and the geographical and historical connections between Pacific Rim cities, Hong Kong provided an extremely attractive lure for federal, provincial and municipal politicians at that time. Political trips, cultural fairs, business seminars, brochures, flyers, pamphlets and the opening of a British Columbia office in Hong Kong were among many of the strategies used by Canadian politicians to attract both capitalists and their capital from Hong Kong (Mitchell 1993). For Vancouver, this multi-faceted strategy proved particularly successful, as many business-people intending to leave Hong Kong were drawn by the relative proximity of the city (in comparison with Toronto), the quality of life (widely touted by the province and city), and the historical ties related to the past migrations of family and friends.[7]

The great majority of the new migrants who came to Vancouver under the investor and entrepreneur categories of the business programme were urban business-people and their families, most having lived in Hong Kong at least ten years (Smart 1994). For many of these business immigrants, the attractions of Canadian cities such as Vancouver were primarily political and social rather than economic. The business programme enticed them with the prospect of an immediate landed immigrant visa and eventual Canadian citizenship. However, their personal resources, business networks and often their fixed capital investments remained primarily in Asia. In addition, aside from investment in real estate, business opportunities were greater in the booming economies of the greater China region than in British Columbia in the late 1980s and early 1990s. The Business Immigration Programme thus demanded entrepreneurs and investors to commit time and resources to doing business in Canada, yet in order to be successful in this pursuit, many immigrants needed to maintain their close ties and expand their opportunities in Hong Kong, Taiwan, and/or China.[8] As a result, a great number of migrants were forced to remain essentially mobile and operate as 'global economic subjects' (Ong 1993), living part-time in Vancouver and part-time in Hong Kong. Because of this widely publicized mobility, wealthy Hong Kong immigrants in Vancouver soon became perceived by many in Canadian society as a sojourning class, part of a fundamentally transnational process of migration, living bi-nationally, and with 'suspect' allegiances vis-à-vis the nation-state.

Banking deregulations and capital flows

The impact of this group of transnational migrants was particularly strong in Vancouver during this time because of their tremendous cumulative wealth. It was the influx of capital that accompanied these investors and entrepreneurs into Vancouver that made this second wave of Hong Kong migrants unique in their ability to affect institutional structures within Chinatown and in the broader society as well (Ng 1999). The exact amounts of capital flows between Hong Kong and Vancouver are not documented by statistical agencies in either city. The business immigrant statistics, however, provide one approximate measure of capital influx. According to *Employment and Immigration Canada*, the amount of estimated funds brought to British Columbia in 1988 (most of the funds brought into the province wind up in Vancouver), was nearly one and a half billion Canadian dollars (Canada 1989). Figures from 1989 show an approximate capital flow of Cdn$3.5 billion from Hong Kong to Canada, of which Cdn$2.21 billion or 63% was transferred by the business migration component (Nash 1992: 3; Macdonald 1990). I consider these figures conservative. Most applicants under-declare their actual resources by a significant margin for income tax purposes.[9] Bankers and immigration consultants I interviewed in Hong Kong in 1991 put the overall numbers as high as five or six billion dollars being transferred from Hong Kong to Canada annually in the late 1980s and early 1990s. Of that amount, nearly one third would be destined for British Columbia (Mitchell 1993; see also Wong 1989).

At the same time that federal immigration laws in the 1980s greatly eased the conditions of entry and citizenship for wealthy business migrants, federal deregulation of the banking industry eased the movement of capital across both international and sectoral borders. Historically, the regulation of Canadian banks took shape under a system known as the 'Four Pillars', which involved the separation of financial activities into the four categories of insurance, banking, securities and trusts. Liberalization of the industry in the 1980s included the removal of the numerous state-based restrictions governing the separation of these financial activities, as well as the termination of ownership restrictions on financial institutions. Tickell writes of this period of reform, which was unprecedented in its speed and in the extent of the transformations that ensued:

> Canadian banks began to pressure Brian Mulroney's conservative government for financial reform that would abolish the Pillars that ensured that the financial system remained functionally and institutionally discreet . . . Accordingly, in 1987 banks were given the power to buy securities brokers; as happened in the UK following the Big Bang in London, brokerage firms rapidly became taken over by larger groups. Four years later, the government allowed banks to take majority of Trusts; allowed them to sell insurance through insurance subsidiaries, and abolished the requirement for them to maintain reserves at the Bank of Canada.
>
> (Tickell 2000: 155; see also Harris 1998)

Following the deregulation and liberalization of the financial system, banks began to dominate all fields of financial activity except for insurance, and quickly began to consolidate partnerships both domestically and offshore (Stewart 1997: 65). Attracting both the financial capital and the social network capital of Hong Kong and other Asian entrepreneurs was a high priority for a number of the largest banks in Canada, and each vied for the new business immigrant customers with strong promotional campaigns. The largest bank involved in facilitating the increasing movement of people and capital from Hong Kong to Canada in the 1980s was the Hongkong and Shanghai Banking Corp (Hongkong Bank).[10] David Bond, the vice-president of the Hong Kong Bank of Canada, its Canadian subsidiary, said of the business investors moving to Vancouver: 'If I was the czar of immigration, I'd send a fleet of Boeing 747s to Hong Kong to pick them up. This is a unique chance to engage in a transfer of human and financial capital that is unprecedented anywhere in the world' (quoted in Claiborne, 1991).

All of the major international banks operating in both Canada and Hong Kong emphasized their global connections and services in order to attract and retain Hong Kong customers. The vice-president of the Royal Bank of Canada, Jim Lawrie, claimed that 'with operations in more than 30 countries, we can provide worldwide linkages for the investment and personal interests of our private banking clients' (quoted in To 1990). As with the Bank of Montreal, the Royal Bank of Canada offered 'premier VIP services' for its Hong Kong clients, including 'a comprehensive package of services to meet all your emigration financial requirements'.[11] Help in real estate ventures – both personal and commercial – was particularly emphasized. Soon after the new immigration regulations of 1986, the Royal Bank executive in charge of private banking operations established an investor immigrant service to help wealthy clients purchase real estate in Canada and to structure five-year offshore tax programmes (Suen 1988).[12]

The rise of the shadow state

Contemporary transnational migration from Hong Kong to Vancouver is markedly different from migrations of the past and reflects the group's powerful economic standing and international connections. In contrast with the bulk of recent scholarship on transnational migration, which focuses on the movements of labourers and the poor, the emphasis on the transnational movements and institutional affiliations of wealthy entrepreneurs affords a different understanding of the role of the state in the degree to which it seeks to incorporate a transnational citizenry into a broader national narrative and agenda, as well as control the capital of those living and working across national borders.

Research that focuses exclusively on the transnational migration of labourers tends to focus on post-colonial states – those states that have been marginalized within the global political economy. In this type of work (e.g. Glick Schiller *et al.* 1995), scholars examine the ways in which new transnational practices are forced on migrants as a result of the marginalization of these states and their citizenry within the global economy. They argue that it is this position of geopolitical subservience that has led to the 'deterritorialized' nation-state, a state which, in order to survive as a legitimate political entity, must control its population across space. In this analysis, the state is posited in a fundamentally adversarial position vis-à-vis the transnational migrant.[13] In a reactive mode, the state adapts to the transnational practices of its citizenry owing to its marginalized status in the global economy and to the importance of economic remittances and political allegiance from those labouring overseas. In an effort to capture the remittances and/or incorporate this group into the networked affairs of the 'home' state, various incentives are offered, including new state-sponsored social services 'abroad' and transnational support institutions.

How does this picture change, however, in the context of a *non-adversarial* relationship between wealthy transnational migrants and non-marginalized states? In what ways are migrants proactively incorporated into nation-building projects and agendas? The answers to these questions are always contingent, nevertheless they can lend important insights into contemporary shifts in the state–society relations of advanced capitalist nations. For example, in setting a neo-liberal course for Canada, Brian Mulroney (with the aid of William Bennett and William Vander Zalm in British Columbia, among countless others) embarked on a major overhaul of the welfare state, involving draconian cutbacks in social service provisioning and the devolution of control from federal authority to the provinces and local political structures. How was a particular kind of transnational migration during this time period one small piece of the much larger project of neo-liberalism, and how did it operate recursively to continually promote this conservative agenda?

With the targeted decline of government activity in the maintenance of the Canadian welfare state, the voluntary sector in Canada became increasingly important in providing social services to needy immigrants and others affected by the steady removal of federal and provincial safety nets. The major contemporary philanthropic and volunteering activities of recent Hong Kong migrants in Vancouver enabled the provincial and federal governments to entrench a neo-liberal agenda through the transfer of responsibility for public services to the voluntary sector, yet without a corresponding loss of legitimacy resulting from an abrupt decline of welfare state provisions. The state was able to privatize and *subcontract* out many services formerly covered under the federal and provincial umbrellas, yet retain firm control of the social service institutions through grant funding, tax remittances and other economic ties.

By facilitating the articulation of global capitals through both the Business Immigration Programme and the deregulation of banking, state officials successfully attracted Hong Kong immigrants to include Vancouver as a key node within a dense network of capital circulation. This type of cross-border phenomenon is not a particularly unusual story in the contemporary world economy. What makes this movement unique is the way in which the liberalization of capital and of the immigration regulations for capitalists furthered the entrenchment of a much broader political agenda. In Vancouver, for example, as government funding for basic services declined, wealthy Hong Kong donors and volunteers stepped into the breach, enabling the continuation of service provisions for the community. It was this type of private financial contribution to specific social services, combined with new forms of public–private partnerships in charity, that enabled the on-going attrition of the welfare state to proceed without greater public resistance. In the following section I chart the course of this attrition in British Columbia over the past decade and a half, and examine the growing connections between government and numerous 'shadow state' institutions involved with charity and other forms of volunteerism.

Canadian neo-liberalism

The rise of neo-liberalism in Canada is evident in a number of areas, including, most importantly, the ratification of the free trade agreements: the Canadian–United States Free Trade Agreement (CUFTA) in 1989, and the North American Free Trade Agreement (NAFTA) in 1993. It is also evident in the debates over the charter and the ensuing constitutional changes initiated by the Mulroney government. Key aspects of the neo-liberal agenda included the decentralization and attrition of federal governance, the accordance of a greater degree of power and control to provincial authorities, the deregulation of banking and other institutions, the privatization of land and industry, the reduction of frictions for the free circulation of commodities, and the provision of various tax and other incentives attractive for business. Taken together, these institutional trans-formations manifested a new direction for Canadian society. The changes promoted during this time in trade, banking, and the bureaucratic organ-ization of government occurred alongside a rhetoric of national deficit and decline, a decline that was firmly linked with the 'excesses' of welfare state provisioning under Trudeau's liberal government.[14]

The quick ratification of CUFTA and NAFTA were the primary markers of the extent to which Canada had already been affected by global restruc-turing in the prior decade. Despite Prime Minister Mulroney's visceral opposition to free trade with the United States that he expressed in 1983,[15] within one year he had become a fervent promoter of CUFTA (Clarkson 1993). CUFTA was ratified following complaints that border tariffs and non-tariff barriers were posing harmful frictions to the circulation of goods and capital. As cross-border investments between the US and Canada had grown in the 1970s, interest in protecting the circuits of Canadian capital from foreign competition had diminished correspondingly. Transnational corporations responding to the increasing globalization of production, particularly vis-à-vis North American production processes, agitated for the free trade agreements; banking network executives involved in the growing flows of foreign direct investment from Canada to the United States between 1975 and 1985 soon followed suit. The pressure of the busi-ness community for a freer circulation of capital and goods dovetailed with the pro-business, anti-governance platform of Mulroney's Progressive Conservative federal government, elected in 1984, and CUFTA and NAFTA both passed within the next decade.

The reduction of friction to the free circulation of capital and commodi-ties that was the major principle behind the free trade agreements was only one feature of the rise of neo-liberalism in Canada. An important corollary to the liberalization of capital was the attrition of governance and the social service provisions associated with the welfare state. The most obvious attack on federal state provisioning and the organizational system of government was evident in the attempted changes to the charter and consti-tution during the 1980s. These changes, while usually discussed in terms of cultural and regional disputes in Canadian politics, especially vis-à-vis the constitutional accords and Québec, were primarily concerned with the manner in which distribution occurs in a federalist system (Jenson 1989). The various disputes and attempted constitutional changes between the 1960s and the late 1980s, including the debates around cultural dualism, regionalism, the Meech Lake Accord and the Charlottetown Accord, did not merely represent struggles of identity, decentralization, and cultural or regional independence, but were more broadly related to the re-ordering of the social and federal-provincial institutional relationships and the reduction of government to make way for the private sector (Rekart 1993; Jenson 1989).

The conservative attack on the provisions of the Canadian welfare state was evident in a number of areas. These included a regressive (and highly unpopular) goods and services tax, the de-indexation of family allowances, more stringent eligibility rules for unemployment insurance, a freeze on federal spending on education and health care, and the extension of a 5% cap on Canada Assistance Plan payments to the 'have' provinces of Ontario, Alberta and British Columbia under Bill C-69 (Rekart 1993: 14). Under the Canada Assistance Plan cap, any increases over 5% in provincial spending on social service programmes would no longer be split equally with the federal government. This cap, which provided a disincentive for provincial funding of social services, was followed by a 1991 budget freeze in federal government payments on Established Programme Funding (EPF) for social services such as medicare and post-secondary education. The initial two year budget was extended through the 1990s.

At the same time that federal funding for services was frozen or capped, the very ability of the government to supply funds was being inexorably eroded. During the 1990s the power of the federal government to tax citizens for social service programmes devolved steadily to the provinces. This downscaling of the federal government's role in social services was particularly important for the formulation of politics in British Columbia. The rise of the Progressive Conservatives in federal politics was paralleled by the growth of a staunchly conservative provincial force, the Social Credit (Socred) party. The Socreds, led initially by Premier Bennett and then William Vander Zalm, fervently embraced the move toward privatization and deregulation. Following Bennett's election in 1983, the party immediately reduced the number of public service employees on the payroll, and cut spending for social services. This was followed by a strong rhetoric of the necessity to re-privatize social services in order to promote maximum efficiency (Rekart 1993: 15–16). Along with the advocacy of the reduction of government involvement, the province actually moved to limit its direct service role in the area of income assistance and child protection. The supply of numerous other social services was also devolved to the private sector and the wider community.[16]

As provincial grants stagnated and in some cases declined, the number of provincial contracts (to private for profit and not-for-profit companies providing selected services) increased greatly. At the same time, earned revenue and fee for service, non-government funds, and funding provided by the social service institutions themselves, began to climb after 1984. By the 1990s, the importance of the voluntary sector in providing crucial services was so great, that the federal government and the voluntary sector launched a joint initiative to explore the possibilities for even tighter connections between them. Joint Tables were formed in the spring of 1999, composed of government officials and sector leaders, who were brought together to discuss how to build a new relationship, strengthen capacity, and improve the government's regulatory framework.[17]

In these meetings, which culminated in a report entitled, 'Working Together: A Government of Canada/Voluntary Sector Joint Initiative', the explicit 'bridging' purpose of the initiative was made clear. In the Executive Summary of the report the authors wrote:

> The federal government and the voluntary sector share a long history of joining forces to achieve mutual goals. In recent years, several factors – for example, changing government roles, increasingly diverse populations, and new social and economic realities – have prompted the government and the sector to seek new ways to work together to better serve Canadians. The purpose of this collaboration is to strengthen the ability of both the government and the sector to achieve their common goal of enhancing the quality of life for Canadians.[18]

The joint initiative was formed at a moment of shifting relationships between the public and private sectors and was clearly an effort by the federal government to formalize and control the relationship of the 'voluntary' sector, the 'vital pillar' of Canadian society.[19] The stated 'Options for an Evolving Relationship', one section of the report, included proposals such as the 'creation of a small secretariat to continue the work of the Privy Council Office's Voluntary Sector Task Force', 'assigning responsibility for the development of the relationship at the ministerial level', 'establishment of a joint Implementation Group to provide direction during the research and consultative stages', and the 'formation of a permanent organization to nurture the relationship'.[20] All of these proposals included the development of a major bureaucratic system of federal control devoted to enhancing the government's 'relationship' with the voluntary sector. In the conclusion, the ultimate goal of 'a new kind of governance' was made clear:

> Now, after decades of working together on a fruitful but mostly *ad hoc* basis, and of pursuing common objectives from sometimes divergent or even opposing positions, the government and the voluntary sector have taken an historic step toward working together to achieve mutual goals. This is good news for Canadians. Canada's long-standing ethic of care calls for a new kind of governance, one in which the voluntary sector and the federal government work together – a collaboration marked by a compassion that helps to create a world where values count, the full range of human activities is encouraged, and every person can realize his or her potential.[21]

The last two decades thus show a profound reworking of the 'partner-ship' between the federal and provincial governments and the voluntary sector. As the government began to withdraw from the provision of direct services, the importance of subcontracting to third parties and of relying on the funding efforts of the agencies themselves increased. The private volun-tary agencies and other third parties began to deliver services on behalf of the government and in lieu of direct welfare provisioning. These heretofore autonomous institutions thus played an increasingly integral role in service provision and, at the same time, they became more and more connected to the government through contractual arrangements and various economic ties such as grants and tax remittances. By the end of the 1990s, this public–private relationship was formally institutionalized and solidified following the release of the 'Working Together' report, which advocated a number of measures for an even tighter 'strategic relationship' between the sectors. The increasingly *semi*-autonomous position of these voluntary associations between the state and civil society thus reflects the underlying foundational changes associated with the privatization of both economic and social institutions and the general attrition of welfare governance in Canada.

Changes in immigration and banking laws in the 1980s made it possible and attractive for a large class of wealthy immigrants to transfer capital and to move to Canada within a relatively short time period. In a recursive process, this group helped to solidify the political positions of those who first designed the changes in the laws, thereby facilitating the on-going transnational movement of both people and capital. Through the process of attracting them and of citizenship formation itself for this group, there developed a feedback loop that worked to entrench the original neo-liberal agenda. Thus, the state-sponsored immigration laws and banking deregula-tions of the 1980s, designed, in part, to capture Hong Kong capital in ways beneficial to Canadian business interests, doubly augmented the neo-liberal project of the articulation of capitals and the attrition of welfare governance.

Cultural citizenship and community networking

If state interests were clearly laid out in favour of the Business Immigra-tion Programme and the articulation of capitals, what was the attraction of philanthropic endeavours in Canada for the new Hong Kong Chinese arrivals? For Hong Kong capitalists seeking to divest their holdings *and* attain citizenship in a stable political region, the Canadian attractions were strong. Despite the immediate garnering of a landed immigrant visa, and the likely conferral of *legal* citizenship, however, there were numerous roadblocks to acceptance on a more local, *cultural* level.[22] Conflicts between the Hong Kong Chinese immigrants and older Anglo and Chinese residents were frequent, particularly around the transformations to the urban environment that were occurring as a result of the rapid influx of capital into the city.[23] In this light, the philanthropy of many Hong Kong immigrants of the last two decades can be seen not only as altruistic, but also as an important social lubricant during a period of high tension and fraught social relations.

The many major donations by Hong Kong immigrants that were made to various Vancouver institutions during this time were perceived to aid in the reduction of racial and cultural frictions, the acquisition of social capital, and perhaps a greater degree of cultural citizenship within the Chinese and wider communities. When high profile contributor David Lam, a Hong Kong immigrant of the 1960s, and the former Lieutenant Governor of Canada, donated a new building for the business school at UBC, he noted publicly in an interview and in a widely circulated video, that philanthropy was a good method of reducing racial friction within the city.

Donations also served within the greater Chinese community as an important form of business networking, helping to increase economic connections through the publicity and social functions offered by the social service agencies themselves. As with Chinese communities worldwide, Vancouver's Chinatown has a long history of social service provisioning via the numerous voluntary associations in the community. Voluntary associations have traditionally provided a key mode of social grouping for immigrants, and although the types of organizations have changed, many of them are still important resources for new Chinese immigrants in overseas societies (Yao 1984). Liu (1998) notes furthermore that, despite the image of voluntary associations as particularist and fundamentally 'un-global' in orientation, some of the organizations have manifested globalizing tendencies through the establishment of worldwide gatherings and linkages with Chinese global business conventions. An affiliation with the associations perceived as 'successful' in the community, can be doubly utilitarian for new immigrants as it holds the promise of an extension of both local and global social and business ties. In this regard, the Hong Kong immigrants' community-based philanthropy of the 1980s and 1990s was a savvy strategy that enabled the new arrivals to become honorary members of key Chinatown associations and to earn a prized position within its system of dense, networked affiliations.

Many of the larger donations by Hong Kong immigrants were directed towards educational facilities, particularly the construction of buildings at the University of British Columbia and Simon Fraser University such as the Chan Centre Concert Hall, the Choi Centre for Asian Studies, and the Ming Pao Centre for Journalism. In addition to the gifts of campus buildings and other infrastructure in the city, a growing number of donations were also made by recent Hong Kong immigrants to the non-profit, social service organization, SUCCESS. These donations did not necessarily make public notice in the wider Canadian society, yet they were important sources of income for the organization and served as the catalyst for its tremendous growth over the next twelve years.

Recent immigrants who donate their time or money to SUCCESS gain legitimacy in the circles of general philanthropy and are also publicly heralded within the Chinese community for their generosity. Forms of publicity for donors include, among other things, a number of fund-raising gala events such as dinners and balls, the dragon walk, and the inscription of names and, in many cases, photographs in newsletters and on a large 'donor wall', in the main lobby of SUCCESS headquarters. By 1999, these 'gala' events were so popular, successful and highly publicized that one dinner/performance fund-raiser in 1999 attracted thousands of guests, each paying over $100 per ticket. The event was publicized worldwide, and included a glossy brochure with individual messages of support from Prime Minister Chrétien, Premier Clark, and Mayor Owen, as well as 39 full-page advertisements from sponsors such as Arthur Anderson, BCTel, the Hong Kong Bank of Canada, and many other corporations catering to the 'transnational' Hong Kong Chinese community.

SUCCESS: a case study

SUCCESS is a highly successful, non-profit social service agency in the Greater Vancouver area focusing primarily on the provision of social services to Chinese immigrants. The society, which is registered as a char-itable organization, was established in 1973 by Hong Kong immigrants to Vancouver. In its early incarnation, SUCCESS was similar in some ways to the early voluntary associations that used to provide mutual aid for Chinese immigrants in the late nineteenth and early twentieth centuries. In those years the clan and regional place associations (*huiguan*) provided services such as capital loans, lodging, the provision of tickets back to China, burial fees, and protection from scams and dishonest dealings within the community (Yao 1984; Crissman 1967; Topley 1960). As SUCCESS has grown in size and popularity, many of these older associations have declined in prestige and funding.[24]

The recent philanthropy and volunteerism of contemporary Hong Kong transnational migrants has enabled SUCCESS to expand its services to accommodate larger numbers of people and a wider geographical area. Spurred on by the major growth of private donations in the late 1980s through the 1990s, the federal and provincial governments massively increased state funding to SUCCESS during the same time period. The exponential expansion of this social service agency, which now operates as a major subcontractor for services previously provided by the government, is a strong example of the rise of a shadow state in Vancouver. The organ-ization's rapid growth has made it beholden to both government funding and private and corporate donations and fees on a massive scale, and it provides many of the core services for immigrants in the greater metro-politan area that were formerly covered under government programmes (including senior housing and hospice care for the elderly).[25]

SUCCESS is now the largest social service provider in Chinatown and one of the largest in all of British Columbia. Core services of the organization include programmes such as New Immigrant Settlement, Family and Youth Counselling, Senior Services, Language and Employment Training and Civic Education. As an institution that provides social services to immigrants (primarily of Chinese heritage) yet maintains an open membership and strong ties with outside social service providers, such as The United Way, SUCCESS also operates as a key bridge between the Chinese immigrant community and the wider host society. The Executive Director, Lilian To, wrote of this primary function, 'In the initiation and implementation of these challenges, we have not lost sight of the essence of our mission, that of "bridging", of building voluntary citizenship, and of providing access and connection for the Chinese community to fully participate in and acquiring recognition from the Canadian community.'[26]

SUCCESS was founded on the basis of a government grant, and from the time of its initial establishment, the organization was anointed by the federal and provincial governments as a privileged subcontractor of social service provisioning for Chinese-Canadian immigrants. It was not until the early 1990s, following the rapid growth of private donations, however, that the organization began to receive a major injection of government funds. In 1989, federal, provincial and municipal grants to SUCCESS totalled just Cdn$246,861. Within a single decade, government grants to the organization topped Cdn$5 million.

The large increases in private funding and in volunteer activities for SUCCESS began in the late 1980s. Between 1987 and 1989 the annual budget of the organization nearly doubled, and the number of staff and volunteers 'increased substantially'.[27] According to the Executive Director in 1989, the 'recent demographic changes in Vancouver', especially the 'influx of immigrants from Hong Kong, Taiwan and students from China' led to the rapid growth during this time period.[28] Mason Loh, the Chairman in 1995, noted that the increasing services offered by the organization were reflecting the great number of immigrants who were coming into the province under the Business Immigration Programme. He wrote, 'Since more than half the immigrants who came to British Columbia last year were from economic categories, we opened our West Broadway Office last year to specialize in settlement and language training services for business-orientated immigrants so that they quickly become contributing residents.'[29] He also mentioned the need to solidify the increasingly 'strong partnership' with the government, the community and the corporate sector.

Between 1989 and 1998 the growth of services and the numbers of people both volunteering and receiving aid was phenomenal. In 1989, 500 active volunteers served approximately 40,000 people. In 1997, 7,200 volunteers served 232,233 people.[30] The types of services provided during this decade also grew exponentially. From what was initially a Chinese mutual aid society, SUCCESS quickly became a full-fledged social service provider for the entire lower Mainland, offering help in many areas of immigrant adaptation and survival. One of the key sectors that was expanded in the 1990s was in the area of job training and employment services. Government grants specifically targeted this sector for funding, with Employment and Immigration Canada providing Cdn$1,278,320 (over one-third of the total of all three levels of government grants of Cdn$3,425,286 given to the organization that year) for the 'Canada Job Strategy' programme in 1994–1995.

Government subcontracting of specific, targeted SUCCESS services is also evident in the consistently high funding of the Immigration Settlement Assistance Programme (ISAP). The ISAP received over $1 million in annual funding from Employment and Immigration Canada between 1993 and 1999. This programme includes numerous services for the elderly and for women, as well as family counselling services. At the same time that the federal government allocated funding for these services in the form of grants made to SUCCESS, funding for similar services directly provided by both the federal and the provincial governments declined precipitously.[31]

Discussion

The primary question posed in this chapter concerned how immigration policy and the process of citizenship formation could operate recursively to reinforce the ideology and material effects of neo-liberalism. In Canada, a special business immigration policy was explicitly targeted by the federal government to attract wealthy Hong Kong business-people, who were, at that time, examining the opportunities for both alternative offshore investment sites and alternative sites of citizenship.[32] The stipulations of the programme, combined with the global economic situation, ensured that many Hong Kong immigrants entering under this programme became essentially 'flexible' citizens, maintaining households in both Canada and Asia.[33]

The business immigration policy was designed to attract people who could contribute to the circulation of capital and networking in Asia, as well as to channel capital and business expertise to Canada directly. It was part of a broader liberalization of finance integral to the neo-liberal movement towards a more laissez-faire Canadian economy and society. The deregulation and deterritorialization of money and credit in the 1980s, alongside the easier cross-border movement of entrepreneurs and investors who controlled some of that money, facilitated the entry of Canada into the fast-moving world of Asian capital networks. On this level, the Business Immigration Programme worked directly to further the goals of global capital articulation and the increasing integration of Canada into the world economy.

At the same time, however, the policy worked on another level as well. The policy itself exacerbated the problems of individual migrants attempting to both attain citizenship in one nation-state, and also maintain global business operations. Business immigrants began to live bi-nationally, and were quickly perceived by older Anglo and Chinese residents as 'sojourners', who were not necessarily committed to the historical memory, values or future of Canadian communities. As a dominant class fraction but a racial minority (one that had experienced major discrimination in Vancouver historically), the Hong Kong Chinese business migrants were able to achieve support from both these constituencies through philanthropy and volunteerism within the Chinese community. The particular organization that best served this double purpose, furthermore, was the one within the community that was perceived as the most modern in its procedural operations, the most entrepreneurial in its grant-getting strategies, the most professional in its *non*-ascriptive membership rules, and the most advanced in its economic and social networking capabilities. SUCCESS thus became the preferred charity of Hong Kong Chinese immigrants in Vancouver, and as a result of their contributions and the succeeding government grants they attracted, it quickly rose to become the key social service provider for immigrants in all of British Columbia.

Although just a minor mutual aid society in 1987, within a single decade SUCCESS became so prominent that when it hosted gala dinner events it attracted both the top Pacific Rim businesses and the top government officials to pay homage. Within a decade it also became a society that crossed ethnic divides, attracting volunteers, charity and publicity from outside the Chinese community. Contributing to the enlargement and pro-fessionalization of SUCCESS thus enabled Hong Kong transnational migrants to attain a kind of 'cultural capital' in the worlds of business and government, and also in both Chinese and Anglo communities. Within the Chinese community, in addition to business-people, many of the most respected lawyers, doctors, and other professionals in the community served on the organization's board, greatly adding to the prestige and social networking possibilities inherent in 'belonging' to the society.

The implications of these processes are many. First, the large charitable contributions and volunteering from the immigrants enabled the govern-ment to abdicate some of its responsibilities for social service provision in British Columbia. At the same time that both federal and provincial govern-ments were cutting back on social service expenditures, particularly in the realm of housing, healthcare and assistance for youth and the elderly, non-profit societies such as SUCCESS increased their provisioning in these very areas. The provincial and local government did not sustain the same loss of legitimacy for the decrease in social service provisioning as it might have if SUCCESS and other institutions had not stepped into the breach during this time.

Second, SUCCESS achieved extraordinary growth in under a decade, moving from an organization with an annual operating budget of approx-imately Cdn$800,000 in 1989 to over Cdn$8.2 million by 1998. This phenomenal growth came in large part because of a spectacular increase in government grants, which totalled just Cdn$277,000 in 1989, but grew to $5.1 million by 1998. At the same time that SUCCESS rose in funding and prestige, many of the other voluntary associations in Chinatown began to wither. The combination of increasing interest and donations from the greater Chinese community, combined with full-fledged government support, made SUCCESS the clear winner among the many social service providers in Vancouver. These combined forces thus effectively worked to reward those voluntary sector organizations that had modernized in ways that dovetailed with a broader neo-liberal agenda. The more entrepreneurial and professional societies, which had already successfully applied for funding and formed partnerships with the government and the corporate sector, emerged as the ultimate victors in the increasingly competitive world of subcontracted social service provisioning. Meanwhile, the many organizations that were denied both community-based and government funding quickly disappeared or became moribund. The rise of a particular type of subcontracting provider paralleled and exacerbated the decline of those Chinese institutional providers that failed to 'modernize' or 'universalize' their clientele and constituency, and generally failed to achieve the appropriate entrepreneurial spirit increasingly advocated by the government.

Third, the public–private partnership that has clearly developed between the state and numerous non-profit organizations such as SUCCESS manifests a new direction for state–society relations. As a major subcontractor for the government, SUCCESS functions in an in-between role that is neither state nor society. Although ostensibly autonomous, it is evident that the charity is accountable to government dictates, and that it must work within prescribed limits in order to win the funding that has become essential to its survival. At the same time, the organization is also beholden to corporate forces, which seed its programmes with donations, while at the same time making it remain an attractive locus for government funds. As an in-between entity, SUCCESS is a good example of the rise of the shadow state in Canadian society. It is a non-government organization that is a partner and subcontractor of the government. It is also strongly reliant on market forces for the continuation of its programmes. Thus SUCCESS exists as an institutional apparatus between the state and the market that is completely *of* the state and the market. As Habermas (1989) has shown, the rise of this kind of semi-autonomous, hybrid organization has vast implications for the extension of the state role into the lifeworld.

Finally, the rise of these shadow state organizations is important to examine vis-à-vis their implications for democratic citizenship. Although SUCCESS is ostensibly run by 'the people', serving in their capacity as volunteers, rather than by 'bureaucrats' working for the government, the boundaries between these categories are increasingly blurred. This has meant a necessary reworking of the framework of citizenship with respect to the concept of active participation in a realm separate from state bureaucracy. It has also meant a shifting of personal identities and social relationships within this framework.[34] Furthermore, although the organizations are developing a major role and correspondent degree of power in society, they are not in any sense democratic in their operations. The semi-autonomous organizations, operating under a new type of public–private partnership, are not elected by their constituencies, nor are they accountable to them. The exponential growth of non-profit social service organizations such as SUCCESS, alongside the decline of democratically accountable government structures, thus spells a movement towards a vastly different form of state–society relations in Canada.

This fundamental shift indicates the long-term impact of micro processes and events such as shifts in immigration laws and the targeted attraction of specific groups of migrants. Although the Business Immigration Programme is ostensibly an economic policy, its numerous ripple effects have been much broader. Entrepreneurs and investors were brought into the Canadian system as economic agents, but they arrived with specific socio-cultural problems, agendas and desires. As wealthy business-people they came as a dominant class fraction, yet they arrived in a city where they were a racial minority, one that had experienced major discrimination historically, and where contemporary forms of racism were burgeoning. In order to be accepted, both culturally and economically, many immigrants became involved in large-scale philanthropic endeavours. Thus the historical and geographical context of the immigration policy, who it attracted, and what their options, strategies and actions were after arrival all greatly affected the ways in which the policy played out on the ground. In this particular case, the process of citizenship formation for the Chinese immigrants, especially the attempt to become cultural citizens networked into established Anglo and Chinese communities, led to actions which dovetailed quite effectively with state strategies of capital articulation and the devolution of direct governance. This, I would argue, was not an anticipated outcome of the original immigration policy, but an unintended consequence of some importance.

In order to further understand the process of neo-liberal entrenchment in Canadian society or elsewhere, more studies of this type must be conducted. Although it is possible that economic policies such as the Business Immigration Programme might lead to consequences which *undermine* a broad neo-liberal agenda, my hypothesis would be that the case study presented here represents the more likely outcome. Studying the impact of transnationalism on neo-liberal entrenchment and shifting state–society relations is useful because transnational migration and other types of cross-border flows often cause moments of rupture in the normative assumptions of society, and thus allow glimpses of hegemonic production in action. Nevertheless, transnationalism (in this case, the transnational movement of wealthy entrepreneurs and their capital), is but one entry point into what needs to be a much broader investigation of the workings of hegemony related to the neo-liberal project that has consumed so much of the world over the past two decades.

Notes

1 This chapter is a slightly revised version of an article previously published in *Economy and Society* (2001). For publisher's information on this journal, see http://www.tandf.co.uk.
2 Quoted in *New York Times*, 27 September 1981. Cited in Wolch (1989: 200).
3 Quoted in Wolch (1989: 200).
4 In 1992, for example, the total emigration from Hong Kong was in excess of 100,000. In 1990, 'fully 66 percent of emigrants of working age and 34 percent of total emigrants could be considered managers and administrators, professionals and associate professional workers' (Skeldon 1994: 30–31). For scholarship on the contemporary Hong Kong–Canada migration phenomenon, see Smart (1994) and Ong (1999). For work on the Hong Kong–Vancouver migration more particularly, see Mitchell (1995, 1997a, 1997b, 1998), Ley (1995) and Li (1994).
5 Statistics show a considerable increase in immigration to Canada from Hong Kong after 1967, burgeoning in the years between 1973 and 1976. (The upsurge in immigration between 1973 and 1976 was probably related to the 1973 regularization of the status of illegal over-stayers in Canada.) The next period of rapid, large-scale migration between Hong Kong and Canada began in 1987, just one year after the expansion and modification of the Business Immigration Programme to include more eligible applicants (Skeldon 1994).
6 In 1991 this was amended so that investors seeking to move to provinces that had already received a significant number of business immigrants (British Columbia, Ontario and Québec) would be required to invest Cdn$350,000 for five years.
7 Although Toronto continued to lead as the major destination point for all Hong Kong immigrants, Vancouver quickly became the leading destination city for business immigrants, a position it maintained through the 1990s.
8 In a series of in-depth interviews with business migrants conducted in the late 1990s for the nation-wide 'Metropolitan Project' on immigration, the UBC geographer, David Ley, found that many who had arrived in Vancouver under the entrepreneur or investor category experienced great difficulties in the Canadian business world and often were forced to return to Hong Kong or Taiwan in order to survive economically. 'Seeking 'homo economicus' transnationally: the strange story of Canada's Business Immigration Programmme', paper delivered at Oxford University, 19 October 2000. Cited with permission of the author.
9 As Robert Puddester, the head of Canadian Immigration in Hong Kong, said in a newspaper interview: 'The more money they have, the less they declare' (quoted in Ben Tierney, 'B.C. now top destination for Hong Kong, Taiwan investors', *Vancouver Sun*, 11 February 1992).
10 In a classic merger of 1986, the Hongkong Bank bought out the Bank of British Columbia and became the Hong Kong Bank of Canada. By 1991 it was the largest of all foreign banks in Canada, with 107 offices, and 16 branches specializing in Asian banking. Between 20 and 25% of the bank's clients were Asian in 1991. See Brian Milner, 'Hongkong Bank finds it's tough on the streets', *Globe and Mail*, 5 August 1991, B3.
11 'Emigrating to Canada?' Royal Bank of Canada brochure, Hong Kong, 1991.
12 Interview with an executive at the Royal Bank of Canada, Hong Kong, 21 May 1991.

13 For Kearney (1991), the adversarial position of the state is sharpened by the transnational practices of the migrants, and new types of conflicts over identities and practices in the no man's land of the border zone emerge that potentially contest the legitimacy and power of the state and its disciplinary apparatuses.

14 For a further discussion of the FTA and its links with neo-liberalism, see Clarkson (1993) and Drache (1993). For more on the charter, see Mandel (1989). On the constitution, a useful source is McBride and Shields (1993). For an overall analysis of the articulation of these dynamics in Canada's unfolding constitutional debates see Sparke (forthcoming).

15 Mulroney said in a campaign speech, 'Free trade with the United States is like sleeping with an elephant. It's terrific until the elephant twitches, and if the elephant rolls over you are a dead man', quoted in Stephen Clarkson, 'Disjunctions: Free Trade and the paradox of Canadian development', in Drache and Gertler (1991).

16 For an analysis of the shifts in government funding and the rise of the voluntary sector in British Columbia in the 1980s, see Rekart (1993: 57–92).

17 The final report of these meetings is entitled, 'Working together: a government of Canada/voluntary sector joint initiative. Report of the joint tables, August, 1999'. It can be found on the web page of the Canadian Centre for Philanthropy at: http://www.ccp.ca/information/documents/joint_table/ gd46eng.htm.

18 Ibid.

19 Ibid.

20 Ibid.

21 Ibid.: 3.

22 The notion of 'cultural' citizenship is discussed in Hannerz (1996), Gilroy (1996) and Ong (1999). I use it here to denote some degree of acceptance into the mainstream values of the Chinese community and/or the wider Canadian society as a whole.

23 For a discussion of some of the conflicts between Anglo residents and the recent Hong Kong immigrants see Mitchell (1993, 1997a), Ley (1995) and Li (1994). For a discussion of some conflicts between second and third generation Chinese residents and the recent immigrants see Mitchell (1998) and Ng (1999).

24 In fact, a number of the older associations have become completely moribund in the last two decades. The earlier functions of mutual aid and the social advantages of networking which they provided have largely been supplanted by the more 'modern' and entrepreneurial voluntary associations such as SUCCESS and the Chinese Cultural Center (CCC). These organizations are perceived as modern in relation to the older associations in that they do not rely on ascriptive (clan or regional place) ties for membership, but are open to all who are willing to pay membership fees to join, and are involved with general community outreach, cultural education, and the provision of social services. They are also considered to be run more 'professionally', with hired staff and in an open democratic process. Although many of the Vancouver clan and regional place associations have declined in prominence, this is not true for all ascriptive associations in overseas Chinese societies (see Liu 1998), and may indicate a strongly negative impact of the competition with SUCCESS and the CCC.

25 Between 1995 and 1998 SUCCESS constructed a $12.2 million, 108-bed Multi-Level Care Facility for seniors funded partially by the provincial government and added a $5 million 26,000 square foot Social Service Centre to accommodate clients in the Chinatown area. This latter project was granted a 58-year land lease at $1 by the city of Vancouver and also given $1 million for the building fund from the provincial government. The city of Vancouver had also granted a long-term lease for construction of a 75-bed extended care facility in Eastern Vancouver in 1989. See the 1989 and 1994–1995 *Annual reports* of SUCCESS.

26　*Annual report* (1989: 8).
27　Ibid.: 7.
28　Ibid.: 8.
29　*Annual report* (1994–5: 4). Business workshops include, 'An introduction to start-ing a small business series, import/export business seminars, buying and selling a business, tax planning for small business, strategic trade talks: success stories, and how to buy a franchise business', p. 40.
30　See *Annual report* (1989: 5) and *Annual report* (1997–8: 20).
31　See the *Canada assistance plan annual reports*, 1993 through 1999, Human Resources Development Canada, Minister of Public Works and Government Services, Hull, Québec.
32　In addition to the worries over the PRC political transition that gripped Hong Kong residents in the 1980s, there was a growing problem of capital over-accumulation for many of the wealthiest residents. In the late 1980s, for example, Li Ka-shing's companies controlled more than 10% of the entire Hong Kong stock exchange. As a result of this dominance, he was discouraged from further local investment by securities regulators. See Mitchell (1995: 374).
33　Aihwa Ong (1999) has written of the constitution of transnational Chinese migrants as 'flexible' in *Flexible citizenship: the cultural logics of transnation-ality*.
34　Brown (1997) has noted with respect to AIDS volunteering in Vancouver, that government-funded subcontracting of AIDS services quickly led to a blurring of the categories of citizen volunteer vs. bureaucrat and to shifting identities and rela-tionships within the tightly-knit AIDS community.

References

Brown, M. 1997 *Re-placing citizenship*. New York: Guilford Press.
Canada 1989. Immigration to Canada: a statistical overview. *Employment and Immigration Canada*, November.
Claiborne, W. 1991.Vancouver: another little dragon in the making. *International Herald Tribune*, 14 May.
Clarkson, S. 1993. Constitutionalizing the Canadian-American relationship, in D. Cameron and M. Watkins eds. *Canada under free trade*. Toronto: James Lorimer and Company, 3–20.
Crissman, L. 1967. The segmentary structure of urban overseas Chinese commun-ities. *Man* 2: 185–204.
Drache, D. 1993. The future of trading blocs, in D. Cameron and M. Watkins eds. *Canada under free trade*. Toronto: James Lorimer and Company, 264–276.
Drache, D. and Gertler, M. 1991. *The new era of global competition: state policy and market power*. Montreal: McGill Queens University Press.
Employment and Immigration Canada 1985. Immigration to Canada. *Public Affairs and the Immigration Policy Branch*, Ottawa.
Gilroy, P. 1996. Route work: the Black Atlantic and the politics of exile, in I. Chambers and L. Curti eds. *The post-colonial question*. London: Routledge, 17–29.
Glick Schiller, N., Basch, L. and Blanc-Szanton, C. 1992. Transnationalism: a new analytic framework for understanding migration. *Annals of the New York Academy of Sciences* 645: 1–24.
Glick Schiller, N., Basch, L. and Blanc-Szanton, C. 1995. From immigrant to trans-migrant: theorizing transnational migration. *Anthropological Quarterly* 68: 48–62.

Habermas, J. 1989. *The structural transformation of the public sphere.* Cambridge: MIT Press.

Hannerz, U. 1996. *Transnational connections.* London: Routledge.

Harris, S. 1998. The politics of financial services liberalization: the case of the Canadian investment dealer industry. *Policy Studies Journal* 26: 526–547.

Jenson, J. 1989. 'Different' but not 'exceptional': Canada's permeable Fordism. *Canadian Review of Sociology and Anthropology* 26: 69–93.

Kearney, M. 1991. Borders and boundaries of state and self at the end of empire. *Journal of Historical Sociology* 4: 52–73.

Ley, D. 1995. Between Europe and Asia: the case of the missing sequoias. *Ecumene* 2: 187–212.

Li, P. 1994. Unneighbourly houses or unwelcome Chinese: the social construction of race in the battle over 'Monster Homes' in Vancouver, Canada. *International Journal of Comparative Race and Ethnic Studies* 1: 14–33.

Liu, H. 1998. Old linkages, new networks: the globalization of overseas Chinese voluntary associations and its implications. *China Quarterly* September, No. 155: 582–609.

McBride, S. and Shields, J. 1993. *Dismantling a nation: Canada and the new world order.* Halifax: Fernwood Publishing.

MacDonald, P. 1990. Canada to trim numbers of independent class visas. *Hong Kong Standard*, 26 January.

Mandel, M. 1989. *The Charter of Rights and the legalization of politics in Canada.* Toronto: Wall and Thompson.

Mitchell, K. 1993. Multiculturalism, or the united colors of capitalism? *Antipode* 25: 263–294.

Mitchell, K. 1995. Flexible circulation in the Pacific Rim: capitalisms in cultural context. *Economic Geography* 71: 364–382.

Mitchell, K. 1997a. Different diasporas and the hype of hybridity. *Environment and Planning D: Society and Space* 15: 533–553.

Mitchell, K. 1997b. Conflicting geographies of democracy and the public sphere in Vancouver, BC. *Transactions of the Institute of British Geographers* 22: 162–179.

Mitchell, K. 1998. Reworking democracy: contemporary immigration and community politics in Vancouver's Chinatown. *Political Geography* 17: 729–750.

Nash, A. 1987. *The economic impact of the Entrepeneur Investment Programme.* Ottawa: Institute for Research on Public Policy.

Nash, A. 1992. The emigration of business people and professionals from Hong Kong. *Canada and Hong Kong Update* Winter: 2–4.

Nash, A. 1993. Hong Kong's business future: the impact of Canadian and Australian business migration programmes, in Y. Yeung ed. *Pacific Asia in the twenty-first century: geographical and developmental perspectives.* Hong Kong: The Chinese University Press, 309–339.

Ng, W. 1999. *The Chinese in Vancouver, 1945–80.* Vancouver: UBC Press.

Ong, A. 1993. On the edge of empires: flexible citizenship among Chinese in diaspora. *Positions* 3: 745–778.

Ong, A. 1999. *Flexible citizenship: the cultural logics of transnationality.* Durham: Duke University Press.

Rekart, J. 1993. *Public funds, private provision: the role of the voluntary sector.* Vancouver: UBC Press.

Rouse, R. 1995. Thinking through transnationalism: notes on the cultural politics of class relations in the contemporary United States. *Public Culture* 7: 353–402.

Skeldon, R. 1994. Reluctant exiles or bold pioneers: an introduction to migration from Hong Kong, in R. Skeldon ed. *Reluctant exiles?* London: M.E. Sharpe.

Smart, J. 1994. Business immigration to Canada: deception and exploitation, in R. Skeldon ed. *Reluctant exiles?* London: M.E. Sharpe.

Smith, M. and Guarnizo, L. 1997. *Transnationalism from below.* New Brunswick: Transaction Publishers.

Sparke, M. forthcoming. *Hyphen-nation-states: critical geographies of displacement and disjuncture.* Minneapolis: University of Minnesota Press.

Stewart, W. 1997. *Bank heist.* Toronto: HarperCollins.

Suen, C. 1988. Canadian Bank sets sights on new immigrants. *South China Morning Post*, 24 October.

Tickell, A. 2000. Global rhetorics, national politics: pursuing bank mergers in Canada. *Antipode* 32: 152–175.

Tierney, B. 1992. B.C. now top destination for Hong Kong, Taiwan investors. *Vancouver Sun*, 11 February.

To, E. 1990. Canadian bank eyes emigrants from Hong Kong. *Business News*, 12 May.

Topley, M. 1960. Immigrants and associations: Chinese in nineteenth century Singapore. *Comparative Studies in Society and History* 3: 41–60.

Wolch, J. 1989. The shadow state: transformations in the voluntary sector, in J. Wolch and M. Dear eds. *The power of geography.* Boston: Unwin Hyman.

Wong, F. 1989. Confidence crisis costing billions. *Hong Kong Standard*, 21 September, 4.

Yao, S. 1984. Why Chinese voluntary associations: structure or function. *Journal of the South Seas Society* 39: 75–87.

Young, M. 1992. *Canada's immigration programme.* Ottawa: Minister of Supply and Services, 13–17.

7 Constructing masculinities in transnational space

Singapore men on the 'regional beat'

Brenda Yeoh and Katie Willis

Gender and transnational communities

As Smart and Smart (1998: 104) note, transnational flows of investment and people are 'made possible by and structured through households, family enterprises, "old boy" networks, cultural understandings and miscommunications. Flows across borders include not only capital and labor, but also gifts, contributions to household expenses, obligations, and cultural influence.' As such, to describe these transnational practices, scholars have moved beyond political economy[1] to consider 'moral economies' or 'social economies' (Smart and Smart 1998: 104). Vertovec's (1999) review of some of the burgeoning work in this area provides a sense of the main focal points of research on transnationalism. The themes he identified include: the social morphology of transnational communities; the type of transnational imaginary or consciousness; the mode of transnational cultural reproduction (as mediated by global media and communications); the activities of transnational corporations and strategies of accumulation of the transnational capitalist class; transnational political activities and activisms; and the (re)construction of place and the emergence of new 'translocalities'. In part because transnational communities, at least in terms of sensibilities if not in form, are seen to trace their genealogy to older 'ethnic diasporas',[2] much of the work has drawn on issues of race, culture and ethnicity, and also ethnonationality, as the basic paradigm informing such analysis, with less attention to other cross-cutting parameters of class and gender. More recent contributions have challenged the essentialism characterizing earlier understandings of (trans)migration (van der Veer 1995; Ong and Nonini 1997). Anthias (1998: 571, 577), for example, suggests that the focus on the link to a 'homeland' central to the 'diaspora problematic' can 'reinforce absolutist notions of "origins" and "true belonging"' and can result in a 'lack of attention to issues of gender, class and generation and to other intra-group and inter-group divisions'. Similarly, Brah's (1994) work on 'racialised gendering' in the context of transmigrant women emphasizes the way in which identities are multiply determined in unstable ways not by 'race' or 'gender' in isolation but by a complex constellation of race, class and gender issues.

As we have argued elsewhere (Yeoh and Willis 1999; Willis and Yeoh 2000; Yeoh *et al.* 2000), negotiating transnational space and the formation of transnational communities are strongly gendered processes. 'Gender' questions feature in at least three ways.

First, as has been established in the older literature on gendered migration, and hence part of the theoretical baggage informing studies on transnational mobilities, the decision to migrate and the whole migratory existence are not simply based on each individual's experiences but strongly influenced by being part of a *family* network. This, for example, has been underscored by Chan's (1997: 195) argument (in the context of the Chinese patrilineal family) that diasporic dispersal is 'often a rational family decision to preserve the family, a resourceful and resilient way of strengthening it: families split in order to be together translocally'. In what Chant (1998: 9) calls the 'household strategies approach to gendered migration', the focus on social relations within households helps us problematize the division of labour and power within households, providing insights as to the 'propensity and freedom of different individuals, according to gender, age and their relationships to other household members, to engage in migration'.[3]

Second, the reproductive sphere, domesticity and households in their various forms are crucial sites for the (re)production and sustenance of transnational communities and mobilities. Unravelling the social relations between 'home' and 'away' as transacted within transnational households, families and communities requires us to problematize the gendered division of labour and power inequalities within these entities. The work, thus far, has highlighted, in particular, the role of women in constructing and maintaining such communities and social networks. Dominant gender relations in most societies stress the importance of women in cultivating social networks, and it is this activity which is crucial in developing migration networks of kin of friends.

Feminist scholars have also noted that gender relations are clearly significant to social processes of identity construction of the group, particularly where this involves notions of 'origins', descent, genealogy or acculturation in the home. As Yuval-Davis (1997: 45) has argued, women especially are expected to represent the 'authentic voices' of a culture, and are 'constructed as the symbolic bearers of the collectivity's identity and honour, both personally and collectively'. Indeed, women are often valued for their feminized roles as 'ethnomarkers' within transnational communities (i.e. as cultural carriers ensuring the symbolic and material maintenance and practice of their respective cultural and ethnic values through their role as mothers) and their gendered identities (defined relationally to the family – as sacrificial and dutiful sisters, daughters, mothers, wives and guardians of family honour).

A third important research arena has stemmed from considering 'nation' and 'migration' as countering, yet interlocking, 'stories', and exploring the way gendered discourses and relations are interwoven into the matrix. It has been argued that 'migration has made the most fundamental challenge to the [nation-]state, making borders porous, attenuating the bonds of citizenship' (Ghai 1994, quoted in Piper 1999). In exploring the 'transgressive fact of migration' (van der Veer 1995) to the project of nation-building, feminist scholars have raised crucial issues of nation, state and citizenship and argued that the gendering and racializing of such migrant flows have further complicated definitions of citizenship and the constitution of civil society. Precisely because the 'transmigrant other' is a gendered subject and precisely because the state articulates nationalism by employing 'genderic' modes, the potentially disruptive absence/presence of female 'transmigrant others' needs to be carefully managed by the state through the politics of inclusion and exclusion. Deconstructing state migration policies and rhetoric relating to the import and export of labour to reveal their ethnicized, classed and gendered connotations continues to form an important research arena in understanding the relationship between 'gender' and 'transnational communities'.

This brief review of the literature offering a gendered perspective on transnational communities indicates that, more often than not, the primary concern in the burgeoning literature has been to (re)instate women – their roles and subjectivities – in the multi-stranded relations at 'home' or the place of sojourn, or in sustaining diverse networks spanning vast spaces. There has been little parallel work on men, not as economic agents (there is of course considerable gender-blind literature on entrepreneurs-as-creators of transnational business networks and empires or expatriate workers sustaining transnational corporations, both categories generally assumed to be male-dominated), but as conscious gendered beings tracing new maps of desire and attachment as they make multiple, circular, return or provisional journeys across transnational space.[4] Our preoccupations thus far have often been with examining women's experiences as 'different' but somehow still assuming that men's must be the norm or the foil against which women's experiences are measured.

A gendered perspective on transnationalism has also encouraged an examination of the ways that transnational mobilities simultaneously reinforce and challenge patriarchy in its multiple forms (Pessar 1999). As Guarnizo (1997: 281) argues, 'instead of being a social equalizer that empowers all migrants alike, transnational migration tends to reproduce and even exacerbate class, gender, and regional inequalities'. A range of studies (Kibria 1990; Hondagneu-Sotelo 1992; Taro-Morn 1995; Lim 1997; Dwyer 1999; Huang *et al.* 2000) have drawn attention to the complexities of the way transmigrant women renegotiate power, showing that, while migration may provide some opportunities for enhancing women's status, such processes are not inherent within migration. While it may be argued that women as transmigrants may build for themselves new roles and new political spaces, it is also clear that because such women continue to 'maintain connections with homelands, with kinship networks, and with religious and cultural traditions' in complex and strategic ways, they may renew patriarchal structures in their new homelands which are at times empowering, and at other times limiting (Clifford 1997: 258–259). In this literature focusing on the intersection between gender and transnational relations, much less has been said about the subjectivities and status of men. Exceptions include Margold's (1995) work linking late capitalist forms of labour control with changes in the lived masculinity of Filipino migrant men in the Arab Gulf countries which argues that state-backed labour controls and constraints on the men's public voice led to a dismembering of masculinity and a reworking of their liminal status as subaltern male bodies. In a different context, Le Espritu's (1999) study of Asian immigrant men (salaried professionals, self-employed entrepreneurs and wage labourers) in the US argues that these men (particularly working-class men) feel that their patriarchal authority has been challenged by the social and economic losses they had suffered in their transition to the status of 'men of color' in a context where immigrant women's employability has been enhanced by the growth of female-intensive industries (see also Westwood 1995). Less has been said about highly skilled male workers, although it has been suggested that in the case of transnational migration associated with upward career mobility, the challenges of pioneering, entrepreneurship and the agility to grapple with newly fluid and somewhat erratic forms of transnational capital, mobility becomes a crucial plank in the construction and sustenance of men's view of the masculine self (Li and Findlay 1996; Lang and Smart, 2000). Insofar as transnationalism creates new subjectivities and consciousness, it is clearly important to map the transformation of personal and collective meanings for both men and women vis-à-vis each other.

Aims and context

In an earlier paper (Yeoh and Willis 1999), we have examined the gender assumptions threaded into the discourses and practices of Singapore's go-regional policy[5] and argued that the transnational space mapped out as a result of regionalizing strategies is a pervasively masculine construction where women participate not as economic agents but are positioned as preservers of the family and moral guardians of the nation. While the state's prime concern with regard to the regulation of male bodies appears to be the production of strong soldier bodies capable of defending the 'vulnerable body boundary' of a small nation (Yeoh 1995/1996: 7), women's bodies are 'constructed as the symbolic bearers of the collectivity's identity and honour, both personally and collectively' (Yuval-Davis 1997: 45). We found the representation of women as the 'authentic voices' of a culture and a nation particularly significant in the 'contact zone' between host and migrant cultures where management and control of cultural difference is called upon. As the symbols and bearers of 'Chinese' virtues and values, Chinese women are expected to be 'traditional', feminine and modest. What

Singaporeans perceive as overly liberal attitude among mainland Chinese women is, thus, interpreted severely as an indictment of Chinese society and a betrayal of the whole of Chinese civilization. As such, Singaporean women are strongly encouraged to accompany their spouses abroad as their presence is represented as necessary to prevent husbands from being ensnared by predatory 'China girls', and hence crucial to preserving the integrity of the Singapore family, community and, ultimately, the nation. As men's proclivity to stray is seen as a 'natural' fact of masculinity when surrounded by the temptations of the other's promiscuity, wives are essential to strengthen their husband's moral armour to ward off danger as the family becomes stretched in transnational fields. In short, transmigrant women are often positioned as stabilizing forces of the 'home' and 'community' – the cultural carriers of 'Asian values', the antidote to *west-oxification* and the preservers and reproducers of the family, the next generation, and the nation, in an increasingly fluid and mobile world. We concluded that, far from offering a level playing field to men and women, Singapore's regionalization drive has done little to destabilize the nation's patriarchal gender norms. In transnationalizing the gender division of family labour, the regionalization thrust has, in fact, further deepened the difference between men and women's roles while diffusing some of the tensions experienced by a nation-in-diaspora.

This chapter turns attention to Singapore men on the 'regional beat', focusing not so much on their role as key players in the web of economic relations but the way in which they maintain or transform gendered subjectivities as they negotiate stretched relations across transnational space. In particular, we examine constructions of the masculine self in relation to (1) their role as transnational entrepreneurs and expatriate workers building economic resources for the family and the nation; (2) their role in nurturing the family's social and emotional ties while navigating in transnational space; and (3) their view of sexual liaisons with mainland Chinese women at the place of sojourn vis-à-vis relationships with their womenfolk back 'home' in Singapore.

Transnational entrepreneurial masculinity

Alongside the view that Singaporeans are, in general, reluctant to work overseas particularly in hardship postings like China given the high 'comfort levels' of home, a number of male interviewees[6] speak of 'going regional' as a toughening up measure, as 'a must to grow our young professionals' vision and to widen their scope of experience', almost as a secular rite of passage for those who wish to succeed in their sphere of work.

For example, Paul who started his own executive search consultancy firm after working for several years as a finance manager for an MNC in Guangzhou likens the China job to 'commando training' and the decision to strike out as an entrepreneur in China to heroic acts of bravery:

The China job is much harder than any job in Singapore. It is like having gone through commando training, you can do anything . . . anything is less than commando work. When the so-called 'China wave' started and our ministers and leaders came to China to lead delegations [to pave the way for private investors], I decided to start my own business as I had the combination of opportunity and experience. That was what drove me on . . . it was a very bold decision to start my own business, very very brave at that time. When I think back, I think I was too brave!

Another interviewee, Bertram, a marketing manager with a Government-Linked Company (GLC),[7] was convinced that, given the gritty realities of the times, Singaporeans need to 'toughen up' and find their niche by developing a more entrepreneurial, risk-taking spirit by venturing into the region:

We need more entrepreneurs out there. We need to toughen up in our performance . . . MNCs are footloose today, if you can get a place as an entrepreneur, you go. It's risky, [but] the real world is like that . . .You go and you find your niche.

Regionalization amounts to acts of courage and risk-taking distinctly associated with men (when prompted, most interviewees would also include single women), with women, as wives, playing a supportive role. With few exceptions, interviewees agree that where the family translocates regionally, men are the lead transmigrants, and 'the wife follows', and 'even if the wife finds a job it is as a result of being there rather than the reason to be there'. It provides an opportunity for Singaporean men at early stages of their career to rapidly chalk up wider experiences and earn their spurs, and in so doing ensure their own career development (as Chiew Chang puts it, an overseas posting translates into 'good resume, good exposure and good money'), even if this is at the expense of their wives:

it was something which I fought for because I thought with this regional thing going on and after growing up in Singapore, it's actually nice to be out of Singapore working in a different environment, dealing with different people . . . I said, why not, just for self-fulfilment and improvement and to broaden my horizon when I'm still young . . . I am glad my wife gave me the support. And I'm glad that she actually sacrificed her career for me because at that time we were newly married. [Yong Seng, whose wife Dorothy gave up her job as a school teacher to accompany him to Beijing]

Some interviewees also capitalized on regional opportunities which presented themselves to make mid-career switches, again either to further their own careers or to increase their earnings, usually with the financial welfare of the family in mind:

> I was mid-career in a military uniform organization, as a military officer. I was on the point of being promoted, but I knew [all too well] the army philosophy of keeping [its officers] young. When this opportunity [of a job in China] came by, I secured the job first and then gave four months' notice. Once I got this job, I prepared my wife mentally that I'll be away for quite long. I told her I don't know what's going to happen, but I [assured her] that I'll give to her financially so she doesn't have to worry. In fact, I'll have more because of the overseas allowance and the cost of living in Suzhou is low. [Bertram]

In navigating transnational space and carving out regional careers, there were differences in views among interviewees as to whether such a form of transnational entrepreneurialism was best undertaken by the individual male striking out on his own, or whether the accompanying family (which will 'go wherever he goes' according to Siew Ling, a 'trailing' spouse) would be an asset providing emotional strength and succour under challenging circumstances. At one end of the spectrum, there were those like Boon Peng (a 30-year-old embarking on a travelling diplomatic career) who saw his family (wife and two-year-old son) as not only integrally intertwined with the relocation demands of his job but a major coping strategy abroad:

> I think one of the things that both of us have found helped us cope with being abroad is family. I think for us, family has always been the source of strength. And we are not about to give up on that. If it is a case of going alone – and I foresee that there will be a phase in our lives when that would happen – I think that will have to take the form of my being based in Singapore and travelling out, maybe travelling out very frequently or travelling out for a week or two and coming back for a few days. But basically home [Singapore] is here – that would probably be the only variation that I would be prepared to accept. I won't take a posting abroad for a year without the family.

In the same vein, others such as Beng Song (a project engineer involved in setting up a new office in Suzhou for his company) were of the view that 'you can only succeed in your business if your family is supporting you'.

At the other end of the spectrum, some male interviewees, particularly those starting out in China and who perceived themselves having to grapple with uncertain work terrains or difficult living conditions, clearly preferred to carve out a space and time away alone in order to focus their energies completely on their jobs, without the encumbrances and distractions of family ties and demands, as well as to shield their families from 'rough times':

I also did not know how I was going to spend my time [in his first year out in China], if it's going to be a rough time, I'd rather suffer those things alone. If she [his wife] comes, she would be a burden to me and that may not be good. I will always have to go back and hear her complain about the dinner. I'd rather go alone, I can work 24 hours. [Bertram]

Family and fatherhood in transnational space

In as much as male identities are defined and honed vis-à-vis the demands and rigours of the regional workplace, they are also simultaneously aligned to the dynamics of the domestic sphere. The role of the state, predicated on ideologies of the 'normal' 'Asian family' incorporating distinct places for men and women in their formulations, has been identified as crucial to the construction of a patriarchal society in Singapore (see, for example, Heng and Devan 1995) alongside the complicity of both men and women (see, for example, Purushotam 1992). We argue that, while the divides of home and work, of the 'private' and the 'public' as embodied in the lives of women and men, have been enduring features of Singapore society, the transnationalization of these lines that divide on a broader canvas illustrates the way gender ideologies are elaborated and reproduced.

First, it is evident that Singapore men, whether at 'home' or 'away', or continually shuttling between the two, have a high degree of success in preserving their immunity from domestic work, and in fact have been able to minimize their roles in that sphere so much so that their physical presence or absence has little effect on the actual mechanics of reproducing everyday life for the family. As several interviewees readily confess, since their encounters with the domestic sphere have always been minimal, or in non-crucial, easily replaceable areas, they are dispensable when it comes to shoring up the domestic front.

As for what goes on at home, there is no difference whether I'm in Singapore or abroad . . . Fortunately, anything related to the domestic area I don't care . . . My wife runs it, controls it, including the purse[-strings]. [Meng Chit, general manager of a pharmaceutical business who travels frequently to China]

. . . OK, the honest truth was I didn't have a great deal of home responsibilities, or I didn't discharge them very well. My wife [formerly working as a medical researcher in Singapore but now a housewife in Suzhou] was really the person who did most of the domestic chores, she still does . . . As for the children, I guess the main difference was I didn't spend as much time with my kids playing over the weekends when I was away a lot. [Ray, engineer who first worked with a government statutory board for several years travelling frequently to China before accepting a posting to Suzhou in a managerial capacity]

What about things like supervising their homework?

I didn't do that even when I was in Singapore. That was my wife's department! [Ray]

Unlike the case of Singaporean women who find their domestic roles more firmly entrenched as a result of regionalization moves (those 'left behind' when their husbands relocate to China find themselves redoubling efforts to shore up the domestic front almost as a single parent; many who accompany their husbands abroad give up paying jobs and careers and become housewives in China, see Yeoh and Willis 1999), Singaporean men continue to enjoy several more degrees of freedom in their engagement with domesticity. As such, domestic work is underscored as a strongly feminized sphere of activities just as spearheading economic regionalization remains a masculinized practice.

As previously argued, 'going regional' is strongly allied to a sense of entrepreneurial masculinity. For married men with children, however, the pursuit of entrepreneurial goals needs to be reconciled with the demands of family ties and responsibilities. In the main, two strategies predominate. First, particularly for those with school-age children, reconciling entrepreneurial ambitions and care-giving responsibilities for the children can only be achieved if husband and wife geographically split in order to preserve the family:

My children are quite big now. They are in secondary school and can take care of themselves. [So when the opportunity for a secondment to the Suzhou office came] . . . I decided to give it a try. It's good experience, to have more exposure and to understand another culture . . . My wife was initially not supportive of me . . . [but] in fact, I was quite determined to come here, so it took just one or two weeks [to persuade his wife], that's all . . .

What about your wife and children coming to China with you?

No, I want her to look after my children. I can't just ignore the children totally and have both of us come here. So letting her come was not an option at all.

  I left it to her [as to whether his wife wanted to leave her school-age children in Singapore with grandparents and fly up to China to accompany him]. It's reverse psychology. The more I say don't come, the wife will be thinking that I must have something to hide. The more I say I leave it to you, she . . . [would vacillate]. In fact, the moment she came up, she felt caught in between – kids here [in Singapore], husband there [in China], she felt split. After three months, six months, she went back [to Singapore to be with the kids] and said she wasn't coming back [to China]. [Bertram]

Second, in the case of a number of interviewees with very young children, going regional presents itself as an ideal strategy to organize family and reproductive activities around the demands of their regional career moves.

It happened that my wife became pregnant and at the same time I'm given this opportunity [of an overseas posting to Suzhou]. Should I stay or should I go? I had two weeks to decide . . . In the end I told her, 'You quit your job *lah*, it's okay. Anyway you have been wanting to quit your job for so long. You quit your job and we go over [to China]. I get this salary increment and an overseas allowance. This would compensate financially [for the wife's loss of income]. You don't have to work'. She was very happy to give up the job but not about me going to China. But I told her it comes together [as a package] and I have to make a decision . . . I decided to go because I was thinking, while the baby is still young, she [his wife] can move over with me. But if say the kid is schooling, then that's totally different altogether. When the kids are still young, I can get four to five years' lead time. I can travel around the world first, chalk up a bit of experience and exposure in different countries'. [Tat Seng, manager with a GLC in Suzhou]

We were keen on an overseas posting because . . . we just like the idea of being able to raise a kid ourselves. I think that was based on the fact that my wife wouldn't be working and so she would be able to stay at home [in Singapore, his wife worked as a school teacher] . . . One of the really attractive thing about working abroad and having a family abroad was that the government was compensating my wife's loss of income with us there. So we would have similar combined income with her not having to work and able to look after our kid at home. [Boon Peng]

From men's perspectives, going regional to fuel career ambitions is eminently reconcilable with family responsibilities, on the premise that the actual tasks of reproducing daily life and caring for children devolved onto their womenfolk. Often, they see their role as fathers and respon-sibility to their family in the traditional terms of strategizing to safeguard and improve the family's income, even if this means, in a world econom-ically driven by regionalizing and globalizing impulses, separation from the family, or alternatively uprooting and transplanting the family as they make each career move.

'Second' families and sexual liaisons

The *Report on Promoting Pro-Family Policies in the Workplace* (Committee on the Family 1996: 16) concluded that, while the problem of 'second families' abroad was exaggerated, 'males posted overseas alone were more exposed to temptations' and 'liaisons of various degrees of seriousness had developed between Singaporean expatriates and the locals'. As has been noted, the process of expanding business into China is characterized by 'systems for engendering trust, making contracts, and keeping in touch with developments [which] involve a range of social encounters between businessmen that are supported by hospitality and escort services' and as a result, 'businessmen [from abroad] may find themselves exposed to opportunities for extra-marital adventures that can be managed far more cost-effectively than would be the case "back home"' (Chang 1999: 72–73). The anxieties that – as a by-product of economic engagement – sexual liaisons with 'the other' in transnational space will rupture notions of the harmonious Singaporean family, nation and homeland is particularly salient in the context of China. The movement of economic migrants to China as part of the regionalization drive is also a form of 'return migration' with many ironic inflections when read in the context of Singapore's history as the product of overlapping diasporas. In the nineteenth and early twentieth centuries, male Chinese sojourners who came to the *nanyang* and set up businesses in Singapore were known to maintain at least two 'homes' and have more than one wife, often a 'first' wife in China, and a 'second' (and possibly 'third' and 'fourth' as well) wife in Singapore. It has been argued that given this 'cultural legacy', extra-marital affairs for the Chinese are 'relatively invisible', and tolerated by Chinese wives, even though in China itself, concubinage and polygamy have been replaced by modern monogamous marriage arrangements since the early twentieth century (Chang 1999: 69). Regionalization reconnects Singaporean Chinese back to China not only in terms of business links but also rekindles the possibility of other historical resonances including the fear of the mainland Chinese woman as 'the other (woman)'.[8]

From a different perspective, Lang and Smart (2000) also pointed out that, in China, 'families have been conscious for many decades that they could use the marriage of a daughter to a Hong Kong-based man or to an "overseas Chinese" to get access to more resources and perhaps emigrate, and daughters are aware of such considerations when the opportunity for such a liaison arises'. In the context of Hong Kong men in China, they argue that extra-marital sexual relationships while in China on business are common and estimate that in the 1990s, there are some 25,000 such men with a mistress or 'second' wife. It has also been reported that 'more and more Taiwanese men doing business in China take two wives – one on each side of the strait' and that this 'unstoppable trend' has led to the setting up of a 'First Wives Club', a non-profit association which provides Taiwanese women whose husbands have had extra-marital relationships in China with legal assistance (*Straits Times*, 19 February 2001).

In the case of Singapore men, most interviewees concurred that while true polygyny is rare, a range of sexual liaisons from keeping a mistress to occasional 'flings' and 'affairs' are common (even though, of course, few included themselves in the headcount; one or two did), although most insist that the Singapore breed is actually better off than their Hong Kong or Taiwanese counterparts. A so-called joke often related to us summarizes the promiscuity pecking order of nationalities – 'out of the ten Singaporeans working in China, eight are having an affair. Out of ten Hong Kong men, ten are having an affair. Out of ten Taiwanese men, twelve are having an affair including those who are travelling in and out and not living there'.

When it came to the question of 'blame', most argue that the state of affairs, while unsatisfactory, was a result of the force of circumstances, citing in particular the man's loneliness away from home and the 'natural' fact borne of economic disparity between the Singaporean man and the 'China girl':

> In China, there are many SMEs [small and medium sized enterprises] out to make some money. You need to sacrifice as a manager, you just go alone. There is . . . the problem of loneliness . . . There will always be this [problem]. Human is just human. And because China is less developed, if you want something naughty, it is quite cheap. And it's a low-entry barrier. In other places, the entry barrier is high, you don't have that kind of money, you don't talk about doing. But the low-entry barrier may induce somebody to go ahead. [Meng Chit]

> I think it's just loneliness and temptation and how willing the environment is. If you are working here on your own, even if you don't search, others come to you, and if you don't find the person repulsive . . . you know it happens . . . I would imagine that many, many men have been approached in some way or another. [Ray]

Others argue that the temptation is particularly strong because a Chinese girlfriend or mistress (often referred to as 'the long-haired Chinese talking and walking dictionary') demonstrates men's virility and economic status, and feeds into men's masculinized sense of self:

> Let's say your handsomeness is 50%, when you come to China you automatically enhance your index. Your handsomeness goes from 50% to 100%! [Philip, entrepreneur in his late forties]

> You know, in Beijing and Shanghai, the dressing of women can be much better than in Singapore? You would be surprised! And you know what? It is [a common view] that if you really want to go and get a Chinese woman, [all you have to do is] take your passport and flash your passport! [Yong Seng]

For those who argue that the second wife phenomenon had been exaggerated, one pointed out that it was possible to develop close and sincere friendships with Chinese women without sexual overtones:

I mean, it is normal that opposite sex are attractive to each other. It's not just for sex. It is kind of natural, when you talk to someone, there is a high chance that you may end up going out with one girl. I mean, don't go tell my wife, but in some places I do have, sometimes, a very close girlfriend. Not necessary that I go to bed with her. No! We are very sincere friends. She treats me like a foreigner, I treat her like a close girlfriend. I visit her family. Sometimes we just talk. [Jong Yau, a manager in an MNC]

Along similar lines, another pointed out that these relatively innocent interactions with Chinese girls provide men a means of coping with the tensions and difficulties of a regionalizing job which is not available to women, hence explaining why men are more capable of surviving the intense pressures of doing business in China compared to women:

You know, for men, they can go to the karaoke, or talk to some beautiful girls, they feel good. You pay 300 bucks and you get somebody to chit chat with you. Then you feel better. Women cannot do that. You look at the stars, you read books, it's very hard. [Philip]

Finally, some argue that not only are sexual liaisons natural and inevitable (given the view that men are not at fault because they are considered naturally promiscuous, or that they cannot help themselves given the force of circumstances), they do not necessarily detract from men's abilities to fulfil their obligations as husbands to their wives back home:

In my opinion, especially as a man, sometimes I think: So what if they have an affair? As long as he looks after his family back home. After all, there's no way, especially in China, that he can bring the girl back. So why do you care? Just ignore it. Most important, he should be responsible to his family. [Jong Yau]

Wives in Singapore should not be so worried. These husbands go to pubs and karaoke lounges because life is very stressful. There's no need to be afraid, they still love their wives, their children, no matter how playful they are sometimes. [Philip]

On the contrary, it would appear that there are also some men who invert the logic and consider having local mainland mistresses a necessity to preserving their virility for the sake of their families and careers. A Taiwanese businessman was reported to have said (*Straits Times*, 19 February 2001):

In China, doing business is tough, so we need an 'inspiring' mainland companion who has different charms from our wives back home to

invigorate our struggles here ... We must not get inebriated lest we
destroy both our family and career.

Conclusion

While generic modes of discourse underlying transnational entrepreneurialism are seldom overtly articulated as plainly as something suited to men's
nature and roles but not to women's, it remains a taken-for-granted assumption. Men are key players in lubricating the construction of the nation's second wing economy while women at best play supportive roles, often as
appendages to men. Conversely, transnational entrepreneurialism and the
regional experience not only prepares men for career advancement but it is
an important testing ground which hones characteristics such as courage and
risk-taking behaviour. Women fit well into supportive roles, either as wives
who are not 'excessively ambitious' (Ray's words), or companions whose
presence demonstrates men's virility or economic status. By stretching the
lineaments of gendered identities on the canvas of transnational space, transnational entrepreneurialism extends and crystallizes male roles as exemplary
fighters, breadwinners, adventurers, husbands, fathers, and lovers, against a
background where women somehow remain sequestered in a supportive,
domestic sphere. Traversing transnational space in this instance seems to be
a hegemonically masculinized enterprise where men and women remain
complicit in the reproduction of patriarchy beyond national shores.

Acknowledgements

The 1997 fieldwork trip was funded by the Lee Foundation (Singapore) and
an HSBC Small Research Grant administered by the Royal Geographical
Society (with the Institute of British Geographers). The 1999 and 2000
fieldwork trips were funded by the Economic and Social Research Council
(Grant No. L214 25 2007). The authors would like to extend their thanks
to these funding bodies, as well as to all the Singaporeans who have helped
them in this research and the postgraduate students in Liverpool and
Singapore who have helped transcribe the interviews.

Notes

1   See Yeung (1998, 1999) for an analysis of the political economy of transnational
    business, with reference to Singapore's regionalization drive. Expanding on
    Eisinger's original notion of an 'entrepreneurial state', Yeung (1999: 264) argues
    that, in recent years, 'the regionalization process has taken on a new degree of
    politicization, as top leaders have become directly involved in the opening-up and
    promotion of business opportunities for government-linked companies and local
    firms' (what Yeung terms 'political entrepreneurship').
2   Tölölyan (1991: 5) describes ethnic diasporas as 'the exemplary communities
    of the transnational moment' while Vertovec (1999: 449) reiterates that 'the

dispersed diasporas of old have become today's transnational communities sustained by a range of modes of social organization, mobility and communication'.

3 More specifically, gender and migration research has highlighted the importance of household and reproductive activities in four main ways: first, migration decisions, although made at a household level, represent inequalities in intra-household power relations and reflect local-level gender relations. Second, the household, or as Zlotnik (1995) terms it 'the family', needs to be considered, as reunification or marriage is an important determinant of migration, particularly to countries of 'permanent immigration'. Third, while most individuals' decisions to migrate for work purposes are linked to improving the economic status of their households, women's labour migration may be constrained by domestic responsibilities, particularly the care of children or the elderly. Finally, access to reproductive services, rather than employment, may prompt household migration. While women and children may remain permanently in the cities with greater access to shelter, services and kinship support, adult men often seasonally migrate outside the cities for agricultural work (Chant 1998).

4 There is, however, a growing literature on the construction of masculinities among male empire-builders, planters and travellers in their contest with tropical nature and people during the colonial era. See, for example, Duncan (2000).

5 Over the past 30 years, economic policy was adapted from an initial focus on export-orientated factory production using cheap labour, to greater value-added industries focusing on service provision, particularly in the financial sphere. However, for the rapid rates of growth to be maintained, the Singapore economy has to keep expanding and developing. Singapore's natural resources are limited, with a small land area and small population. These resource limitations have led the government and private sector to view investment outside the national boundaries to be of crucial importance. While Singapore companies have always been involved, to some degree, in foreign investment, it is only since 1986 and particularly since 1992 that this policy has been heavily promoted. 'Going regional' involves investment in South and East Asia and is an example of how the processes of globalization have led to an increasingly complex web of international economic flows, and a fragmenting of the previous core–periphery divisions. Singapore has become the node of a regional economy, acting as a conduit for non-Asian funds coming into the region, as well as Singapore firms investing directly in regional economies (see Yeoh and Willis (1997) and Willis and Yeoh (1998) for further details).

6 The arguments are grounded mainly in research materials garnered from in-depth interviews with about 80 male Singaporean migrants (or potential migrants) to China (including Hong Kong) collected between 1997 and 2000.

7 These are large, locally owned enterprises, including land development agencies and telecommunication companies, where the Singapore government has majority ownership.

8 Anxieties about Singapore men being 'ensnared' by mainland Chinese women while working in China are mirrored by what has been called 'the China bride phobia', the perception that China brides (Chinese nationals who marry Singapore men and move to Singapore) are 'gold-diggers or schemers who use marriage as a stepping stone to obtain permanent residence or citizenship' in Singapore (*Sunday Times*, 13 August 2000).

References

Anthias, F. 1998. Evaluating diaspora: beyond ethnicity? *Sociology* 32: 557–580.
Brah, A. 1994. *Cartographies of diaspora: contesting identities*. London: Routledge.

Chan, K.B. 1997. A family affair: migration, dispersal, and the emergent identity of the Chinese cosmopolitan. *Diaspora* 6: 195–213.

Chang, J.S. 1999. Scripting extramarital affairs: marital mores, gender politics and infidelity in Taiwan. *Modern China* 25: 69–99.

Chant, S. 1998. Households, gender and rural-urban migration: reflections on linkages and considerations for policy. *Environment and Urbanization* 10: 5–21.

Clifford, J. 1997. *Routes: travel and translation in the late twentieth century.* Cambridge, MA: Harvard University Press.

Committee on the Family 1996. *Report on promoting pro-family policies in the workplace.* Singapore: National Advisory Council on the Family and the Aged.

Duncan, J.S. 2000. The struggle to be temperate: climate and 'moral masculinity' in mid-nineteenth century Ceylon. *Singapore Journal of Tropical Geography* 21: 34–47.

Dwyer, C. 1999. Veiled meanings: young British Muslim women and the negotiation of differences. *Gender, Place and Culture* 6: 5–26.

Guarnizo, L.E. 1997. The emergence of a transnational social formation and the mirage of return migration among Dominican transmigrants. *Identities* 4: 281–322.

Heng, G. and Devan, J. 1995. State fatherhood: the politics of nationalism, sexuality and race in Singapore, in A. Ong and M.G. Peletz eds. *Bewitching women, pious men: gender and body politics in Southeast Asia.* Berkeley: University of California Press, 195–215.

Hondagneu-Sotelo, P. 1992. Overcoming patriarchal constraints: the reconstruction of gender relations among Mexican immigrant women and men. *Gender and Society* 6: 393–415.

Huang, S., Teo, P. and Yeoh, B.S.A. 2000. Diasporic subjects and identity negotiations: women in and from Asia. *Women's Studies International Forum* 23: 391–398.

Kibria, N. 1990. Power, patriarchy and gender conflict in the Vietnamese immigrant community. *Gender and Society* 4: 9–24.

Lang, G. and Smart, J. 2000. Migration and the 'second wife' in South China: toward cross-border polygyny. *International Migration Review* 36: 546–569.

Le Espritu, Y. 1999. Gender and labor in Asian immigrant families. *American Behavioral Scientist* 42: 628–647.

Li, F.L.N. and Findlay, A.M. 1996. Your move or mine? an investigation of gender and migration amongst Hong Kong professional couples. Centre for Applied Population Research, Research Paper 96/5. Department of Geography: University of Dundee.

Lim, I.S. 1997. Korean immigrant women's challenge to gender inequality at home: the interplay of economic resources, gender and family. *Gender and Society* 11: 31–51.

Margold, J.A. 1995. Narratives of masculinity and transnational migration: Filipino workers in the Middle East, in A. Ong and M.G. Peletz eds. *Bewitching women, pious men: gender and body politics in Southeast Asia.* Berkeley: University of California Press, 274–298.

Ong, A. and Nonini, D. 1997. Towards a cultural politics of diaspora and transnationalism, in A. Ong and D. Nonini eds. *Ungrounded empires: the cultural politics of modern Chinese transnationalism.* London: Routledge, 323–332.

Pessar, P.R. 1999. Engendering migration studies: the case of new immigrants in the United States. *American Behavioral Scientist* 42: 577–600.

Piper, N. 1999. Gender, labour and citizenship: female migrant workers in Japan. Paper presented at the 'Gendered mobilities in Asia' conference, Chinese University of Hong Kong, Hong Kong, 24–26 November.

Purushotam, N. 1992. Women and knowledge/power: notes on the Singaporean dilemma, in K.C. Ban, A. Pakir and C.K. Tong eds. *Imagining Singapore*. Singapore: Times Academic Press, 320–361.

Smart, A. and Smart, J. 1998. Transnational social networks and negotiated identities in the interactions between Hong Kong and China, in M.P. Smith and L.E. Guarnizo eds. *Transnationalism from below*. New Brunswick: Transaction Publishers, 103–129.

Straits Times 2001. First Wives Club, 19 February.

Sunday Times 2000. China Brides: have they become wives of last resort? 13 August.

Taro-Morn, M. 1995. Gender, class, family and migration: Puerto Rican women in Chicago, *Gender and Society* 9: 712–726.

Tölölyan, K. 1991. The nation-state and its others: in lieu of a preface. *Diaspora* 1: 3–7.

van der Veer, P. 1995. Introduction: the diasporic imagination, in P. van der Veer ed. *Nation and migration: the politics of space in the South Asian diaspora*. Philadelphia: University of Pennsylvania Press, 1–16.

Vertovec, S. 1999. Conceiving and researching transnationalism. *Ethnic and Racial Studies* 22: 447–462.

Westwood, S. 1995. Gendering diaspora: space, politics and South Asian masculinities in Britain, in P. van der Veer ed. *Nation and migration: the politics of space in the South Asian diaspora*. Philadelphia: University of Pennsylvania Press, 197–221.

Willis, K. and Yeoh, B.S.A. 1998. The social sustainability of Singapore's regionalisation drive. *Third World Planning Review* 20: 203–221.

Willis, K. and Yeoh, B.S.A. 2000. *Gender and migration*. Cheltenham: Edward Elgar.

Yeoh, B.S.A. and Willis, K. 1997. The global-local nexus: Singapore's regionalisation drive. *Geography* 82: 183–86.

Yeoh, B.S.A. and Willis, K. 1999. 'Heart' and 'wing', 'nation' and 'diaspora': gendered discourses in Singapore's regionalisation process. *Gender, Place and Culture* 6: 355–372.

Yeoh, B.S.A., Huang, S. and Willis, K. 2000. Global cities, transnational flows and gender dimensions: the view from Singapore. *Tijdschrift voor Economische en Social Geografie* 91: 147–158.

Yeoh, B.S.E. 1995/1996. The regulation of bodies: Singaporean men, unpublished Academic Exercise, Department of Sociology: National University of Singapore.

Yeung, H.W.C. 1998. The political economy of transnational corporations: a study of the regionalisation of Singaporean firms. *Political Geography* 17: 389–416.

Yeung, H.W.C. 1999. Regulating investment abroad: the political economy of the regionalization of Singaporean firms. *Antipode* 31: 245–273.

Yuval-Davis, N. 1997. *Gender and nation*. London: Sage.

Zlotnik, H. 1995. Migration and the family: the female perspective. *Asian and Pacific Migration Journal* 4: 253–271.

8 A European space for transnationalism?

Alisdair Rogers

> It is precisely in the name of European values that Estonia needs a secure
> border . . . Our border is the border of European values.
>
> (Estonian President Lennart Meri, March 1993,
> cited in Graham Smith (1999))

A transnational discourse and research associated with the phenomenon
were initially established in the Americas and, later, Asia-Pacific. But,
particularly if also judged by press coverage and public debate, this is
perhaps less so within Europe. This may be surprising given the region's
long history of various non-national social and cultural formations,
including the classic diasporas. Attempts to refine a social scientific definition and analysis of transnationalism have mostly taken the Americas as
their starting point. This raises the question of just how 'transnational'
transnationalism is. This chapter proposes both that there is scope for a
more macro-regional approach to transnationalism, and that there are good
grounds for expecting European space to differ from the Americas. Using
the concepts of migration order and migration configuration, it suggests
some basic distinctions derived from history, politics and geography.
Eastern and Western European varieties of transnationalism can be distinguished, and within the European Union there are both internal and external
forms. The chapter, then, considers whether these several kinds can, in fact,
be considered part of a single process, an emerging European *mobility order*
described by a geography of concentrically defined regions that stretch
beyond the continent itself and shaped, above all, by the economic and
geopolitical aspirations of the European Union.

An exemplary episode of transnationalism

One episode in particular seems to exemplify the emergence of a European
mobility order, where migration, security, human rights, diasporas and
inter-state relations collide. It is the case of Abdullah Ocalan, leader of
the Kurdish Workers' Party (PKK), and his flight into captivity.[1] Under

the threat of Turkish invasion, Syria expelled Ocalan in November 1998. He fled to Moscow via Greece and Armenia, where he went into hiding with the support of Vladimir Zhirinovsky, the ultra-nationalist Russian politician. When rumours of his presence spread, both Turkey and the US State Department urged the Russian government to deport him. He entered Italy on a false passport, was arrested and detained under house arrest. Italy refused to hand him over to Turkey, because Turkey could execute Ocalan, but neither did it offer him asylum. Despite there being a warrant for his arrest on terrorist charges in Germany, Bonn was reluctant to cause unrest among German Kurds (numbering around 500,000) by bringing him to justice.

On 16 January 1999, Ocalan left Italy, there being no charges against him. He flew to Russia but was prevented from going through customs and passport control, allowing the authorities honestly to inform Turkey that he had never entered Russian territory. He then flew to Greece, on to Minsk in Belarus and, along the way, tried to land in Amsterdam to present himself to the Permanent Court of Arbitration in The Hague. Belgian jet fighters prevented him landing there and he was refused permission to re-fuel in Switzerland. He may have touched down in Milan airport before flying on to Greece where, again, his plane was isolated on the runway. It appears then that the Greek authorities persuaded him to seek asylum in South Africa, smuggling him into the Greek embassy in Nairobi. But the city was full of US and Israeli intelligence agents, following the bombing of the US embassy the previous July. US agents tipped off Turkey, whose commandos seized Ocalan on his way to the airport on 15 February.

Widespread demonstrations, embassy occupations and civil unrest of all kinds were immediately sparked throughout Kurdish communities, not just in Europe but also in Central Asia, Australia and the Philippines. These demonstrations, which were allegedly coordinated and organized, graphically revealed the Kurdish diaspora presence in European cities in Germany, Netherlands, UK, France and elsewhere. Ocalan was detained on a Turkish prison island and later sentenced to death. While on trial, the European Union appealed for clemency and requested observer status at the proceedings (both denied), part of a sustained diplomatic effort to save his life. He is currently serving a life sentence in a Turkish prison, his death sentence having been commuted.

European Union territory was hermetically sealed against Ocalan, as he bounced between airport runways, kept in zones of uncertain sovereignty and even challenged in airspace. Having been forced out of the EU and the zone of transit countries he was not even safe in an embassy in Africa. Yet, having been the victim of the European mobility regime, the EU then pleaded that he be granted civil rights. It was made clear to the Turkish authorities that the death penalty did not accord with 'European values', and was incompatible with eventual membership of the Union. These

developments may seem paradoxical or hypocritical, but they are consistent, after a fashion. Human rights, among other values, follow a geography
of concentric zones, in which everyone should be in their rightful place.
What is the form of this geography of security, rights, and movement and
how does it shape transnational activities?

The case for a macro-regional approach to transnationalism

Based on the regular digest of news sources compiled for *Traces*, available
on-line from the ESRC 'Transnational Communities' programme web-site,
little attention is paid to transnationalism (however defined) in the European
press. It is not simply that there is comparatively little use of the term 'transnationalism' in papers and news agencies, aside from references to
transnational corporations. It is more that, with some exceptions, the
kinds of processes, relations, and phenomena we might wish to describe
as transnational receive scant publicity. A similar point might be made
about published research on transnationalism in Europe, although this is
becoming less so over time. The key texts and exemplary cases of transnationalism have been drawn from either the Americas or the Asia-Pacific
region (for example, Basch *et al.* 1994; Glick Schiller *et al.* 1992; Ong and
Nonini 1997; Portes *et al.* 1999; Portes 2001; Smith and Guarnizo 1998),
as have many of the sceptical reactions and corrections to transnationalism
(for example, Foner 1999). There are few European contributions to a
recent reader on *Migrations, diasporas and transnationalism* (Vertovec and
Cohen 1999). Notable exceptions include Hannerz (1996) and Faist (2000).
This suggests that there may be a case for considering the macro-regional
dimension of transnational research and discourse.

   Katharyne Mitchell (1997) advocates 'bringing geography back in' to
studies of transnationalism, diaspora and hybridity. Exploring the macro-
regional dimensions of transnationalism is *one* part of this process. First,
there are naive geographical questions. One might ask of any phenomenon,
what are its spatial distribution, relative location and so forth. Second, a
more regional approach fits into the various efforts to distance transnationalism (and globalization) from the emphasis on deterritorialization
given to it both by the pioneering work of Glick Schiller, Basch and
Blanc-Szanton and, in a different sense, by some approaches rooted in
cultural studies (for example, Appadurai 1996). In their desire to move
away from the kind of bounded entities and concepts which characterized
standard migration research, such as community or world systems theory,
Glick Schiller *et al.* (1992) have been faulted. As Guarnizo and Smith
(1998: 12) suggest, 'the image of transnational migrants as deterritorialized,
free-floating people represented by the now popular adage "neither here nor
there" deserves closer scrutiny'.

Setting aside for the moment the questionable conflation of material, empirical, everyday and spatial suggested by this exchange, it is possible to distinguish a number of 'localizing strategies' in current studies of transnationalism. Although Appadurai (1996) writes of translocalities, Michael Peter Smith (1999) uses the same term in a more sociological way to refer to the rural villages, small towns, metropolitan districts and provinces connected by transnational ties. The significance of locality and trans-local relations is confirmed by much ethnographic research (for example, Riccio 2001; R.C. Smith 1998). A second and related localizing move links transnationalism with global cities, and their repositioning in relation to nation states (Sassen 1998; Smith 2001). Both these scales are sub-national, as if the conceptual and empirical shift away from the nation-state level could lead to only two polar opposites, global and local, with nothing in between. The studies in *Ungrounded empires* (Ong and Nonini 1997) convey a rich sense of the range and diversity of the sites, zones and regions of Chinese transnationalism. But it seems that the supra-national level plays only a minor part.

Third, and carrying on from this point, another research priority has been suggested in 'comparing practices of migrants and states vis-à-vis trans-migration in different broadly geo-political regions (e.g. Latin America and the Asia-Pacific) to determine if differences within regions are greater than differences between regions' (Guarnizo and Smith 1998: 28). But what is being compared, and are these regions alike?

As well as suggesting a macro-regional approach in general terms, there might be good grounds for considering transnationalism in regions other than the Americas. Appadurai (1986) once noted that in anthropology there were certain gatekeeping concepts which typified each major region, such as lineage or segment in Africa, caste in South Asia, or the manipulation of bodily substances in Melanesia. He meant that not only did it seem natural to study key concepts in paradigm regions, but that these regions were understood through the lens of such concepts: 'the burning issues of anthropological theory are regionalized, so that a particular region comes to more general theoretical prominence in terms of certain issues' (Fardon 1990: 26). One consequence of this, he warns, is that 'as certain kinds of theorizing in anthropology become cryptophilosophical, the original place of origin of ethnographic descriptions becomes quite irrelevant' (Appadurai 1986: 361). This suggests that we ought to scrutinize the relations between general concepts and their geographical origins.

Given that the founding definitions of transnationalism derived from empirical studies in the Americas, it might be questioned whether the core features of the concept are general or more particular to that one region. Or, does transnationalism only appear now because of the historical accident of the world's richest country (the US) being adjacent to one of the world's poorest (Mexico)? Is transnationalism an accident of geography or a global process, albeit uneven in its extent and effects?

A macro-regional focus, therefore, contributes to the general grounding of the study of transnationalism in the relations between spatial and temporal scales, while at the same time establishing its necessary and contingent factors and providing some basis for comparative analysis. Within geography there has been a stress on relational conceptions of space in the understanding of globalization, notably from Massey (1999). This implies, among other things, that the world should neither be conceived of as comprised of homogeneous spatial units (for example Huntington's 'civilizations') nor as a borderless, frictionless and absolute space across which rush and spin the flows and networks of globalization and transnationalism. This prompts a regional perspective, but only if the constructed and contested nature of the region in question is also acknowledged.

American and European transnationalism compared

Are there good grounds for thinking that American and European transnationalism would differ in any way? At the most abstract level, it may be that European migration and transmigration patterns have been affected as much by geopolitical developments as by economic globalization or any revolution in information and communication technologies. The collapse of the USSR and the further integration and expansion of the European Union have no obvious correlates in the Americas, although civil wars and unrest in Central America may be linked to Cold War politics. Second, there is a marked demographic contrast between the European Union and the US. According to a UN report (United Nations 2000), even at current levels of immigration, the EU will not replace either its total population or its working age population (scenario I). By contrast, the US will continue to grow and, by 2050, its population will surpass that of the EU 15. For the 47 countries of the whole of Europe to maintain the size of their working age population by 2050, they would require three times the current level of net immigration. The demographically driven demand for labour in Europe will undoubtedly affect both future migration and transmigration and future policy on population mobility.

These two contrasts alone are strong enough to suggest that European transnationalism may differ from American. But further comparative analysis will require a more refined understanding of what exactly is being compared. What is 'Europe' in this case? Two concepts, both derived from established migration systems approaches, suggest ways of proceeding: 'migration orders' as detailed by Nick Van Hear, and 'migration configurations' as suggested by Frank Pieke.

Van Hear (1998) draws from the literature of forced migration to compose a concept of *migration order* appropriate to understanding transnational communities. Such orders include four domains: (1) root causes or structural background; (2) proximate causes such as business cycles; (3) precipitating factors which trigger a migration event, such as the onset of war or sudden economic collapse; (4) intervening factors, which affect whether a migration flow is continued or not, including transport, communication and *migration regimes*, or the attempts by national and international entities to manage migration. Shifts from one order to another may be gradual, 'transitions', or sudden, 'crises'. For example, the break up of the Soviet Union marked one transition for the USSR and East-Central Europe. For Van Hear, it marks a transition from immobility to mobility or a 'transition from regulated mobility to increasingly disorderly movement' (1998: 38). Another example would be the shift from being an immigration country to being an emigration country, for instance in southern Europe. Van Hear emphasizes that states are not autonomous actors in such transitions, but that they are also made 'by the strategies and decision-making of individuals and households, and through the development and working out of their networks' (1998: 58).

In the context of studying Chinese international and internal migration as a single process, Pieke (2000) suggests that research should shift from migration as the core variable to migration configuration. A *migration configuration*:

> includes flows of information, goods, money and other resources. Institutions and networks within the migration configuration shape interaction across different sites, such as kinship groups, friendship and home community networks, emigration and immigration officials and commercial human traffickers, other ethnic groups at a particular destination, airlines, railways and shipping companies, and law firms, human rights groups, and anti-immigration activists.
>
> (Pieke 2000: n.p.)

Pieke intends that a configuration should be more actor-centred than a system, and should embrace all forms of mobility. It is not immediately clear what constitutes a migration configuration, although he suggests that a diaspora from one region of China or expatriate migration might be examples. (He also speculates that such configurations might be part of a Chinese *world system*, in which Europe is a migration frontier.) The point is that migration, including transnational migration, should be placed in a larger, possibly regional, context sensitive to the whole range of mobility.

Although neither of these two concepts is necessarily regional, let alone spatial, they point towards a framework for comparison. Furthermore, both place migration in a context of mobility as a whole, including the role of migration regimes (law enforcement, immigration rules, etc.). Both indicate that economic and technological forces alone cannot account for either the onset of movement nor its continuation, for example how migrants become transnational communities.

Using Van Hear's typology of domains, a number of potential differences between Europe and the Americas can be sketched out:

1 Root or structural factors include the legacy of imperialism and colonialism on European and colonized states, the collapse of multi-national empires in the twentieth century, the geopolitical relations between Christianity and Islam, and the long history of emigration. The process of nation-state building differs systematically between old societies and settler societies, but also within Europe between the more class-stratified nation states of the North and West and the organic nation states of the South and East (Mann 1999). In turn, this has affected the development of contrasting modes of citizenship and reactions to ethnic or cultural difference. One possible consequence of this, relevant to transnational politics for example, is the relative closure of European legislatures and executives to diaspora lobbying.[2] Another is the apparent significance of religion, notably Islam, as a marker of difference and a foundation for new or revived transnational communities. Demographic factors, notably ageing populations, belong here, along with differences in labour markets and employee mobility.

2 Proximate causes and triggering events are, by definition, more particular to places and less relevant to comparison. They include such events as the wars in Yugoslavia, the earthquake in Turkey and the decision of Hungary to let East Germans have access to the West, leading ultimately to the fall of the Berlin Wall.

3 Intervening factors, by contrast, are significant in the contrast between Europe and the Americas. In general, affluent European societies have done their best to exclude migrants and refugees in the past two or more decades and show every sign of continuing to do so. This contrasts with the US and Canada. In addition, there is the generally lower level of mobility within Europe compared with much of North America, the result of the uneven diffusion of technology and the slower pace of deregulation for air transport, telecommunications and so forth. Cheap travel and telephone calls, so vital to transnational connections, have not sprung up evenly and contemporaneously. Although Ukrainians, for example, only require a visa to cross into the Czech Republic to find casual work, the $50 passport fee is still beyond many people. And although Med TV was available by satellite throughout Europe, few Kurds could afford a dish (Wahlbeck 1998). That the EU itself is taking a lead in the regulation of e-commerce, telecommunications and air travel both suggests convergence and promises greater mobility for the average EU citizen. Another point of comparison might be the differential development of commercial money transfer facilities (now big business in the Americas).

The collapse of the Soviet Union and the economic and political integration of the European Union are the two major political forces influencing transnational migration above and beyond economic globalization and technological change. I have suggested that these geopolitical factors hold the key to differentiating between American and European transnationalism. Yet, they also appear to distinguish between broadly Western and Eastern European migration orders. I wish to maintain this distinction for now (despite its Cold War undertones), but later speculate on how the two are linked in an emerging single European mobility order.

'Eastern' transnationalism

In his survey of forced migration, Van Hear (1998) notes that diasporas are made, un-made and re-made, and the same may be said of transnational communities after the fall of the Soviet Union. When Portes, Guarnizo and Landolt define transnationalism as 'occupations and activities that require regular and sustained social contact over time across national borders' (1999: 219), they are referring to people moving across borders. But in Eastern and Central Europe there is a corresponding history of borders moving across people and their communities. This shakes up the region's many cross-border transnational communities. There is also a dark history of ethnic cleansing, forced migration, expulsion and forced assimilation (Mann 1999), with ramifications for transnational connections. In the years after 1914, for example, transnationals were as likely to be armed soldiers as economic migrants.

The types of this regional transnationalism therefore include:

1 'Made diasporas', notably the five million people forced from Yugoslavia, the vast majority of whom have not returned, including the exodus from Kosovo and Albania. Further afield are those fleeing civil violence in Algeria and south-eastern Anatolia, many of whom pass through the region.

2 'Stranded minorities' such as the 25 million ethnic Russians left inside the successor states to the USSR but outside the Russian Federation, among whom a strong sense of community and a willingness to engage in collective political action has been slow to develop (G. Smith 1999). Yet, this potential transnational community has become a significant thorn in bilateral relations between Russia and some Baltic States for example. Relations between Russia and Latvia deteriorated during 1998 over the latter's citizenship laws and the commemorative activities of the Latvia SS Legion. By contrast, the stranded post-1919 Hungarians, of whom there are 1.6 million in Romania and around 350,000 in Serbia, have been able to revive many transnational connections since 1989. There are also renewed levels of cultural and political life between Lithuanians, Belorussians and Ukrainians in Poland and their respective national homelands.

3 'Unmade transnational communities'. Of the 17.7 million Germans living east of Germany and Austria in 1945, only 2.6 million remain: 11.7

million fled, and 3.2 million died in war or massacre (Mann 1999). Between 1989 and 1999 alone, the number of ethnic Germans in Romania's Transylvania region plummeted from 114,000 to 17,000. But among some Germans formerly of the Sudetenland, there are loud demands for compensation from the Czech government for the loss of property.

4 'Thawed exiles'. Exile communities from the Soviet era have begun to get involved in their homelands from abroad, such as Czech exiles in the US campaigning for restitution and voting rights or even, in the cases of Lithuania and Latvia, actually returning to become President.

5 'Crossed out border communities', for example along the Estonian– Russian border, the so-called 'Ikea curtain'. The river Narva flows between the towns of Narva in Estonia and Ivangorod in Russia. Until 1991 there was easy movement between them, but now Narva has cut off the water supply and sewage facilities to its debt-strapped neighbour and the border is enforced. As James Meek (*Guardian*, 4 February 1999) describes it: 'short commutes to work became daily trips abroad. The quick walk across the bridge to the shops became a winding path past a chain-link fence topped by barbed wire, with queues at two customs posts and two passport controls.' The irony is that the majority of Narva's inhabitants are, themselves, ethnic Russians.

6 'Remade diasporas', such as the returning Bulgarian Turks, of whom 350,000 fled to Turkey from the mid-1980s in response to coercive assimilation. Now many are returning.

In addition to these explicitly geopolitical types of transnationalism, political and economic dislocation since 1989 in Eastern and Central Europe have resulted in a thoroughgoing transition from 'regulated immobility to increasingly disorderly movement', as Van Hear puts it. A specifically transnational element is subsumed within this wider context. The dimensions of these changes have been best described by Wallace *et al.* (1996, see also Wallace 1999). Without using the term itself, they document the migration order for the region since 1989. Rather than the anticipated 'flood' from East to West there has emerged a much wider field of mobility. It is travel, not just migration, that is on the increase. And alongside the movement of people there are flows of goods, meeting new consumption demands, and capital investment. Moreover, the majority of moves are short distance and cross-border, between neighbouring countries. Many are of short duration, like the enforced prostitution of migrant women across the Czech/Austrian and Polish/German borders (Organisation for Security and Cooperation in Europe 1999). Wallace concludes that 'the opening of borders, allowing for free communication between countries, resulted not so much in globalization as in *regionalization*' (1999: 206).

Among the types of movers are: forced migrants; transit migrants from Africa, China and the Middle East; labour migrants; postmodern migrants, such as young Americans in Prague; tourists and border traders; and suitcase peddlers. Many of these, of course, correspond with the kinds of transnationals described in the Americas. And they are linked with ethnically defined niches and networks, as Wallace *et al.* (1996: 277) explain: 'the ethnicization of these trading relations is an important element in making such long range communication possible in countries where telecommunication infrastructure and travel facilities are below average'.

They have emerged as the result of geopolitical change, but are also linked to developing civil societies where corruption and the black market flourished. If traffickers in human beings, arms and drugs (increasingly using the same networks, routes and criminal organizations) are added to this list, then it becomes clear that the future development of civil society is also in question. The transition to greater mobility, including transnationalism, may be a central fact shaping governance, authority and security in Eastern and Central Europe for the next decade or more.

'Western' transnationalism

The Western European variant of transnationalism contains two varieties. One is much like the economically driven transnational migration described by Portes, Guarnizo and Landolt (1999), which also extends to social and political connections of all kinds. The other is more peculiar to the European Union: transnationalism as emerging within, and making use of, EU economic and political space. This is the sense in which the EU institutions themselves use the term 'transnational'.

There are, of course, many studies of the classic diasporas in both Eastern and Western Europe, including Greek, Irish and Italian. But, in addition, a growing body of research reveals the presence of the full range of transnational processes, activities and communities. These include regular trading, hometown associations, remittances, periodic returns for festivals and holidays, diaspora lobbying, satellite broadcasting, among many other things. Nonetheless, such studies have focused on a small number of exemplary cases, usually linking one homeland and one European country of destination. The exemplary cases include Maghrebis in France (Cesari 1998; Vasile 1997); Turks and Kurds in Germany (Caglar 1995; Østergaard-Nielsen 1998); Senegalese and Moroccans in Italy (Grillo *et al.* 2000); and South Asians in Great Britain (Gardner 1995). They rarely examine or compare transnational communities and relations in different European countries from the same origin. There is also scope for cross-regional comparisons between the Americas, Asia-Pacific and Europe.

The second variety is what was once termed supra-nationalism within the European Union. In EU documentation, for example in the Leonardo da

Vinci vocational training programme or Culture 2000, 'transnational' refers to activities within EU space as a whole, beyond the national scale but more across or between nations than standing above them. This space is occupied by migrants 'from above' and 'from below'. From above, the EU has created institutions that stimulate and facilitate organization across the 15 member states and encourage lobbying in Brussels and Strasbourg. The main example for migrants is the Migrants' Forum, an umbrella body for nationally defined migrant and ethnic lobbies. Although it has not generally been regarded as successful (see Danese 1998), some authors sense the possibility of new, post-national forms of citizenship empowering migrants at the EU level and actively demanded by migrant organizations (Kastoryano 1998). Directorate General I has funding for joint ventures between migrant communities and their homelands, particularly as part of the Union's Mediterranean programme (Danese 1998). In this way, the two varieties of European transnationalism are linked, raising questions as to whether one is an alternative to the other, or whether they are compatible.[3]

From below, some transnational groups have formed European-wide organizations, although not just confined to the EU but also including the Organisation for Security and Co-operation in Europe and the Council of Europe. Well-known examples include Jews and Roma, but there are others. Minghuan (1998) and Christiansen (1998) record the proliferation of Chinese associations since 1945. While the European Federation of Chinese Organisations receives backing from Beijing, the rival Association of Taiwanese Chambers of Commerce is supported by Taiwan. According to these authors, Chinese migrants think of themselves as going to and living in Europe, rather than any one particular European country. They are organized at this level, also through family associations. Note, however, that unlike EU nationals resident in other EU countries, non-EU nationals do not enjoy the full rights of citizenship. European Union territory continues to differentiate between these two potential kinds of transnationals.

Towards a single European mobility order?

> Free movement within the EU could some day begin just west of Minsk
> (Koslowski 1998)

Are these many varieties of transnationalism linked together through the development of a single European mobility order? I use the term *mobility order* to avoid confusion with Van Hear's and Pieke's concepts (which nonetheless inspire the term), and to emphasize the significance of mobility of all kinds in understanding transnational movement and transactions. I also want to refer to something located at a larger or higher regional level than migration orders. This order partly rests on the economic and demographic contrasts within the wider region. It is also the consequence of policies undertaken not just by the European Union, but also by the other supra-national organizations in the region, among them the Council of Europe, the Organisation for Security and Co-operation in Europe (OSCE) and the Western European Union (WEU). Whether these organizations are pulling in the same direction or whether they conflict remains to be answered. But it does seem clear that the European Union is hegemonic (recall that its 15 members are also members of the other organizations). At the same time, there are significant fractures within the European Union along state lines and between various institutions of governance.

Following the 1997 Amsterdam Treaty, immigration and asylum moved from the third to the first pillar of the EU and came under the competence of the Commission. Since then there have been slow but certain moves towards a coherent, though not common, policy in this area. A single EU migration and asylum policy is some way off, even though the principles have been outlined many times since 1997 (for example Commission of the European Communities 2000). The simplest way to understand what this order might be is to consider the Austrian government's proposal to the K4 Committee of the European Union in July 1998 and later discussed by the Justice and Home Affairs Council of Ministers and the Tampere inter-governmental conference held in October 1999. The Austrian proposal suggested organizing EU migration and asylum policy in a series of concentric zones extending more or less across the world. The innermost zone of EU countries abiding by the Schengen Treaty have agreed to co-ordinate both immigration control and policing, and permit free circulation across their common borders.[4] Beyond this are the EU members who have either not yet signed or who are not intending to sign the Treaty. Nonetheless, all 15 constitute the space of EU transnationalism (as defined earlier), although actual migration and labour mobility between them appears surprisingly low. Only around five million persons, or 1.5 per cent of the EU's population, reside in an EU country other than the one of their birth, for example. (This is around one-third of the total number of non-EU nationals resident in the 15 states.) There is, of course, a higher level of transnational commuting short of change of residence. Policies on asylum, cross-border policing, dual citizenship, etc. are converging slowly and unevenly. There are differences between states intent on full harmonization and states content with just co-ordination.

The second zone consists of aspirant members of the European Union, within the so-called 'buffer zone'. The price to pay for eventual membership by Estonia, Poland, the Czech Republic, Slovenia, Hungary, Malta and Cyprus is greater EU influence now over migration, visa, asylum and border policies, as well as economic and social affairs in general (Koslowksi 1998). The EU no longer regards them as a potential source of unwanted immigration, but policies in these areas will be expected to fall into line with the EU. They are deemed safe countries as far as refugee and asylum policy is concerned. Under provisions announced by the EU Justice and Home Affairs ministers in 2000, citizens of these countries will not be eligible for freedom of movement to other EU countries immediately upon joining. They will face restrictions for at least two years and possibly as many as seven, as Spain, Portugal and Greece did in their day. The EU's influence can be benign, for example the PHARE and TACIS programmes fund NGOs in Central Europe to tackle the rising problem of human trafficking, female and child prostitution. And there are also bilateral relations. For example, Germany funds Poland to reinforce its border controls with Russia, Ukraine and Belarus. Once more or less open for 35 years, the tightening of these borders has infuriated thousands of cross-border traders. The EU finances the electronic passport-reading devices at Poland's new border posts.[5]

As part of the pre-membership process, aspirant states may also be obliged to loosen ties with their diasporas. Hungary, for example, has been required to drop all claims to Romanian territory and cease involvement in the affairs of the ethnic Hungarians living there. They fear the coming of stricter border controls in line with Schengen. Other cross-border populations likely to be affected are Poles in Belarus and Belarusians in Poland. Political and administrative intervention in the full range of mobility policies places EU influence at the centre of governance throughout the second ring. It may also impact on relations between states. In both ways, the conditions for transnational communities are affected.

Transit countries, the third zone sketched out at Tampere, include countries no longer regarded as a source of unwanted immigration. They include North Africa, the rest of Central and Eastern Europe (including prospective but not immediate candidates for EU membership), Turkey and Russia. EU relations with some of these transit countries, notably in North Africa, formally link migration, trade and development together, for example through the 1995 Barcelona Declaration. But these connections are not backed up by the lure of eventual membership. The EU relies more on diplomatic procedures to exert influence in this circle. An example of diplomatic co-operation in this region is the meetings held between EU and Turkish high-level police officers to address a sudden upsurge in Kurdish refugees entering Europe in early 1998. These meetings were inconclusive and marked by friction between the parties over the role of the PKK in the exodus.

The Tampere conference spelled out policies for 'co-development' with countries in this region (Commission for the European Communities 2000). These partnership agreements between governments aim to link migration and development, to reduce push factors in the countries of origin and to consider the effects of remittances and brain drain on development in general. Of significance to transnational communities is a commitment to enable individuals to move back and forth between the EU and the country of origin without losing their status in the host country. Eventual return to the country of origin is among the aims of co-development.

Although EU influence is less direct in this zone, many transit countries are members of the Council of Europe and the Organisation for Security and Co-operation in Europe (OSCE), both of which have their own interests in mobility. Like the EU, these interests place migration within a wider concern for transnational activities including human trafficking, drug smuggling and terrorism. The OSCE's field missions in the Balkans for example, are regarded by the organization as a vital part of its Task Force on Trafficking in South East Europe. The OSCE provides funding, support and expertise for training border and judicial authorities as far away as Kyrgyzstan (Organisation for Security and Cooperation in Europe 1999). It also mediated the relations between Croatia and the Croat diaspora in Bosnia-Hercegovina (the 11th constituency) by supplying many of the 350 observers to the parliamentary elections in January 2000. Also in this region, the EU and Council of Europe have intervened on behalf of minority ethnic or ethno-national groups when under threat from majority or ruling ethnic groups. Examples of groups assisted under the 1997 European Convention on nationality include the Roma in Slovakia, but also Russians in Latvia and Lithuania. The Council of Europe has been noticeably more active in advancing the rights of Roma than the EU, suggesting that there are significant differences between the various supra-national organizations.

It is difficult to separate the elements of a mobility order in this zone from wider concerns for European political and cultural hegemony. The close and evolving connections between the politics of mobility and politics of security in this zone are summarized in remarks made by Javier Solana, High Representative of the EU for Common Foreign and Security Policy to a meeting of the Western European Union:

> Globalization has brought with it a wide range of transnational challenges, many of which were unheard of a generation ago. The threat of terrorism, international drug-dealing, money-laundering, the spread of AIDS: all these present us with new, 'globalized' problems and new responsibilities ... As the Union enlarges, and as we face new challenges in the next century, we have to be prepared to take more responsibility for regional security, particularly in those areas bordering the Union where we have direct interests at stake. We also have to be prepared, where necessary, to use all legitimate means to project security and stability beyond our borders. And we need to be able to *assert our values* of humanitarian solidarity and respect for human rights in all areas where people's lives depend on relief assistance.
>
> (Solana 1999, emphasis added)

The final outer sphere consists of countries still regarded as being sources of unwanted immigration, and against whom the full range of EU immigration policies are to be directed. But this includes more than the devices of exclusion. In February 2000 the EU announced its £8.5 billion aid and trade package for 71 poorer countries in Africa, the Caribbean and the Pacific – a new agreement replacing the Lome convention (1975). For the first time, the EU will attach conditions to aid relating to migration. Recipients will be required to take back illegal immigrants entering from their territory, even if they are not citizens.

The order outlined above is not conclusive, and the European Commission and the governments of member states are still debating and negotiating the form that a mobility order will take in the context of EU enlargement. Since Tampere for example, the pressures for some kind of EU skilled migration programme, possibly involving a green card, have grown. Some states – the UK and Germany – have already embarked on their own schemes. But I do suggest that the several forms of transnationalism can be placed within the context of differing zones such as those outlined above. Transnational communities and transnational movement can also be related to the full range of mobility patterns and policies. Elements of a common European migration regime – legislation, training, protocols, etc. – may therefore be built into a wider mobility order, which extends from technical assistance for border policing through to regional co-operation in security and law enforcement. It is driven by a hegemonic European Union, but not without countervailing influence, for instance from Turkey over Kurds.

Because the 15 member states are intent on lifting internal barriers to the movement of people and the circulation of goods, they require not only strengthened surveillance of collective external borders, but also intervention in the surrounding states of aspirant EU members and transit countries – the buffer zone. Intra-EU transnationalism, the second variety of the 'Western' transnationalism mentioned above, would appear to be at the expense of extra-EU transnationalism, the first variety. But this paradox may be more apparent than real, for two reasons. First, by hardening the EU's external walls the fifteen are driving cross-border activities underground. Often this means criminal organizations (Organisation for Security and Cooperation in Europe 1999), which are sometimes entangled with networks supplying arms and drugs. It is as if the EU is actively helping to make the transnational monster it fears on its eastern borders. Second, by elevating some transit countries into potential members and pushing the effective external border eastwards, a new tier of states is being drawn into the intra-EU transnationalism. But by beefing up the eastern borders of the aspirant members, trafficking routes have been driven to the north (across the Baltic) and to the south, through the Balkans, Morocco and Tunisia. Transnational problems are, thereby, more widely regionalized.

In any case, it is difficult to gauge the impact of the mobility order on transnational migration and communities. Not all migrants are transmigrants and not all cross-border moves are transnational. The various policies and programmes described as a mobility order set the conditions under which individuals, families and communities make their decisions. Staying put, commuting, suitcase trading, migrating permanently or living transnationally are different options. It seems unlikely that the mobility order will simply have the stated effect of successfully managing all movement.

Conclusion

The key theoretical challenge for human geography in particular, but also social science in general, is how to jointly theorize networks, scale and difference (Rogers *et al.* 2001). Theories of transnational communities and related empirical research have understandably concentrated on flows and networks, and to a lesser extent localities. This chapter has argued that, as part of a move to include scale in this field of study, the macro-regional level is worth investigating. The ground-breaking research on transnationalism was based on empirical anomalies observed in research on migration to the US, as well as the observations of globalization in Asia-Pacific. Concepts and definitions based on the experience of these world regions are equally applicable elsewhere. But, I have also suggested that there are certain distinctive characteristics of transnationalism in Europe. These partly derive from two general features, geopolitical change and demographic ageing. The mix of transnational networks and communities throughout Europe is varied, although a crude contrast can be made between West and East. Particularly in Eastern Europe, it makes sense to view transnational social processes as components of a wider transition from one migration order to another, involving higher levels of mobility of all kinds. People and borders both move.

But, as well as accounting for the varieties of transnationalism, I go on to speculate that they are linked at a macro-regional level through the influence of the EU on migration regimes. This influence is, in part, a consequence of the EU's moves towards internal freedom of circulation, transnationalism in the sense of greater integration of states and movement between them. But it is also a consequence of its larger geopolitical ambitions, including enlargement to the east and a common voice on foreign affairs. Four zones are recognized. The EU itself (Schengen and non-Schengen); the aspirant members of the former buffer zone, such as Poland and Slovenia; the transit zone of Eastern and Central Europe, Turkey and North Africa; and the ACP developing countries, for the first time bound in agreements with the EU on migration and repatriation policy. In the outer zones, particularly the middle two, the EU interacts with other supra-national organizations (OSCE, Council of Europe), and transnationalism becomes integrated into larger security concerns. These are also the areas where 'European values' are imposed and contested, and where the contradictions between the espousal of human rights and the imposition of constraints on movement are most glaring. The reluctance of the EU (and possibly the OSCE) to fully recognize that greater restrictions on migration into the EU or back and forth across its external borders drives migrants underground into the hands of transnational traffickers is a serious problem. The contradiction was clearly evident in the fate of Abdullah Ocalan. But it equally applies to the hundreds of thousands of people trying to enter the region each year, many enduring personal suffering and abuse of their human rights, in open conflict with 'European values'.

Notes

1 For fuller details see *Traces* issues 4 and 5 at http:www//transcomm.ox.ac.uk/ traces. This account draws upon contemporary press reports that may not contain the full story.
2 Some authors have suggested that there are successful instances of diaspora lobbying, for example, by Turks and Croats in Germany (Østergaard-Nielsen 1998), or by Kashmiris in Britain (Ellis and Khan 1998). But these are probably out-numbered by failures. The Greek-Cypriot lobby in the UK is the largest in Parliament, but has conspicuously failed to shift policy. The success of French-Armenians in persuading the National Assembly to recognize the Armenian genocide has caused friction between France and Turkey.
3 For example, Danese (1998) argues that the Senegalese in Italy have strong home-town organizations but weak representation at the EU level. This is because there is no Italian-level organization among Senegalese. Their activities and efforts are subsumed under Mouridist religious brotherhoods.
4 The Schengen Treaty countries include Austria, Belgium, France, Germany, Italy, Luxembourg, the Netherlands, Portugal and Spain, with Denmark, Sweden, Finland, Norway and Greece at various stages of complying with the Treaty.
5 The EU has also invested in the physical infrastructure of mobility. Part of the $1.8 billion aid package promised to southeastern Europe in March 2000 includes funding for bridges and roads, e.g. a new Danube bridge between Romania and Bulgaria, and better crossings between Macedonia and Kosovo.

References

Appadurai, A. 1986. *The social life of things: commodities in cultural perspective.* Cambridge: Cambridge University Press.
Appadurai, A. 1996. *Modernity at large: cultural dimensions of globalization.* Minneapolis, MN: University of Minnesota Press.
Basch, L., Glick Schiller, N. and Blanc-Szanton, C. 1994. *Nations unbound: transnational projects, postcolonial predicaments, and deterritorialized nation-states.* New York: Gordon & Breach.
Caglar, A. 1995. German Turks in Berlin: social exclusion and strategies for social mobility. *New Community* 21: 309–23.
Cesari, J. 1998. Diasporas of transnational networks in the context of globalization. Conference paper MIG/40, Integrating Immigrants in Liberal States, European University Influence Florence, 8–9 May.
Christiansen, F. 1998. Chinese identity in Europe, in G. Benton and F. Pieke eds. *The Chinese in Europe.* Basingstoke: Macmillan, 42–63.
Commission of the European Communities 2000. On a community immigration policy, Brussels 22 November 2000, COM(2000) 757 final.

Danese, G. 1998. Transnational collective action in Europe: the case of migrants in Italy and Spain. *Journal of Ethnic and Migration Studies* 24: 715–33.

Ellis, P. and Khan, Z. 1998. Diasporic mobilisation and the Kashmir issue in British politics. *Journal of Ethnic and Migration Studies* 24: 471–88.

Faist, T. 2000. *The volume and dynamics of international migration and transnational social spaces.* Oxford: Oxford University Press.

Fardon, R. 1990. Localizing strategies: the regionalization of ethnographic accounts, in R. Fardon ed. *Localizing strategies.* Edinburgh: Scottish Academic Press, 1–41.

Foner, N. 1999. What's new about transnationalism?: New York immigrants today and at the turn of the century. *Diaspora* 6: 355–76.

Gardner, K. 1995. *Global migrants, local lives: travel and transformation in rural Bangladesh.* Oxford: Clarendon Press.

Glick Schiller, N., Basch, L. and Blanc-Szanton, C. eds. 1992. *Towards a transnational perspective on migration.* New York: New York Academy of Sciences.

Grillo, R., Riccio, B. and Salih, R. 2000. Here or there? Contrasting experiences of transnationalism: Moroccans and Senegalese in Italy. Centre for the Comparative Study of Culture, Development and the Environment, University of Sussex.

Guarnizo, L.E. and Smith, M.P. 1998. The locations of transnationalism, in M.P. Smith and L.E. Guarnizo eds. *Transnationalism from below.* New Brunswick, NJ: Transaction, 3–34.

Hannerz, U. 1996. *Transnational connections.* London: Routledge.

Kastoryano, R. 1998. Transnational participation and citizenship: immigrants in the European Union. Transnational Communities Programme Working Paper WPTC-98–12.

Koslowski, R. 1998. European migration regimes: emerging, enlarging and deteriorating. *Journal of Ethnic and Migration Studies* 24: 735–49.

Mann, M. 1999. The dark side of democracy: the modern tradition of ethnic and political cleansing. *New Left Review* 235: 18–45.

Massey, D. 1999. Imagining globalization: power-geometries of time-space, in A. Brah, M.J. Hickman and M. Mac an Ghaill eds. *Global futures.* Basingstoke: Macmillan, 27–44.

Minghuan, L. 1998. Transnational links among the Chinese in Europe: a study of European-wide Chinese voluntary associations, in G. Benton and F.N. Pieke eds. *The Chinese in Europe.* Basingstoke: Macmillan, 21–41.

Mitchell, K. 1997. Transnational discourse: bringing geography back in. *Antipode* 29: 101–14.

Ong, A. and Nonini, D. eds. 1997. *Ungrounded empires: the cultural politics of modern Chinese transnationalism.* London: Routledge.

Organisation for Security and Co-operation in Europe 1999. Trafficking in human beings: implications for the OSCE. ODIHR background paper 1999/3 for the OSCE Review Conference, September 1999.

Østergaard-Nielsen, E. 1998. Diaspora politics: the case of immigrants and refugees from Turkey residing in Germany since 1980. D.Phil. thesis, Faculty of Social Studies, University of Oxford.

Pieke, F.N. 2000. At the margins of the Chinese world system: the Fuzhou diaspora in Europe, project description. ESRC Transnational Communities Programme http://www.transcomm.ox.ac.uk/wwwroot/pieke.htm.

Portes, A. 2001. Introduction: the debates and significance of immigrant transnationalism. *Global Networks* 1: 181–93.

Portes, A., Guarnizo, L.E. and Landolt, P. 1999. The study of transnationalism: pitfalls and promise of an emergent research field. *Ethnic and Racial Studies* 22: 217–27.

Riccio, B. 2001. Disaggregating the transnational community: Senegalese migrants on the coast of Emilia-Romagna. ESRC Transnational Communities Programme Working Paper WPTC-01–11.

Rogers, A., Cohen, R. and Vertovec, S. 2001. Editorial. *Global Networks* 1: i–iii.

Sassen, S. 1998. *Globalization and its discontents*. New York: New Press.

Smith, G. 1999. Transnational politics and the politics of the Russian diaspora. *Ethnic and Racial Studies* 22: 500–23.

Smith, M.P. 1999. New approaches to migration and transnationalism: locating transnational practices. Keynote address to the conference New Approaches to Migration: Transnational Communities and the Transformation of Home, University of Sussex, Brighton, 21–2 September.

Smith, M.P. 2001. *Transnational urbanism: locating globalization*. Oxford: Blackwell.

Smith, M.P and Guarnizo, L.E. eds. 1998. *Transnationalism from below*. New Brunswick, NJ: Transaction.

Smith, R.C. 1998. Transnational localities: community, technology, and the politics of membership within the context of Mexico-US migration, in M.P. Smith and L. Guarnizo eds. *Transnationalism from below*. New Brunswick, NJ: Transaction, 196–238.

Solana, J. 1999. The development of a common European security and defence policy: the integration project of the next decade. Address at the EU Commission/ Institut für Europäische Politik Conference, Berlin, 17 December.

United Nations 2000. Replacement migration: is it a solution to declining and ageing populations? Population Division of the Department of Economic and Social Affairs.

Van Hear, N. 1998. *New diasporas*. London: UCL Press.

Vasile, E. 1997. Re-turning home: transnational movements and the transformation of landscape and culture in the marginal communities of Tunis. *Antipode* 29: 177–96.

Vertovec, S. and Cohen, R. eds. 1999. *Migrations, diasporas and transnationalism*. Cheltenham: Edward Elgar.

Wahlbeck, Ö. 1998. Transnationalism and diasporas: the Kurdish example. ESRC Transnational Communities Programme Working Paper WPTC-98–11.

Wallace, C. 1999. Crossing borders: mobility of goods, capital and people in the Central European region, in A. Brah, M.J. Hickman and M. Mac an Ghaill eds. *Global futures: migration, environment and globalization*. Basingstoke: Macmillan, 185–209.

Wallace, C., Chmouliar, O. and Sidorenko, E. 1996. The Eastern frontier of Western Europe: mobility in the buffer zone. *New Community* 22: 259–86.

Index

Figures given in *italics* indicate pages containing figures or tables.

.